LUDICS IN SURREALIST THEATRE AND BEYOND

Taking as its point of departure the complex question about whether Surrealist theatre exists, this book re-examines the much misunderstood artistic medium of theatre within Surrealism, especially when compared to poetry and painting. This study reconsiders Surrealist theatre specifically from the perspective of ludics—a poetics of play and games—an ideal approach to the Surrealists, whose games blur the boundaries between the "playful" and the "serious."

Vassiliki Rapti's aims are threefold: first, to demystify André Breton's controversial attitude toward theatre; second, to do justice to Surrealist theatre, by highlighting the unique character that derives from its inherent element of play; and finally, to trace the impact of Surrealist theatre in areas far beyond its generally acknowledged influence on the Theatre of the Absurd—an impact being felt even on the contemporary world stage. Beginning with the Surrealists' "one-into-another" game and its illustration of Breton's ludic dramatic theory, Rapti then examines the traces of this kind of game in the works of a wide variety of Surrealist and Post-Surrealist playwrights and stage directors, from several different countries, and from the 1920s to the present: Roger Vitrac, Antonin Artaud, Günter Berghaus, Nanos Valaoritis, Robert Wilson, and Megan Terry.

Vassiliki Rapti is Preceptor in Modern Greek in the Department of The Classics at Harvard University, USA, where she is also serving as Research Fellow in Greek Literature and Language Pedagogy at the Harvard Center for Hellenic Studies (Washington, D.C.).

ASHGATE STUDIES IN SURREALISM

Series Editor:
*Gavin Parkinson, The Courtauld Institute of Art,
University of London, UK*

With scholarly interest in Surrealism greater than ever, the Ashgate Studies in Surrealism series serves as a forum for key areas of Surrealist inquiry today. This series extends the ongoing academic and popular interest in Surrealism, evident in recent studies that have rethought established areas of Surrealist activity and engagement, including those of politics, the object, photography, crime, and modern physics. Expanding and adding various lines of inquiry, books in the series examine Surrealism's intersections with philosophical, social, artistic, and literary themes. Potential subjects to be examined in the context of Surrealism include but are not limited to: nature; queer studies; humor and play; science; theory in the 1950s and 1960s; the New Novel; Surrealist activities beyond Paris.

Proposals are welcomed for both monographs and essay collections dealing with the above subjects or with discussions of Surrealism in other aspects and genres. Monographic writings on artists and writers who have been generally overlooked by English-language scholarship (for instance, Victor Brauner, Toyen, Jorge Camacho) would also fall within the scope of this series.

LUDICS IN SURREALIST THEATRE AND BEYOND

Vassiliki Rapti

ASHGATE

Published by
Ashgate Publishing Limited
Wey Court East
Union Road
Farnham
Surrey, GU9 7PT
England

Ashgate Publishing Company
110 Cherry Street
Suite 3–1
Burlington, VT 05401-3818
USA

http://www.ashgate.com

British Library Cataloguing in Publication Data
Rapti, Vassiliki.
    Ludics in Surrealist theatre and beyond.—(Ashgate studies in surrealism)
    1. Surrealist games. 2. Experimental theater. 3. Surrealism   (Literature) 4. Comic, The.
    I. Title II. Series
    792'022—dc23

The Library of Congress has cataloged the printed edition as follows:
Rapti, Vassiliki.
    Ludics in surrealist theatre and beyond / by Vassiliki Rapti.
        p. cm.—(Ashgate studies in surrealism)
    Includes index.
    ISBN 978-1-4094-2906-7 (hardcover : alk. paper) 1. Theater—History—20th century. 2. Experimental theater. 3. Surrealism (Literature) 4. Breton, André, 1896–1966—Influence. I. Title.

    PN2189.R37 2013
    809.2'91163—dc23
                                                                              2012034194
ISBN 9781409429067 (hbk)
ISBN 9781472412263 (ebk—PDF)
ISBN 9781472412270 (ebk—ePUB)

MIX
Paper from
responsible sources
FSC
www.fsc.org
FSC® C018575

Printed and bound in Great Britain by the
MPG Books Group, UK

To Andreas.

Contents

LIST OF ILLUSTRATIONS

So I am inclined to distinguish between the essence and the inessential in a game too. The game, one would like to say, has not only rules but also a point.

—Ludwig Wittgenstein

ACKNOWLEDGMENTS

This book is the final product of my long commitment to surrealist theatre. My interest in the subject began in 2000, and evolved considerably from those beginnings, in particular thanks to the "apprenticeship" I served under the author Nanos Valaoritis. The "last Greek Surrealist" has helped me tremendously by so generously entrusting to me all his unpublished archives and kindly permitting me to work on them and publish them in part. Moreover, during our endless telephone discussions for more than a decade now, he has enlightened me on various issues that I would otherwise not have noticed. For all this and more, I am profoundly grateful to him.

I would also like to express my gratitude to my mentor Stamos Metzidakis and my colleagues Stratos Constantinidis and Olga Taxidou for their stimulating intellectual exchange throughout the book project.

I am also grateful to my colleagues at Harvard University, especially Kathy Coleman, Ivy Livingston, John Duffy, Michael Herzfeld, Rhéa Karabelas-Lesage, Greg Nagy, Panagiotis Roilos and Mark Schiefsky, who along with the staff of the Department of the Classics, Teresa Wu and Alyson Lynch, secured me an inspirational research environment.

Special thanks are also due to all those affiliated with several public and private foundations that supported this project over the years, especially the Greek State Scholarship Foundation, the Alexander S. Onassis Public Benefit Foundation and Washington University in St. Louis.

I am also grateful to many of my friends who supported me over the years in many ways, in particular, to John Anton, Diane Miles-Touliatos, Jane Loe, Jerry McAdams, Vinia Tsopelas, Julia Dubnoff, Anna Stavrakopoulou, and Eva Prionas, for their constant care, and the late Venetia Gavrielatou for being an inexhaustible source of wisdom and encouragement.

My thanks also are extended to Amy Debrecht, Nicole Miller, and Susan Kapit-Husserl for their comments on stylistic matters at various stages of preparation of my manuscript. My warmest thanks also go to Katalin Mitchell for granting me permission to search the Robert Wilson Archives at the American Repertory Theater and to use the pictures from the production of Robert Wilson's *Alcestis* that have been included in Chapter 4. In relation to the same chapter, I am most grateful to Günter Berghaus for his kind permission to use the illustrations from his production of Antonin Artaud's *Jet de Sang*. I am indebted to Megan Terry, JoAnn Schmidman, and Sora Kimberlain for granting me permission to use four illustrations from the Omaha Magic Theatre in Chapter 5, one of which appears on the cover of this book. Megan Terry's generosity extended to the invaluable comments she provided on the way she approaches games; I found all her commentary truly enlightening. I would like to thank Tonda Marton for putting me in touch with Megan Terry. I would like to express my gratitude to Pella Publishing Co., and McFarland & Company, Inc. for granting me permission to include here parts of my articles on ludics, first published in their journals *Charioteer* and *Text & Presentation*, respectively. Special thanks are also due to all those affiliated with several public and private foundations that supported this project over the years, especially the Greek State Scholarship Foundation and the Alexander S. Onassis Public Benefit Foundation. I am also grateful to many of my friends who supported me over the years in many ways, in particular, to John Anton, Diane Touliatos, Jane Loe, Vinia Tsopelas, and Eva Prionas, for their constant care, and the late Venetia Gavrielatou for being an inexhaustible source of wisdom and encouragement. I am deeply grateful to Melanie Stowell for her diligent treatment of my manuscript. Without her excellent and conscientious work, this book could not have been completed. I wish to thank Ashgate Publishing, especially Meredith Norwich, Margaret Michniewicz, Beatrice Beaup, Emily Ruskell and Jonathan Hoare, for all their help, as well as the Studies in Surrealism series editor Gavin Parkinson of the Courtauld Institute of Art. Last but not least, I am grateful to my family, particularly to my mother and parents-in-law, my sisters and my husband Andreas, for their patience, support and love, and to our daughter, Katerina Maria, who in her own way helped facilitate the completion of this project.

LIST OF ABBREVIATIONS

The following abbreviations are used for this study's most frequently cited works:

CW   *Collected Works*

OC1   Œuvres *complètes*, vol. 1

OC2   Œuvres *complètes*, vol. 2

INTRODUCTION: DOES SURREALIST THEATRE EXIST?

The question whether surrealist theatre exists or not is neither rhetorical nor self-explanatory. Rather, it is crucial to the unraveling of our understanding of this theatre. To be sure, theatre has not received the attention it deserves within Surrealism—a movement which officially traces its roots to 1924 in France, and which advocated the absolute freedom of human beings, the omnipotence of dreams, and the pursuit of the marvelous. J.H. Matthews pointed out in 1970 that theatre "has been the least developed mode in Surrealism" ("Surrealism" 239). Six years later, Annabelle Henkin Meltzer was more categorical and warned scholars not to have any illusions: "Surrealism had not sought to develop an aesthetic for the theatre, but rather had abducted a literary genre for its own purposes" (*Dada* 167). She further elaborated: "Just as the surrealist text itself is often difficult to grapple with, on the theoretical level the reader will have to struggle with the absence of a consistent and consecutive approach to drama as well as the absence of a unified program for the stage" (ibid.). The statistics that Philip Auslander offered a few years later confirmed Henkin Meltzer's remarks: only 17 surrealist plays were staged in Paris, their performances covering merely 30 nights in a period of two decades between the two World Wars.[1] Such conspicuous neglect becomes even more marked when compared to poetry and painting, the two pillars of this movement, as Ruby Cohn poignantly remarked already in 1964: "Although poetry and painting were rocked to their foundations by the Surrealist explosion of the imagination, the theatre of the time was virtually untouched" ("Surrealism" 159).[2] Two years later, Michael Canney would note on the occasion of the art exhibition "Surrealism: A State of Mind, 1924–1965," presented by the Art Gallery at the University of California, Santa Barbara: "We are perhaps only now beginning to appreciate how great the influence of Surrealism has been upon post-war art" (no page, Foreword).[3] Since then, it has become commonplace to acknowledge the pervasive influence of Surrealism in popular culture, reflected in the countless reproductions of works of art by Salvador Dali or Max Ernst among many other surrealist artists. Yet, this is not the case when it comes to surrealist theatre. The controversial attitude of the leader of Surrealism, André Breton, toward theatre is not the only reason for such oversight, but it is without doubt a major factor, and the one most commonly recognized by scholars. Martine Antle, in *Cultures du surréalisme: les représentations de l'Autre* (2001), for example, confirms this fact when she emphasizes Breton's ambivalent attitude toward theatre and his "peu de goût pour les planches" (82) [his small interest in the stage]. The scholar who addresses this issue in most detail, however, is Henri Béhar, whose views will be discussed in detail in the next chapter.[4]

Whether responsibility for theatre within Surrealism never becoming fully fledged lies entirely with Breton, or only in part, as this book aspires to address, the fact remains that surrealist theatre is missing as a separate category from almost all extant dictionaries of theatre, due either to a lack of official support or to a misconception about the incompatibility of Surrealism with the stage. Martin Esslin, for instance, argues that surrealist theatre lacked "the qualities that would have been needed to create a real surrealist drama" (*Artaud* 348). Therefore, at best, whenever it is mentioned, surrealist theatre is subsumed under the "avant-garde" or "experimental" theatre and, in some cases, it is confused with the Theatre of the Absurd. With the exception of *The Penguin Dictionary of the Theatre*, which confirms that "unlike Dada, Surrealism expressed itself little in drama" (261), and that "Artaud was for a while associated with the movement" (261), almost all other major dictionaries of the theatre,[5] including *The Oxford Companion to the Theatre*, Patrice Pavis's *Dictionary of Theatre*, and Alfred Simon's *Dictionary of Contemporary French Theatre*, do not include a separate lemma for "Surrealist Theatre," nor even for "Surrealist Drama," at all. Thus, for anyone who takes the authority of the dictionaries as a given, a negative answer to our initial question as to whether surrealist theatre exists or not, would be inevitable. Nevertheless, surrealist theatre does exist, mainly "as the result of individual initiatives outside the surrealist movement," as Béhar states (*Étude* 30), and other prominent experts of Surrealism have shown.[6] In this light, the term "surrealist theatre," as distinct from "surrealist drama"—in the sense that it goes beyond the limits of the page and reaches the stage—needs further elucidation. What is "surrealist theatre" and what are its characteristics? Where and when did it make its appearance and for what time span? These issues will be addressed here, starting with an attempt to define the term "surrealist theatre." By this term, I refer to any theatrical work that claims to be surrealist, and which has been put on stage (thus going beyond the limits of the page), independently of the consent of the leader of Surrealism, André Breton. For if Breton's approval must be necessary for any theatrical work to be considered surrealist, then such a theatre would indeed not exist, given Breton's overall hostile attitude toward theatre (despite his own early theatrical attempts during his Dadaist phase). Finally, if there is a theatrical work that does not make any overt claim of connection to Surrealism, yet arguably bears traces of it, I prefer to classify it as an epigone to surrealist theatre. As such, one should talk about the influence of surrealist theatre, one that has indeed exceeded both the national borders of the parent country of Surrealism—France—and the temporal borders of the movement's historical moment, which officially expired in 1968, two years after André Breton's death.[7] I must add here that, as such, the influence of the surrealist theatre is a key issue for its much-needed reconsideration.

Among those who have raised this issue, Henri Béhar devoted himself to the study of Dada and surrealist theatre. His works, *Roger Vitrac: Un reprouvé du surréalisme* (1966), *Étude sur le théâtre dada et surréaliste* (1967), and *Théâtre ouvert sur le rêve* (1980), to name but a few, which "helped considerably to rethink the place that the theatre occupies within the Surrealist thought and esthetics" (Antle, *Cultures* 81), are at the origins of my study. Also, J.H. Matthews' book *Theatre in Dada and Surrealism* (1974), Gloria Orenstein Feman's work *The Theater of the Marvelous: Surrealism and the Contemporary Stage* (1975), and David G. Zinder's work *The Surrealist Connection: An Approach to a Surrealist Aesthetic of Theatre* (1976), all constitute great contributions to the study of surrealist theatre. Equally important is the anthology of translated French surrealist plays, edited by Michael Benedikt and George E. Wellwarth, *The Avant-Garde, Dada, and Surrealism. Modern French Theatre: An Anthology of Plays* (1964). Finally, monographs or articles on surrealist theatre, written by Martine Antle, Annabelle Henkin Meltzer, Anette S. Levitt, Philip Auslander, and Albert Bermel, to name but a few, combine to prove that surrealist theatre does exist as a separate category in the history of theatre and deserves special attention.

It is easy to attribute the dismissal of surrealist theatre to its "failure" as a theatrical genre. Antle, for example, points to the ambiguous status of the surrealist theatrical text as the primary reason for such a failure (*Cultures* 82). This holds true particularly when the surrealist theatrical text is judged—as has often been the case—through the lens of Aristotelian theory and its basic qualitative components of plot, character, thought, diction, melody, and spectacle. None of these elements necessarily apply to surrealist theatre. Moreover, its profoundly anti-mimetic nature, due to its much-sought "surreality," in other words, the meeting place of opposite categories, poses a great obstacle for surrealist theatre to be considered successful by the standards of conventional theatre. Thus, in the eyes of some critics, as Mark Bennison states, "surrealist plays are formless, nonsensical, and meaningless. At best, they are interesting; at worst, sophomoric jokes" (190). However, a closer look reveals unusual merits that encompass its revolutionary shock value aimed at the attack of reason. Anna Balakian's following words bear evidence that, already in 1975, there was room for reconsideration of surrealist theatre:

> Some years ago, … I reread the fragmental plays that the surrealists had created in the early phase of their cenacle and came to the conclusion that *surrealism produced nothing more than a blueprint for theater. That was before Gloria Orenstein launched on her global and exhaustive investigation of the flowering of the terrain*, vaguely delimited but fertile, which the surrealists had seeded and their followers cultivated (quoted in Orenstein Feman xiii; my emphasis).

Today, almost 35 years later, despite an accumulated bibliography on the field of surrealist theatre—a field that flourished in the late 1960s and 70s due to the emergence of experimental theatre and the exploration of its affinities with surrealist theatre—there is still room for reconsideration of the latter. Martine Antle's study *Cultures du surréalisme* (2001) is a recent example. Focusing on the disregarded media of theatre and photography, Antle reviews Surrealism's multicultural aspects and shows how these media are "fontamentaux pour une compréhension de l'alterité dans le surréalisme" (179) [fundamental for a comprehension of alterity within Surrealism]. She proposes a re-reading of Breton's *Nadja* among others, and demonstrates how its theatricality determines the self's quest for identity. Most important of all, Antle demonstrates "how pervasive Surrealism has become in contemporary popular culture by showing how it has fallen into the public domain within, and outside of Europe, and how it continues to thrive there and to play a fundamental role on a bigger scale" (Conley 4).

A reconsideration of surrealist theatre would not only challenge the idea about its mimetic character, but also demystify André Breton's controversial attitude toward theatre. Furthermore, it would differentiate surrealist theatre from other experimental theatre going on at the same time and would trace the influence of surrealist theatre to areas far beyond its more generally acknowledged influence on the Theatre of the Absurd, as it imbues even the contemporary, postmodern stage.[8] With regard to the Theatre of the Absurd, for instance, which "strives to express its senselessness of the human condition and the inadequacy of the rational approach by the open abandonment of rational devices and discursive thought" (Esslin, *Theatre of the Absurd* xix–xx), Eugene Ionesco admits that Surrealism dazzled and liberated him. So he was not surprised to be considered by the great surviving Surrealists as the most successful practitioner of Surrealism. In an interview with Edith Mora in 1960, he observed: "When he (Philippe Soupault) and Breton and Benjamin Péret saw my plays in 1952 and '53 they did indeed say to me, 'That's what we wanted to do!' But I have never belonged to their group, or to the neosurrealists, although the movement interested me" (Ionesco, *Notes* 120).

Puzzled by the distinct nature of surrealist plays, which do not seem to fall into the category of mimetic theatre in the Aristotelian sense, but rather follow the ludic[9] organizational principle, I believe one might usefully look at surrealist theatre through the lens of this theory of play and games. For surrealist theatre displays a gamut of ludic strategies that were destined for ample use by the contemporary postmodern stage in general. Therefore, given the importance attributed to play and games by the Surrealists themselves, I would argue that examining surrealist theatre through the lens of ludic theory is a safe path to use in reconsidering surrealist theatre in general, and in the further exploration of its deep impact on contemporary theatre. As Stamos Metzidakis claims,

> Dès que l'on dit "surréalisme," on évoque la notion d'une activité ludique. Pour cette raison, bien des critiques n'ont jamais pris les surréalistes au sérieux. Ils prétendent que ceux-ci ne faisaient que jouer à des petits jeux linguistiques dont la majorité était incompréhensible ("L'Apothéose de l'erreur" 7).

> [From the moment we say "Surrealism" we evoke the notion of a ludic activity. For this reason, several critics have never taken the Surrealists seriously. They pretend that these latter did nothing but play small linguistic games, the majority of which were incomprehensible.]

Unlike these critics, I believe with Metzidakis that it is substantial to take surrealist ludic activity seriously, for it was the equivalent of rebellion for them: "the message [the word 'jeu'] strove so desperately to communicate was the refusal to be serious about a social order and a set of values that were believed discredited by history" (Toloudis 149). Originally introduced as a source of fun and a means of bonding by showing their group's common interests, their experimental games quickly developed into a significant research area for the Surrealists. In his work *Donner à voir* (1939), Paul Eluard offers the following vivid description of the way surrealist games reinforced solidarity among the players:

> How many evenings did we spend lovingly creating a race of cadavre exquis! ... All cares were banished, all memory of our poverty, of boredom, of the outside world. We played with imagery and there were no losers. Everyone wanted his neighbor to win, and to continue winning even more, until he had everything. No longer did revelation need food. Its features disfigured by passion seemed far more beautiful than anything revelation can tell us when we are alone, for when we are alone we are struck dumb by our vision (quoted in Gershman 55).

Discovering a new vision stemming from their so-called dialogue games,[10] Surrealists soon used them to learn about and put into motion the mechanisms of the psyche. As early as 1924, the *Manifesto of Surrealism* mentioned play in the form of "disinterested play of thought," next to "the superior reality of certain forms of previously neglected associations" and "the omnipotence of dream" (Breton, *Manifestoes* 26). Thirty years later, Breton explained why Surrealism placed such a great importance on play activity. "Play," as opposed to "seriousness," reflected the desire of the Surrealists "to break with all obsolete antinomies such as action versus dream, past versus future, reason versus folly, high versus low, etc." (quoted in Garrigues 217).

It is indeed imperative to treat surrealist ludic activity as a research tool, since it has been considered such by the Surrealists themselves, particularly from the moment they invented their own games. To the Surrealists, as Herbert S. Gershman states, "surrealist games were a method by which they might detach themselves from the world, a gesture meaningless in the context of 'ordinary' life, but pointing toward a social distinction—and suggesting a distinctive metaphysical look" (51). Furthermore, the same scholar adds, the surrealist games "were a gesture of defiance directed at the world of reality, a thumbing of the nose at adult (utilitarian) logic, a retreat to a paradise where the liberty so loudly proclaimed in other spheres could not possibly obtain. ... The game, in short, is a formal construction which shuts out one reality while creating another, more nearly ideal one" (51-2). It is as such that I view each surrealist play, that is, as a game that shuts out a limited reality and creates another, more ideal one that has been called "surreality." Yet, this new ideal reality in which opposite categories conflate is not a fiction, but the outcome of an active engagement on behalf of the participants-players. In the words of Freud and Huizinga: "the opposite of play is not serious activity but reality" (Slovenko and Knight 9).

Such a view obviously stands in sharp contrast to the view of surrealist plays as generally "mimetic," as we find in Martin John Bennison's otherwise important dissertation, "Aesthetic Principles in Representative Surrealist Plays" (1971). There he claims, "in the main, the Surrealist plays discussed are mimetic" (190). By "mimetic play," he refers to "an object, sufficient or complete in itself that arouses certain emotions and completes or realizes these emotions. Plot is the chief principle of formal organization in the mimetic play" (192). And Bennison concludes, "[i]n essence, therefore, surrealist dramas do not differ in aesthetic foundation from previous drama in Western culture" (190); he even leaves room for didacticism in some of the surrealist plays, which can be seen as another motivation for mimesis. To make the claim that surrealist drama is accepted as an integral part of the Western dramatic canon inaugurated by Aristotle's *Poetics* according to which mimesis is the fundamental mode of art (1447a) that refers to the imitation of human action and external reality, is to diminish the revolutionary character of surrealist drama. Bennison attempts to equate surrealist drama with the Western dramatic canon in order for it to be more easily accepted. However, surrealist drama, like any avant-garde drama, defies this canon and its value lies precisely in such defiance. "No longer interested in the imitation of external reality, [it] turned to the imitation of personal experience which, it felt, was more truthful, more profound, and even more universally significant than any form of art that had preceded it" (Zinder 1). Thus, surrealist drama has been created in reaction to any previous form of Western drama, whether Greek classical drama, French neo-classical drama, realistic and naturalistic drama, or psychological drama, all of which comply with the illusionistic principle. Its main difference lies in its defiance of the world of external reality and in its attempt to amplify it, by actualizing the world of dream on stage, not necessarily in an idealized form, but in all its depth, no matter how cruel it might be. Such amplification of the stage is the result of a different view of the use of language, which goes against the logical use of language and therefore of a coherent use of reality. From this point of view, although imitation may be used in surrealist dramas as one of their ludic strategies, it is never as a faithful representation of reality, but rather one that despises it or, at best, attempts to transform it by transporting the participants to another world.

Thus, unlike Bennison, who sees surrealist drama as a mimetic drama with all the components of Aristotelian dramatic theory, I argue, rather, that by foregrounding the play-concept that is considered free activity *par excellence*, surrealist drama is *methectic*, that is, initiative, participatory, and ritualistic. In other words, surrealist drama does not *represent* but rather *re-presents*, in the sense that an event or a series of events is not shown figuratively on stage but is actually reproduced in the action. It thus defies *mimesis* and instead encourages *semiosis*, a process whereby something functions as a sign that may reinforce the sense of a total theatre where the unification of opposites occurs. Through such a process, both the actors and the audience engage in a game as a lived experience, and thus overcome the obstacle of the stage's inherently mimetic nature and the notion of a world divided between the stage and the auditorium. This kind of theatre has its own lucidity and brings to the fore notions that are common in the postmodern stage: the play of dreams, sexuality, drives, or phantasms; intertextuality; intermediality, i.e.: the integration of aesthetic concepts from different media (particularly from the cinema) into a new context; non-linearity; superposition; visuality; bodied space as the site of signs; the transformation principle; poeticized language; the active participation of the audience.

Ludic theory thus provides the principal vocabulary for this study, combined with some notions borrowed from a variety of other disciplines such as semiotics and performance analysis, the psychoanalysis, and philosophy of language, all of which provide useful tools for my analysis of individual plays. As regards the specific ludic theory that I follow here, since there is a great variety of theories related to the play-concept, and in order to narrow my approach, I was initially guided by Mihai I. Spariosu's seminal study *Dionysus Reborn: Play and the Aesthetic Dimension in Modern Philosophical and Scientific Discourse* (1989). In Spariosu's history of play in philosophy and science since the eighteenth century, the concept of play is linked to a Western mentality revolving around a set of rational and pre-rational concepts. It was the pre-rational concept of play that best fitted surrealist theatre, given the outspoken hostility of the Surrealists toward reason. My main approach was then further channeled by Johan Huizinga's well-known study *Homo Ludens: A Study of the Play Elements in Culture* (1938), which stressed the essentially irrational and ritualistic character of the play, in which culture arises and unfolds *in* and *as* play, and which Breton hailed in 1954 as complying with the surrealist beliefs with regard to play. For Huizinga, human play is indeed "irrational" (4) and "always belongs to the sphere of festival and ritual-the sacred sphere" (9). Combining "strict rules with genuine freedom" (22), the world of play belongs to "the world of the savage, the child and the poet" (26), while its quintessentially creative character is intimately related to language. Attributing several key aspects to play, Huizinga defined play as free, disinterested, limited in time and space, orderly, displaying an element of tension, fostering a play-community, and finally, extra-ordinary, in the sense of being distinct from real life.

In addition to Huizinga's work, I also benefited from the insights of several other studies that themselves re-examined *Homo Ludens*, such as the study *Les Jeux et les hommes* (1958), conducted by the ex-Surrealist, Roger Caillois. In this study, Caillois puts forward a new typology of games that tries to correct Huizinga's view of them as essentially competitive or *agon*-based, disregarding entirely the element of chance. In Caillois' view, games should be classified under the following four general categories: *agon* (contest), *alea* (chance), *mimicry* (imitation), and *ilinx* (vertigo). I used his classification in this study, particularly since it incorporated a new dimension that is seminal for the Surrealists, namely chance—best expressed in the notion of the *hasard objectif* (the objective chance), which itself includes both premonitions and striking coincidences. Objective chance is more specifically defined as "the discovery of the natural link existing between personal subjective automatism and universal automatism ... between personal unconscious, collective unconscious, and even cosmic unconscious" (Carrouges 7). Susan Laxton's dissertation, "Paris as Gameboard: Surrealist Ludic Practices" (2004), explored the factor of chance in the ludic activities of surrealist painters, through their experiments with drawing on the basis of the surrealist game "cadavre exquis" [exquisite corpse]: "a self-consciously constructed process for stimulating an 'automatism-effect'" (386).

While many concepts drawn on in Laxton's work, including her article "The Guarantor of Chance", where she concentrates on the "exquisite corpse" surrealist game, were influential to this project, I preferred instead to concentrate on the surrealist game "one-into-another" (defined below), because of its proximity to the ludic model employed here according to which play inhabits two interlocking realities conceived as two communicating vessels to use Breton's terms, provided one is able to retrieve their hidden correspondences. Although it was invented much later than the original effervescence of surrealist theatre, even a posteriori this game exemplifies the main theoretical ludic pillars of the genre. Besides, the surrealist ludic activity was only theorized retrospectively,[11] thanks to the efforts of Emmanuel Garrigues, who compiled the compendium *Les Jeux surréalistes* (*Archives du surréalisme*, no. 5, 1995). The game "one-into-another"[12] was invented by Breton and Benjamin Péret and was published in *Médium* (no. 2, February 1954 and no. 3, May 1954), "as a way of systematizing an important area of Surrealist thought, that of metaphor, analogy and the 'image'" (Gooding 145). It relies upon the idea that any object is "contained" within any other object, once one can isolate some of its—color, structure, or dimensions—that can also apply to the other object. In other words, it refers to the coupling of two terms of reality not normally associated with one another and is intended to signify the possibility of relations existing in the world other than those usually perceived. A different sort of causality is asserted, or at least hinted at, exemplifying the principal surrealist idea of the reconciliation of contradictory forces, as well as the disinterested play of thought. In a sense, in "one-into-another" there is an enigma of sorts in search of its own solution by means of play. As Philippe Gréa puts it, "less famous than the exquisite cadavers, it is based on a particular use of the threaded metaphor and consists in an enigma that has to be cracked by the players" (91). On the basis of interpretive semantics, this scholar demystified the inner logic of this game by foregrounding the semantic foundations of the game and the mechanisms that lead to the discovery of the solution. According to him, "l'un dans l'autre forms what can be called a semic complex" (ibid.), while "a rule of optimality eventually paves the way towards the answer" (ibid.).

Another influential study from which I borrowed the term "ludics" in the sense of the poetics of play and games, is Warren Motte's study *Playtexts: Ludics in Contemporary Literature* (1995), in which he revisits Huizinga's *Homo Ludens* through a critical analysis of its two main revisions, namely, Caillois' *Les Jeux et les homes* (1958) and Jacques Ehrmann's study "Homo Ludens Revisited," included in the special issue of *Yale French Studies*, entitled *Game, Play, Literature* (1968). In this study, Ehrmann offers a model of play as economy, communication, and articulation. Play for him is thus a dynamic economic system characterized by motion and creativity. Embracing this model, rather than Huizinga's or Caillois' play models, Motte developed the concept of literary ludics, according to which every text is the product of a playful activity among the author, the reader, and the text, during which one appropriates language to oneself, simultaneously and playfully constructing an idiolect. Thus, Motte's thesis also bears the mark of Ludwig Wittgenstein's notion of "language-game," as developed in his *Philosophical Investigations*, according to which, as Motte glosses, "each sort of utterance may be thought of as a game, guided by its own set of rules" (13), and that "these games are varied yet bear nonetheless certain mutual resemblances" (ibid.). This "family" resemblance, Motte argues, "can be accounted for by the attitude with which we approach these activities, an attitude that is—in varying degree—ludic in character" (14). By appropriating certain of Ehrmann's and Wittgenstein's ideas, Motte questions idealist formulations of play, and targets the opposition of play and seriousness that lurks behind both play models of Huizinga and Caillois. Warren Motte embraces Wittgenstein's axiom that all game has a "point" (an axiom that appears on page 150 of *Philosophical Investigations*, which Motte quotes on page 15 of *Playtexts*).

Embracing this idea myself, which we retrieve in Huizinga's model uttered as "all play means something" (1), I have embarked on an endeavor similar to Motte's; I attempt a construct of surrealist dramatic ludics in the same way that Motte offers a construct of literary ludics, where every single literary piece he examines may be considered as a playtext in which a variety of diverse ludic strategies is materialized. Likewise, in this book, every single representative play I examine may be considered as a stage game that materializes the "one-into-another" ludic principle. My departure point comes from Breton's text *Nadja* (1928), which is also among the variety of seminal texts examined by Motte, specifically as a terrain in which Breton materializes diverse ludic strategies. Interestingly, *Nadja* does constitute my departure point in this book in one of its specific moments wherein Nadja invites her interlocutor to engage in a game of her own. This being the focal point of my rereading of *Nadja*, it affects this book's organization as follows:

Chapter 1 presents the seminal surrealist game "one-into-another" in *Nadja* and Jean Pierre Palau's infamous play *Les Détraquées* (*The Derouted*), in an effort to formulate André Breton's implicit dramatic theory as it emerges from some of his major writings, in particular from *Nadja*, "Le Discours sur le peu de réalité" ("Discourse on the Paucity of Reality," 1924), and, of course, his manifestoes of Surrealism. What this dramatic theory consists of, how it is related to the concept of play and the surrealist game "one-into-another," in particular, and how this implicit dramatic theory accounts for Breton's controversial attitude toward theatre, constitute the main issues addressed in this chapter. It must be stressed that this chapter goes beyond Orestein Feman's findings in the introductory part of her study *The Theatre of the Marvelous: Surrealism and the Contemporary Stage* (1975), in which she undertakes a similar endeavor. Orenstein Feman attempted to define Breton's dramatic theory through a succinct intra-textual analysis and astutely concluded that "theater could one day become the medium par excellence for surrealist expression" (18). More specifically, this chapter traces the first official implementation of Breton's implicit ludic surrealist dramatic theory on stage. The latter is reconstructed on the basis of a re-reading of *Nadja* that joins two of its moments: Nadja's invitation to play, addressed to the narrator/Breton, and the latter's task to play the performance analyst as a deeply troubled spectator, facing the staging/re-staging of Palau's play *Les Détraquées*. The interweaving of these two moments demonstrates how Breton is taught by Nadja how to play a mimicry game and how he himself is transported by this game to the terrain of the aforementioned spectacle which he recalls. He engages thus in a voluntary activity that totally absorbs him in a quasi-ritualistic manner: in the process he becomes a performance analyst/ spectator guided by desire and is situated at the interface of two realities: one, in which he challenges his memory, and another, in which he re-experiences the feelings that troubled him in front of the spectacle of *Les Détraquées*. This absorption was made possible due to the major force of desire.

A ludic theory that challenges the spectator in this way was paradoxically first implemented on stage thanks to the efforts of two ex-members of Surrealism. I refer to the staging of Vitrac's *The Mysteries of Love: A Surrealist Drama* (1924) under Antonin Artaud's direction in the Théâtre Alfred Jarry in 1927—the subject of my second chapter. The chapter also showcases how Breton's ludic dramatic theory reached its peak in the Greek playwright Nanos Valaoritis's self-conscious experimentation with surrealist games after joining the surrealist group in its latest phase, specifically in his play *The Nightfall Hotel* (1957), modeled after Vitrac's *The Mysteries of Love*. Through a comparative analysis of these two thematically similar plays that center around "mad love," this chapter demonstrates how both these plays are structured after Breton's concept of the surrealist dialogue-game and how they bring the matter of language into play even when applied to the stage, thus remaining faithful to the basic tenets of Surrealism. To render my thesis even more plausible, these plays are examined through the lens of Breton's surrealist credo, as well as in light of some seminal theoretical texts, signed by both Vitrac and Artaud and published during the period 1927–30, heavily influenced by Breton's ideas. I refer, in particular, to the seminal text "Le Théâtre Alfred Jarry et l'hostilité publique" ("The Alfred Jarry Theatre and Public Hostility") and some excerpts from Valaoritis's books, written in Greek, Για μια θεωρία της Γραφής (*For a Theory of Writing*) (1990) and Για μια θεωρία της Γραφής Β (*For a Theory of Writing B*) (2006) that illustrate the development of the reception of Breton's ludic ideas.

Chapter 3 departs from the idea that ludic activities, in many surrealist plays, are guided by rules, and argues that surrealist theatre ingeniously places the inherent logic of games into the service of the irrational, in order to become a tool of subversion of the social order. More precisely, the rule-bound ludic activity of the Surrealists led to the exploration of the unconscious and of chance, to the point where genuine freedom meets with reason-bound rules. In fact, the Surrealists express their desire to disassociate reason from its common conception as the opposite of nonsense and try to treat it as a communicative vessel with nonsense. Nonsense then becomes meaningful as an attempt to reorganize language according to the rules of play. Take, for instance, the so-called "one-into-another" game, which is the culmination of surrealist ludic activity. Anna Balakian describes this game, which explores the mechanism of analogy, as follows: "[it is] the power of seeing in each object two or an infinite quantity of others, the range and number dependent on the power of desire and obsession" (quoted in Orenstein Feman 23). This basic rule functions as a guarantor of freeing the players' imagination to the point that it supports the irrational, since it encourages improvisation and free association. Such a freedom of imagination is characteristic of children's behavior. In fact, as Freud points out, "(the child) finds enjoyment in the attraction of what is forbidden by reason. He now uses games in order to withdraw from the pressure of critical reason" (125–6). Huizinga appeals to the same concept when he states, "really to play, a man must play as a child" (quoted in Motte 12). It thus became necessary to expand the use of surrealist games to that of children's games in this chapter, particularly since they are also widely incorporated in surrealist theatrical output. This chapter offers a comparative reading of three plays that showcase how their diverse ludic strategies become tools of social disruptiveness: Vitrac's play *Victor ou les enfants au pouvoir* (*Victor or Children in Power*, 1928) and its loose adaptation by Valaoritis, entitled *Henriette où est-elle passée?* (*Henriette, Where Did She Go?* 1957), as well as Valaoritis's *Les Tables rondes* (*The Round Tables*, 1957). All these plays feature children as their protagonists, who play with language and children's games in an extremely intelligent manner that turns the world of adults upside down. Furthermore, taking the ludic strategies employed in his model (*Victor or Children in Power*) a step further, Valaoritis, in his play, *The Round Tables*, plays with language's patent nonsense and creates something new from it. While Vitrac uses games as a means of revealing the problem of human expression, Valaoritis uses them as an end in itself, to show that a theatrical work conceived as a game is far more interesting than any merely mimetic play.

Chapter 4 takes its cue from Louis Aragon's idea that the theatrical work of postmodern artist Robert Wilson constitutes the fulfillment of Surrealism. From here, it seeks to identify the affinity of Wilson's work with Surrealism on the basis of the pioneering gamut of ludic strategies that he uses on stage. This chapter, through a comparative approach, offers representative examples of Wilson's stage games from several of his theatrical works, particularly from *Le Regard du sourd* (*Deafman Glance*, 1967), the seeds of which can be traced back to Antonin Artaud's early experiment *Le Jet de sang* (*The Spurt of Blood*, 1927). Sharing a similar process in their respective attempts to reinvent the language of the stage, both men deal with the action on stage as an ongoing, thrilling game, in which both actors and audience are wholeheartedly engaged as players, and during which language is transformed into images, thus placing at the foreground a visual rather than a verbal logic. If the surrealist mode of playing with images as exemplified in Artaud's *The Jet of Blood* resembles improvisation, Wilson's play with language resembles a more sophisticated, rule-bound game, despite its intended, careful advanced planning. In an effort to better illustrate Artaud's conceptualization of the stage in his *Jet de sang*, I look at one of its multiple contemporary stagings that seems to do justice to it in all respects. I refer to its staging at Wickham Studio Theatre in Bristol, UK, under the direction of Günter Berghaus that took place February 14–17, 1996. The accompanying pictures of this performance will, I hope, help the reader visualize that materialization of Artaud's surrealist stage ludics.

The final chapter focuses on another seminal American playwright, Megan Terry, whose theatrical work, both in theme and style, is driven by the ludic principle, particularly in her so-called transformation plays that best express her ties to surrealist theatre. In the span of a long and successful career as a playwright and stage director, Terry never stopped experimenting with the concepts of play and games both on the level of stage language and that of the actors' body movements in an ultimate attempt to interrogate the function of the ever-elusive "self" within the framework of a feminist agenda. Focusing on four of Terry's transformation plays—*Calm Down Mother: A Transformation for Three Women* (1965), *Keep Tightly Closed in a Cool Dry Place* (1966), *Comings and Goings: A Theater Game* (1966), and *Objective Love* (1980)—this last chapter offers a demonstration of post-surrealist ludic stage techniques primarily operating on the level of the actors' bodies, and the way these techniques challenge the notion of reality, the nature of identity of the character, and the nature of the relationship between the stage and auditorium.

In conclusion, in this book, I focus exclusively on the ludic strategies employed in surrealist theatre and in plays that bear clear affinities with Surrealism. Considering it as essentially ludic and transformational, surrealist theatre has a life of its own and is separate from experimental and avant-garde theatre.

What distinguishes it from the latter is its focus on the aesthetic category of the "marvelous" in the context of the developmental stages of surrealist games, animated by the same spirit that infuses children's games. As such, surrealist theatre has greatly intruded upon and infused the contemporary stage, bringing with it the leader of Surrealism to be once more ahead of his time in his re-imagining of the stage for future generations.

Notes

1   For more details on this issue, see Auslander, "Surrealism in the Theatre."

2   For more details, see Cohn, "Surrealism and Today's French Theatre."

3   This exhibition lasted from February 26 to March 27, 1966.

4   For a more detailed discussion of this issue, see Béhar, *Étude*, 30.

5   Here are some representative ones: *The Oxford Companion to the Theatre*, Patrice Pavis's *Dictionnaire du théâtre* and Alfred Simon's *Dictionnaire du théâtre français contemporain*.

6   The following three articles were also particularly influential to the present study: Levitt, "Roger Vitrac and the Drama of Surrealism," Bermel, "Artaud as Playwright," and Metzidakis, "L'Apothéose de l'erreur."

7   See, Schuster, "Le Quatrième chant."

8   I use the term "postmodern" in Ihab Hassan's sense, that is, as a new aesthetic formation, characterized by the openness of elements such as "'play', 'chance', 'dispersal', 'combination', 'difference', and 'desire'" against the closure and rigid organization of elements linked with modernism such as, among others, "'form', 'hierarchy', 'mastery' and 'determinacy.'" See Malpas, *The Postmodern*.

9   The word "ludic," more common in French than English, is associated with the activity of playing games. It comes from the Latin word *ludus*. Johan Huizinga comments, with regard to *ludus*: "In remarkable contrast to Greek with its changing and heterogeneous terms for the play-function, Latin has really only one word to cover the whole field of play: *ludus*, from *ludere*, of which *ludus* is a direct derivative. We should observe that *jocus*, *jocari* in the special sense of joking and jesting does not mean play proper in classical Latin. Though *ludere* may be used for the leaping of fishes, the fluttering of birds and the splashing of water, its etymology does not appear to lie in the sphere of rapid movement, flashing, etc., but in that of non-seriousness, and particularly of 'semblance' or 'deception.' *Ludus* covers children's games, recreation, contests, liturgical and theatrical representations, and games of chance. In the expression *lares ludentes* it means 'dancing'" (35).

10   Although the first surrealist game, called "Liquidation" and published in *Littérature* in March 1921, was based on Breton's concept of dialogue as two simultaneous monologues, the Surrealists decided only in March 1928 to name their games "dialogues." Both the rules and the texts they produced were published under the title "Dialogue in 1928" in *La Révolution surréaliste* of the same year. They published other games in subsequent issues until September 1962 and collected them in a volume edited by Emmanuel Garrigues in 1995. In addition to the "Dialogue in 1928" the following forms of this game appeared in various journals: "The Dialogue in 1929" (*Varietés*, June 1929) and "The Dialogue in 1934" (*Documents*, spec. issue, June 1934). These were published by Emmanuel Garrigues along with "The Dialogue

in 1952–1954" and "The Game of Syllogisms." In the "dialogue" the participants were seated around a table without looking at each other, and wrote questions and responses on a circulating piece of paper. Their various sentences were then assembled and the result was always funny and puzzling. A version of this game is the famous "cadavre exquis" (exquisite corpse).

11   See Jean Paul Morel's relevant remark: "these fixed theoretical elements were, besides, established in their majority retrospectively and a posteriori." This information was diffused by the electronic list Melusine through which Jean-Paul Morel's French original version of his article "Les Jeux surréalistes" appeared and which would be published in Portuguese in the collective volume *O Surrealismo* (2004).

12   Breton explains the creation of this game in "Perspective cavalière" (1970): "En quête d'un exemple pour faire valoir ce que je défendais, j'en vins à dire que le lion pouvait être aisément décrit à partir de l'allumette que je m'apprêtais à frotter. Il m'apparut en effet, sur-le-champ, que la flamme en puissance dans l'allumette 'donnerait' en pareil cas la crinière et qu'il suffirait, à partir de là, de très peu de mots tendant à différencier, à particulariser l'allumette pour mettre le lion sur pieds. Le lion est dans l'allumette, de même que l'allumette est dans le lion. [In search of an example to assert what I defended, I came to say that the lion could be easily described from the match that I was going to rub. It appeared to me indeed, over-the-camp, that the flame in power in the match 'would give' in a similar case the mane and that it would suffice from that moment onwards from very few words tending to differentiate to specify the match in order to put the lion on foot. The lion is in the match in the same way that the match is in the lion.] (Breton, 1970, p. 53)" (quoted in Gréa).

1

The surrealist game "one into another" in *Nadja* and *Les Détraquées*: Reconstructing André Breton's ludic dramatic theory

Nous demeurons quelque temps silencieux, puis elle me tutoie brusquement: "Un jeu: dis quelque chose. Ferme les yeux et dis quelque chose. N'importe, un chiffre, un prénom. Comme ceci (elle ferme les yeux): Deux, deux quoi? Deux femmes. Comment sont ces femmes? En noir. Où se trouvent-elles? Dans un parc ... Et puis, que font-elles? Allons, c'est si facile, pourquoi ne veux-tu pas jouer? Eh, bien, moi, c'est ainsi que je me parle quand je suis seule, que je me raconte toutes sortes d'histoires. Et pas seulement des vaines histoires: c'est même entièrement de cette façon que je vis."* ...

*Ne touche-t-on pas là au terme extrême de l'aspiration surréaliste, à sa plus forte idée-limite? (André Breton, *Nadja* in *OC1* 690).

[We remain silent for a while, then she suddenly addresses me using tu: "A game: say something. Close your eyes and say something. Anything, a number, a name. Like this (she closes her eyes): Two, two what? Two women. What do they look like? Wearing black. Where are they? In a park ... And then, what are they doing? Try it, it's so easy, why don't you want to play? You know, that's how I talk to myself when I'm alone, I tell myself all kinds of stories. And not only just silly stories: actually, I live this way altogether."* ...

*Does this not approach the extreme limit of the surrealist aspiration, its furthest determinant? (Howard 74).][1]

Introduction

The above quotation, depicting a young female protagonist named Nadja playing—and explaining—a spontaneous game with words, will be the focus of this chapter. The asterisked footnote that accompanies the passage raises it to a significant moment among the myriad snapshots that comprise André Breton's *Nadja*. First published in 1928 and then again in the 1963 Gallimard edition, this *sui generis* text is like a ludic cryptogram, made up of images, anecdotes, photographs, and text, arranged in a kind of constellation that invites the reader to interpret along with its narrator/author the signs of the marvelous that intrude in his daily life. Likewise, this chapter undertakes a similar act of interpretation, in an effort to elucidate the above-mentioned footnote's rather rhetorical question; the question endows Nadja's confession about practicing and experiencing her game as a way of living with the aura of the extreme limit of the surrealist aspiration.[2]

In an attempt to grasp what is at stake in this footnote, it is necessary to make a detailed examination of the main parameters involved in the female protagonist's game, and discuss some of the main surrealist tenets that this game apparently touches upon. By undertaking such an endeavor, it is my hope that the unexpected revelatory power of Nadja's game for her interlocutor will be equally revelatory for our understanding of Breton's enigmatic attitude toward the theatre. Such a detailed examination of Nadja's game will not only shed light on the importance granted by the narrator/author to the *play* itself, but ultimately mark the starting point for a reconstruction of the implicit in this dramatic theory of the leader of Surrealism. In other words, I examine Nadja's game of questions and answers closely in the hope of grasping Breton's ludic dramatic theory, which is never explicitly stated yet fully informs his work.

This game, I argue, may be seen as a model-stage that shows Nadja playing/ acting according to the rules that Breton lays out in his prolific writings. Nadja's play reflects Breton's major ideas about language and its surrealist use, along with its relation to the images and the position of the self before "surreality," as he had expressed them in 1924 in the *Manifesto of Surrealism*, and in the "Introduction au discours sur le peu de réalité" ("Introduction to the Paucity of Reality.") Both texts, along with *Nadja*, are seminal to our attempt to reconstruct Breton's implicit ludic dramatic theory. For Nadja's game constitutes a rudimentary ludic/ dramatic moment, in which notions such as play and game, dream, theatre and spectatorship, self-analysis and subjectivity are enigmatically interconnected. In this schema, concatenate circles encapsulate the fundamental surrealist *modus vivendi*, namely, that of the *coincidentia oppositorum*.

This chapter thus sets out to lay bare all the possible hidden layers of Nadja's game that unfolded in a taxi, on the second day after her acquaintance with the narrator/author of *Nadja* (October 5, 1926). This game started as a spontaneous language game, and soon went on to take on the form of mimicry, and ultimately became an associative type of play that led the parties involved to a transformational experience. This seemingly "simple" moment invites a reading that brings forth all the main surrealist tenets as formulated by Breton himself in his major theoretical writings, besides *Nadja*, all of which have the potential to be applied to the stage as a playground that brings together two realms of reality. To better grasp all these layers, we must meticulously analyze the above excerpt and unfold its multifarious connections step by step. To this end, next to ludic theory in general, and some of the tools of psychoanalysis (including the well-known Lacanian notions of the *imaginary* and the *mirror stage*), a brief look at Breton's position towards the theatre in relation to his major beliefs about the use of language and the image is necessary.

Revisiting André Breton's scattered remarks on the theatre and the stage

It is noteworthy that even before launching himself as the author of the *Manifesto of Surrealism* in 1924, André Breton had already appeared in the public sphere as both a playwright and an actor. I refer to his Dadaist experiments *S'il vous plaît* (*If You Please*, 1920) and *Vous m'oublierez* (*You Will Forget Me*, 1920)— both included in the Gallimard edition of his famous *Magnetic Fields*—written in collaboration with Philippe Soupault by means of automatic writing. These were short skits in which he himself performed with his friends during the Dada evening at the Théâtre de l'Œuvre on March 27, 1920, and which, despite their humor, he soon discarded as being filled with "an infantile skepticism" (*OC1* 1176).[3] *S'il vous plaît*, according to Breton, treats the theme of the seduction game in four forms in each one of its four acts: artistic, commercial, amorous, and theatrical (*OC1* 1175). *You Will Forget Me*, which deals with "the conflict of the ideas of conservation and reproduction" (ibid.) features characters-objects: specifically, an umbrella, a gown, and a sewing machine placed next to an unknown person. Breton's *Poisson soluble* (*Soluble Fish*), published along with the *Manifesto of Surrealism* (1924), is also the outcome of automatic writing. *Soluble Fish* contains one of the most revealing theatrical scenes. Two women and two men act as Lucie, Helen, Mark the poet, and Satan in a stage setup consisting of a giant gyroscope that revolves around its vertical axis, with one point resting on the edge of a glass. The character dialogues challenge logical coherence within a normal syntax. The value of these dialogues lies in the extraordinary poetic images they create, while Satan's final words prefigure a new form of theatre: "Ladies and gentlemen, I am the author of the play that we have just had the honor of performing for you. The clockwork is of little importance, *the symbols in this new form of theater being no more than a promise*" (*Manifestoes*, Seaver and Lane 100; italics mine). His later work, *Amour fou* (*Mad Love*, 1937), as well as many of his poems, also abound in references to the stage and theatrical magic. In short, while Breton's attitude toward the stage remains quite controversial, it is as if he played a game with constantly changing rules. At least, as Gloria Orenstein Feman states, "a superficial perusal of his works would indicate a negativism toward theatre—or at best an indifference to it as an art form. This attitude turned to outright hostility when it came to Breton's clash with Artaud over the theatre in Alfred Jarry's presentation of the *Dream Play* by Strindberg" (17–18), as we will see in more detail in the next chapter.[4] However, incidents such as Breton's clash with Artaud should not be taken to account definitively for Breton's negativism towards theatre; for this negativism might simply be the result of his dissatisfaction with the practice of theatre up to his time: it was bound to the representational and illusionistic principle, which was incompatible with the absolute freedom that he sought everywhere. Besides, for him, any involvement with professional theatre meant inexcusable compromises, such as the one that forced the leaders of the Théâtre Alfred Jarry, Antonin Artaud and Roger Vitrac, to yield to "unworthy commercial instincts, to the extent of wanting to produce surrealist plays in the framework of the professional theatre" (Esslin, *Antonin Artaud* 331). Thus, one must truly scrutinize Breton's prolific writings to come to a conclusion with regard to his debated anti-theatricality. For, as Orenstein Feman stresses,

> [a] careful exploration of Breton's writings reveals that there is an intimate linkage in his mind between surrealism and theatrical form. This subterranean analogy, which likens the dream or the inner life of the psyche to the theater, is a recurrent underlying motif, suggesting the interpretation that theater could one day become the medium par excellence for surrealist expression, for it is one art form in which imagination can become reality and where *I* can become an *other* (18).

Along the same lines, I believe that Breton envisioned an idealized version of theatre, which prevented him from giving it its full potential and resulted in a constant deferral of its materialization to the future. Keeping this idealized version at the back of his thoughts, he held that new form of theatre perpetually unrealized or, to quote his own words, he kept it as "a promise of the future." Hence his infamous claim in *Nadja*, for instance, that the only play written for the stage worthy of recollection was Pierre Palau's *Les Détraquées*, performed by Le Théâtre des Deux Masques in February 1921. A claim that denies an entire theatrical tradition in this way is clearly anti-theatrical, particularly given the fact that the quality of Palau's play has been questioned, as we will discuss in detail shortly. Unsurprisingly, this challenging statement has prompted several different interpretations among scholars of surrealist theatre.

Henri Béhar, first of all, the scholar who has most devoted his life to the study of surrealist theatre, wrote a provocative article, entitled "The Passionate Attraction: André Breton and the Theatre." He owes the title of his article to the following note, written by Breton in *Nadja*, with regard to the actress Blanche Derval, who played one of the two female protagonists in Palau's *Les Détraquées* and whom he greatly admired:

> Qu'ai-je voulu dire? Que j'aurais dû l'approcher, à tout prix tenter de me dévoiler la femme réelle qu'elle était. Pour cela, il m'eût fallu surmonter certaine prévention contre les comédiennes, qu'entretenait le souvenir de Vigny, de Nerval. Je m'accuse là d'avoir failli à l'attraction passionnelle (*OC1* 673).

> [What did I want to say? That I should have approached her, that at every price I should have attempted to reveal the real woman she was; to do this, I ought to have overcome certain reservations against actresses who maintained the spirit of Vigny, of Nerval. Here I reproach myself for having failed to yield to this passionate attraction.]

In the expression "passionate attraction," used by Breton about the actress Blanche Derval, Henri Béhar saw Breton's attitude toward the theatre:[5]

> I very willingly see it as the ambivalent sign of his attitude toward theatre. On the one hand, he expects from it a revelation, or at least a great find ...

> ... But, on the other hand, there is the irrevocable condemnation found in "Introduction au discours sur le peu de réalité" of the two masks .... The theatrical game is impossible from both sides ("Passionate Attraction" 18).

What Béhar had traced as an obstacle in "Introduction au discours sur le peu de réalité" was Breton's overall reaction against the imitative principle of the theatre. More precisely, this was the moment when Breton imagined donning a suit of armor, in order to discover some of the consciousness of a fourteenth-century man. In his failure to do so, he exclaims:

> Ô théâtre éternel, tu exiges que non seulement pour jouer le rôle d'un autre, mais encore pour dicter ce rôle, nous nous masquions à sa ressemblance, que la glace devant laquelle nous posons nous renvoie de nous une image étrangère. L'imagination a tous les pouvoirs, sauf celui de nous identifier en dépit de notre apparence à un personnage autre que nous-même (*OC2* 266).

> [Oh eternal theatre, you require, not only in order to play the role of another, but even in order to suggest this role, that we disguise ourselves with its likeness, that the mirror before which we pose returns us to a foreign image of ourselves. The imagination has every power except that of identifying ourselves, despite our appearance, to a character other than ourselves (Muller and Richardson 317).]

In these words Breton explicitly confronts the notion of theatre as mimesis, highlighting its permanent artificiality: an artificiality which is manifest in the persistent discrepancy between the self and its impersonations on stage. Employing the familiar mirror metaphor—a favorite among the Surrealists—he faults theatre for a lack of genuineness and, thus, of truthfulness and effectiveness. Breton could not, of course, anticipate the path-breaking theories about the formation of the self that Jacques Lacan (despite Breton's impact on him), would later develop.

Surrealism's influence on Lacan is well documented; as Stamos Metzidakis states, Lacan, who was to provide structuralism with a radically new language and a rewriting of the sign, "was largely inspired by the automatic writing to which André Breton held all his life" ("Breton's Structuralism" 38). Also, the same scholar continues, Breton was interested in "the [same] eternal quest for, and renewal of, desire as Lacan"; indeed, there are striking similarities between Lacan and early Surrealism with regard to the "probing of the id" and the "stretching of the limits of the ego" (ibid. 39). Yet, in his seminal study, "The Mirror Stage as Formative of the Function of the 'I' as Revealed in Psychoanalytic Experience" (1949), which, interestingly, refers to Breton's "Introduction au discours sur le peu de réalité,"[6] and which informs my own project, Lacan maintains his distance from Breton. He argues for the child's "méconnaissance" (miscognition, misconstruction of the self) in front of the mirror—in the sense of a false image of wholeness—as a prerequisite for knowledge. This, I believe, could amply apply to surrealist theatre, for it is a theatre of *imagos* that seeks to transform both its actors and spectators through identification. In Lacanian terms, identification is "the transformation that takes place in the subject when he assumes an image—whose predestination to this phase-effect is sufficiently indicated by the use, in analytic theory, of the ancient term *imago*" (Sheridan 2).

Being unaware of the seminal role that the notion of "méconnaissance" plays for the infant in front of the mirror, and of the possible application of this concept to the theatre in general, Breton continued his attack against theatre. In his view, theatre unacceptably calls for such a misconstruction of the actor's self, since the actor has to assume the role of the "other." Thus, Breton closes his "Introduction au discours sur le peu de réalité" with a more categorical declaration-confession against disguise: "Je n'aime pas qu'on tergiverse ni qu'on se cache" (*OC2* 266) [I don't like either procrastinating or hiding]. Breton's denial of *mimesis*, which is a prerequisite for the stage, poses a great impediment in our effort to reconstruct Breton's dramatic theory, as Béhar also acknowledges. However, as this chapter will demonstrate, this obstacle is not insurmountable. Rather, it may be seen as a necessary precondition for establishing a more solid basis for our endeavor. The denial of representation, as exemplified in the actor's false identification with the image of the "other," may not necessarily mean negation of the theatre; rather, it may mean the beginning of a transformation, a new conception of this medium, one that refers to a would-be-non-mimetic theatre. After all, we must keep in mind that Breton embraced the image of the "demain joueur,"[7] in the sense of "the player of tomorrow." In this case, emphasis is placed on the future as capable of playing with its past, allowing for reconsideration and constant reevaluation. One has only to recall the following words from the *Second Manifesto of Surrealism* (1930):

> Il est normal que le surréalisme se manifeste au milieu et peut-être au prix d'une suite ininterrompue de défaillences, de zigzags et de défections qui exigent à tout instant la remise en question de ses données originelles, c'est-à-dire le rappel au principe initial de son activité joint à l'interrogation du demain joueur qui veut que les cœurs "éprennent" et se déprennent (*OC1* 801).

> [It is normal for Surrealism to manifest itself at the center and perhaps at the cost of an uninterrupted series of faints, zigzags and defections that require at any moment questioning its original data, that is to say, recall the initial principle of its activity attached to the interrogation of tomorrow's player, according to which the hearts "are infatuated" and then cease to be infatuated.]

This statement made by Breton appears here like a safety valve for our endeavor; we can reconsider his work on the basis of the transformative principle of "the player of tomorrow" which determines Surrealism's position at every moment, including the disposition of Surrealism toward theatre. It is interesting to notice here how this ludic principle betrays Breton's aspiration to originality, as Metzidakis has defined the latter term, as "a 'backwards' or inward-looking model of the concept [of originality]" (*Difference Unbound* 150). If, for Surrealism, it is mandatory to question their original tenets [la remise en question de ses données *originelles*]—an action informed by the ludic principle of change—we can assume that Breton's own contradictory views on the theatre simply reflect a deeper, problematic issue on the question of theatre; one that derives from his desire to achieve "a singular *presentation* of a different reality, a more holistic, anterior existence" (ibid. 151). Once Breton's dramatic theory is reconstructed in light of such an issue, it will then be possible to offer a clearer explanation for his overall neglect of theatre, and thus to provide a better account of the so-called "failure" of surrealist theatre.

Another scholar who has focused on the intimate link between the ludic principle and theatricality in Breton's work is Warren Motte. In his study *Playtexts: Ludics in Contemporary Literature* (1995), he treats *Nadja*, among other texts, as a "playtext," in the sense of being "animated by a strong ludic spirit" (27). Motte argues that this anti-literary narrative is the outcome of the author's playful experimentation with a variety of literary ludic strategies, including make-believe theatrical techniques, to the point that a conflation arises between the words "ludic" and "theatre":[8]

> In the theater, after all, everything is play. Nadja herself is intimately and explicitly associated with the theater. She is compared to the actress Derval (64), even to the point of physical resemblance; she chose her own name, as an actress chooses her stage name (66); she lives "somewhere near the Théâtre des Arts" (94). Before she actually appears in the text, Breton alludes to her imminent "entrée en scène" (rev. ed. 69) (46).

He suggests, in this manner, that Nadja will be a player on the textual stage (ibid.). Breton himself, Motte continues, "speaks of the scenes" of Nadja's past life and denotes certain of her actions as "même jeu" [same game], a locution that closely resembles the stage directions according to which Nadja takes on various fictional poses (ibid.). In short, Motte concludes, "Nadja *plays* constantly; that is, she acts and she plays, in both senses of these two words. This playful spirit is clearly part of her attraction to Breton, part of the seduction she exercises upon him: 'Try it, it's so easy, why don't you want to play?'" (ibid.). This peculiar linguistic game of Nadja's, that transforms her at once to a performer/auditor and takes her to another reality, attracts Breton to the point that he is finally involved in the game, despite his initial reluctance. As Motte argues, Breton plays the game of transforming Nadja to *Nadja*: "Breton's game finally, is one of expropriation and domestication, and its stake is the authoritative circumscription of *convulsive* beauty within the limits of a text" (47).[9] Also, in Marguerite Bonnet's view, thanks to its "subtle play of the blanks," among other games, *Nadja* becomes something more than a book: "le lieu d'une mutation décisive du livre, où se modifie son rapport avec la vie" (*OC1* 1502) [(It is) the place of a decisive mutation for the book where its rapport with life is modified].

The peculiar fusion of play and life in *Nadja* reflects Breton's fascination with Nadja, who also constantly fuses life and play. This fusion—or rather *confusion*, in Nadja's case, due to her insanity, which nevertheless for Breton and the Surrealists is seen "as the extreme point of genius" (Wylie 100)—offers the key to taking Motte's thesis a step further and starting the reconstruction of Breton's dramatic theory. While Motte saw in *Nadja* a displacement of sexuality into textuality, this study sees Breton's vision for the theatre in Nadja's game, a vision that started as a fascinating game, only to be abandoned, like Nadja herself, after she has served "as a catalyst in Breton's discovery of self" (ibid.).[10] This abandonment was due to the unattainability of the rules for one of its players, one who became a game-spoiler, namely, the narrator/Breton himself. In effect, I see Nadja's game as a "free play" *par excellence* in the realm of language, which encapsulates Breton's overall dramatic theory. In other words, I view Nadja's game as an early actualization of Breton's beliefs regarding language and the game's rapport with images and the self within "surreality." In the following pages, I proceed with a close reading of Nadja's game, in order to test it by means of both intratextual and intertextual references; but first, I will take a closer look at Nadja's overall ludic tone.

The overall ludic tone of *Nadja*

Ever elusive, *Nadja* has never ceased to raise controversy among its critics. Michel Beaujour's seminal article, "Qu'est-ce que *Nadja*?" ("What is *Nadja*?"), offers an appealing viewpoint: *Nadja* is an anti-novel that submits itself to the "jeux du désœuvrement, de l'errance et du hasard" (780) [the games of idleness, of wandering and of chance]. Furthermore, Beaujour suggests that we see *Nadja* "comme un jeu de cartes que l'on peut battre et déployer en un nombre de réussites, comme un parcours au long duquel ses pas le conduisent maintes fois, et toujours différent …" [like a game of cards that we can shuffle and unfold in a number of successes, like a trajectory whose steps guide it many times, and always different …]. This approach to *Nadja*, as both the author's and the reader's playful trajectory, is indeed able to bring forth the "marvelous" of one's daily life.

Whether *Nadja* was written as a treatise on the "marvelous," or as the first prose elaboration of the theory of the "marvelous" that Breton presented in his *Manifesto of Surrealism* (1924) (Burke 41), one thing remains undeniable: this is a preeminently autobiographical text,[11] at least in Philippe Lejeune's sense of the term. In Lejeune's view, autobiography is defined as a "[r]etrospective narrative written by a real person concerning his own existence, where the focus is his individual life, in particular the story of his personality" (4). Thus, in *Nadja*, Breton focuses on his individual life after experiencing a challenging sequence of strange incidents, inexplicable coincidences, and unexpected occurrences, among which is his decisive encounter with an enigmatic young female figure named Nadja; dwelling in the borders between insanity and reality, she wholly captivates the narrator, Breton, who names his peculiar, jointly verbal and visual narrative after her. He is strangely attracted to this inspiring, Sphinx-like creature, an incarnation of the Celtic mythic figure of Melusina,[12] who "represents the union of opposites, and hence the reconciliation of the world of desire with that of reality" (Matthews, *Theatre* 8), and he is fascinated by "the sense of the marvelous" that this unique creature is able "to release in him" (ibid. 9)—an experience that forces him to play a part in Nadja's game and thus, ultimately, to undergo a transformational experience in the sense of a reexamination of his self. It is no wonder, then, that *Nadja* opens with the existential query: "Who am I?" which could also be translated as "Whom am I following?" making still more explicit the narrator's self-alienation and the feeling he has that he is haunted by another self, or rather that he is haunting someone else. This idea of the "one" inhabiting the "other" and vice versa (and, in consequence, the idea of an actor assuming both the subject and the object) is fundamental in *Nadja*. It is exactly this concept of "one into another" that Nadja's game so boldly and successfully stages, thus making Breton the narrator/author include it in his daily magic and raise it to the level of the "idea-limit" or "further determinant" (in Howard's translation), a seminal point which will be soon revisited. It is also interesting to note that this game remains unaltered between the first edition of *Nadja* in 1928 and its 1963 Gallimard edition, bearing proof of this moment's value for the narrator/author of this text.

This narrative "pris sur le vif" [taken alive],[13] which amply uses ludic strategies by enlisting the miscellaneous aleatory encounters in the narrator's life, also leaves room for Nadja's free play with words. This free wordplay seals Nadja's second encounter with the narrator/author on October 5, 1926, and, more importantly, is granted a special significance thanks to the author's footnote: "Ne touche-t-on pas là au terme extrême de l'aspiration surréaliste, à sa plus forte *idée-limite*?" (*OC1* 690) [Does this not approach the extreme limit of the surrealist aspiration, its *furthest determinant*? (Howard 74)]. Thanks to this footnote in this peculiar narrative, the voice of the narrator can be differentiated from that of the author. More specifically, due to the interval that separates the actual time of the narrated events and the time of their narration, one could argue that the two voices correspond to two different personas of the same person, distinct, yet inextricably connected, affecting each other like two communicating vessels. These two personas are those of the player and the narrator/author, respectively, another aspect of the ludic strategies that Breton applies in *Nadja*. Another playful element to notice here is the way in which Breton blurs the boundaries between Nadja's voice and his voice. In an attempt to recapture a moment of the past, the narrator gives voice to Nadja, quoting her in her invitation to him to play. Then he comments on that moment, by expressing a value judgment, summarized in the content of the footnote. This fascinating unification of voices in the vivid narrative present tense is the result of the retelling of an event that fuses the barriers between dialogue and monologue—another hybrid form that Breton cherished and practiced since his famous *Les Champs magnétiques* (*Magnetic Fields*, 1919).[14]

Let us return now to the "idea-limit" that appears in Breton's footnote and notice first the demonstrative pronoun *this*—in the French text, it is "là," meaning "there"—which refers to Nadja's fusion of *playing* her word game while also *performing* it, and *experiencing* it as reality on a repeated basis. This fusion of Nadja's may constitute, according to *Nadja*'s author, the ultimate surrealist aspiration, its "idea-limit" or "further determinant," in the sense of fusing the imaginary with reality. It is Breton's rhetorical question in the footnote, which approximates with Surrealism's "idée-limite" Nadja's vivid playing/acting experienced as reality, that constitutes this chapter's point of departure. Detecting a tangible version of Breton's lifelong quest for "surreality" in Nadja's fusion of a word game with acting/living, both as an actress and as a listener/viewer, this chapter explores the implicit theatrical elements in Nadja's game in light of André Breton's overall surrealist beliefs, and primarily the so-called notion of surreality, better clarified two years after *Nadja* in the *Second Manifesto of Surrealism* (1930). Here is Breton's famous definition of "surreality":

> Tout porte à croire qu'il existe un certain point de l'esprit d'où la vie et la mort, le réel et l'imaginaire, le passé et le futur, le communicable et l'incommunicable, le haut et le bas cessent d'être perçus contradictoirement. Or, c'est en vain qu'on chercherait à l'activité surréaliste un autre mobile que l'espoir de détermination de ce point (*OC1* 781).

> [Everything tends to make us believe that there exists a certain point of the mind at which life and death, real and imagined past and future, the communicable and the incommunicable, high and low cease to be perceived as contradictions. Now, search as one may one will never find any other motivating force in the activities of the Surrealists than the hope of finding and fixing this point (*Manifestoes of Surrealism*, Seaver and Lane 123–4).][15]

In other words, Nadja's seemingly simple game that relies on the evocative power of language, like a predecessor of the famous surrealist game "exquisite corpse," reveals Breton's desire for a more profound unity—the point at which reality fuses with the imaginary—and illustrates his own notion of theatricality. The fusion that was a fervent hope for the Surrealists is a "given" for Nadja, manifested in her natural ability to blur the imaginary with the real, thus almost effortlessly reaching Surrealism's "idée-limite" or "sublime point," as Mary Ann Caws defines it:

> [S]urrealism's "sublime point" is convergence actualized, the meeting place of opposite categories, whereas one of its privileged games and several of its privileged images are based upon the notions of flux and crossing-over, of substances and sentiments and perceptions merging into others, of the imaginary mixing with the real (xiiv–xiv).

Nadja's game is a privileged one, based on the notions of flux and crossing-over, while her effortless achievement of this mixing of opposites is undeniably what attracts Breton to her and it. This seemingly simple game, composed of fragmentary questions and answers, bears interesting analogies with the famous, collective surrealist game "exquisite corpse,"[16] while it is also a harbinger of the "one into another"[17] surrealist game that made its appearance later on, and which we will revisit below. The "exquisite corpse" was a collective surrealist game that took its name from its first question-answer—le cadavre-exquis-boira-le-vin-nouveau [the exquisite-corpse-will-drink-the new-wine]—and was officially introduced in issue 4 of *Le Surréalisme au service de la Révolution* on December 19, 1931, although the Surrealists had already practiced it in the form of the game of the "small pieces of paper." According to this rule, a paper that contains a hidden question circulates among a circle of friends, to be followed by an answer, always creating surprising and funny results. Nadja's game follows exactly the same pattern as the "exquisite corpse" later did; the only difference is that the pattern unfolds in her imagination, rather than on small pieces of paper, thus both equating her imagination with an invisible writing material, and splitting Nadja herself into the various players. The fusion of reality with the imaginary (the latter understood in the Lacanian sense as "the world, the register, the dimension of images, conscious or unconscious, both perceived and imagined") is an ideal that the leader of Surrealism constantly sought in the notion of "surreality" (*Écrits* ix, trans. Sheridan), a notion that can be activated only by means of a surrealist use of language.

André Breton on language

Language, Breton boldly claims in the *Manifesto of Surrealism*, "a été donné à l'homme pour qu'il en fasse un usage surréaliste" (*OC1* 334) [Language has been given to man so that he may make Surrealist use of it (Seaver and Lane 32)].[18] A surrealist use of language is best exemplified in the form of dialogue, yet dialogue that bears none of the elements of conventionally conceived dialogue, which is marked by "the exchange and reversibility of the *communication*" and which "is often considered to be the fundamental and exemplary form of drama" (Pavis, *Dictionary* 98). Nor does surrealist dialogue have any relation to Mikhail Bakhtin's "dialogism," which refers to the polyphonic heterogeneity of a discourse. Instead, surrealist dialogue has a function of its own:

C'est encore au dialogue que les formes du langage surréaliste s'adaptent le mieux. Là, deux pensées s'affrontent; pendant que l'une se livre, l'autre s'occupe d'elle, mais comment s'en occupe-t-elle? Supposer qu'elle se l'incorpore serait admettre qu'un temps il lui est possible de vivre tout entière de cette autre pensée, ce qui est fort improbable. Et de fait l'attention qu'elle lui donne est tout extérieure; elle n'a que le loisir d'approuver ou de réprouver, généralement de réprouver, avec tous les égards dont l'homme est capable. Ce mode de langage ne permet d'ailleurs pas d'aborder le fond d'un sujet. Mon attention, en proie à une sollicitation qu'elle ne peut décemment repousser, traite la pensée adverse en ennemi (*OC1* 335).

[The forms of Surrealist language adapt themselves best to dialogue. Here two thoughts confront each other; while one is being delivered, the other is busy with it, but how is it busy with it? To assume that it incorporates it within itself would be tantamount to admitting that there is a time during which it is possible for it to live completely off that other thought, which is highly unlikely. And, in fact the attention it pays is completely exterior; it has only time enough to approve or reject—generally reject—with all the consideration of which man is capable. This mode of language does not allow the heart of the matter to be plumbed. My attention, prey to an entreaty, which it cannot in all decency reject, treats the opposing thought as an enemy (Seaver and Lane 34).]

In other words, dialogue in Surrealism is bereft of the conventional functions of progressive exchange of information, communication, and pleasure of argumentation. Thus, it would be in vain to search for any solid logic in it. Instead, one should consider dialogue as composed of two distinct soliloquies and follow each of them separately, in order to experience the acrobatics of the characters' imaginations, and the poetry that it elicits:

Le surréalisme poétique, auquel je consacre cette étude, s'est appliqué jusqu'ici à rétablir dans sa vérité absolue le dialogue, en dégageant les deux interlocuteurs des obligations de la politesse. Chacun d'eux poursuit simplement son soliloque, sans chercher à en tirer un plaisir dialectique particulier et à en imposer le moins du monde à son voisin. ...

Les mots, les images ne s'offrent que comme tremplins à l'esprit de celui qui écoute (*OC1* 336).[19]

[Poetic Surrealism has focused its efforts up to this point on reestablishing dialogue in its absolute truth, by freeing both interlocutors from any obligations of politeness. Each of them simply pursues his soliloquy without trying to derive any special dialectical pleasure from it and without trying to impose anything whatsoever upon his neighbor. ...

The words, the images are only so many springboards for the mind of the listener (Seaver and Lane 35).]

This use of dialogue triggers the stimulating free play of imagination, which, in turn, bears a revelation—obviously quite different from what one expects of dialogue in the theatre. The value of dialogue does not lie in its significance as a communicative act but in the enchanting, evocative power of its images.

In other words, what matters is not what is said, but what is projected/seen through the fleeting signifiers uttered by the interlocutors. This effect can better be illustrated by the technique of image-building, also used in Surrealism. Image building was defined by Pierre Reverdy and wholly embraced by Breton in his *Manifesto of Surrealism*:

> L'image est une création pure de l'esprit. Elle ne peut naître d'une comparaison mais du rapprochement de deux réalités plus ou moins éloignées. Plus les rapports des deux réalités rapprochées seront lointains et justes, plus l'image sera forte—plus elle aura de puissance émotive et de réalité poétique (OC1 324; italics his).

> [The image is a pure creation of the mind. It cannot be born from a comparison but from a juxtaposition of two more or less distant realities. The more the relationship between the two juxtaposed realities is distant and true, the stronger the image will be—the greater its emotional power and poetic reality (Seaver and Lane 20).]

Anna Balakian, who studied surrealist imagery in poetry and painting extensively, offers some astute observations; referring to the surrealist metaphor, she argues that "instead of being based on analogy, [it] is derived from divergence and contradiction" (*The Road* 120). As Martin John Bennison sums up, rather than being a private image that evokes associations and meanings within the writer's mind, for Anna Balakian "the surrealist image was a means of provoking sight or creating thought first within the reader's mind; in effect, the Surrealists reversed the process of image or metaphor composition" (101–2). The result of such a free-for-all treatment of both dialogue and image in surrealist writing is a sequence of images, scenes, and visions, with no apparent connection among them, which led to "an intensified use of all known mental faculties and the exploration of latent ones" (Balakian, *The Road* 149). This kind of unrestricted use of language is equally stressed in the "Introduction sur le discours sur le peu de réalité,"[20] where Breton also emphasizes a need for the liberation of language:

> Qu'est-ce qui me retient de brouiller l'ordre des mots, d'attenter de cette manière à l'existence toute apparente des choses! Le langage peut et doit être arraché à son servage. Plus de descriptions d'après nature, plus d'études de mœurs. Silence, afin qu'où nul n'a jamais passé je passe, silence!—Après toi, mon beau langage (OC2 276).

> [What keeps me from messing up the order of the words, from challenging in this way all apparent existence of the things? Language is able and must be freed from its servitude. No more descriptions after nature, no more studies of morals. Silence, so that I pass where no one before has even passed, silence! After you, my beautiful language!]

Breton clearly expresses here the need to be finished with the old-fashioned descriptions based on nature and morality studies; in doing so, he also stresses the search for a fundamentally new approach to language that will challenge the limits of reality and inspire an extraordinary lucidity.

Nadja's game, emerging as it does within the realm of language and make-believe, is, in effect, like a mirror, which reflects this surrealist use of language; a mirror, which also challenges the limits of "the little bit of reality,"[21] as it leads its players to an in-formation of the "I," thus expanding its perception of reality.

The value of this game rests in its power to awaken the players' imaginations by bringing them face to face with a cluster of images the assumption of which *in-forms* the self, as understood in Lacanian terms: "'giving *form* to' something—whether it be the intuitive form of an imprint as in memory, or the form that guides the development of an organism" (Muller and Richardson 28).[22] Lacan traces the genesis of the imaginary ego back to the mirror stage of child development. The imaginary is understood here as the idealized ego formation. With her game, Nadja, like an analyst, breaks the fascination of the imaginary so as to allow the symbolic order of the unconscious to speak. By announcing that she has made the discovery of the otherness of the self in her endless impersonation of a series of other selves, she leads her playmate to a derangement of all senses. An analysis of the circumstances in which this curious game unfolds can elucidate the implicit theatrical elements in Nadja's game and thus help in our reconstruction of Breton's fragmented dramatic theory.

Unfolding Nadja's game

Although Nadja's peculiar game appears simple at first glance, it is more convoluted than it appears precisely because of the way she plays it—combining a surrealist use of language with the imitative principle that is quintessential for the theatre. The game follows just one rule: the participants must surrender to the evocative power of words. Their surrender will enable them to experience "the marvelous" before a series of images that emerges from a new grouping of the words, one that defies (logical) syntax and inaugurates its own logic. The "marvelous" is understood here in the sense that Aragon gave it in *Le Paysan de Paris* (1926), that is, as the "apparent lack of coherence" (Burke vii): "[l]a réalité est l'absence apparente de contradiction. Le merveilleux, c'est la contradiction qui apparaît dans le réel" (250) [[r]eality is the apparent absence of contradiction. The marvellous is the eruption of contradiction within the real (Watson Taylor 217)]. Thus, in *Nadja*, the "marvelous" "is acting upon indefinable emotions, not 'things,' thus it is sensed through 'emotions felt' rather than through 'things seen'" (Burke 46). Breton also believed that only the "marvelous" is beautiful. A non-linear, enigmatic imagination seems to be a prerequisite for both players in Nadja's game—an element that immediately attracts the narrator/Breton. Such an imagination is very close to that of a child's, and Breton wholly embraced childhood imagination as a way to attack reason. His inclusion in *La Révolution surréaliste* in October 1927 of a relevant excerpt from Sigmund Freud's "La Question de l'analyse par les non-médecins" is indicative of Breton's interest in children's imaginations, as opposed to that of adults: "Les choses dans lesquelles le 'moi' infantile, épouvanté, avait fui, apparaissent souvent au 'moi' adulte et fortifié comme un simple jeu d'enfant" (quoted in Garrigues 27) [The things in front of which the infantile "ego," frightened, has escaped, usually seem to the adult and fortified "ego" like a children's game].[23] In her interlocutor's eyes, Nadja seems to be an infant-woman, as it were, who plays a children's game in a childlike way.

In fact, all the major elements of play, as both Johan Huizinga and Roger Caillois described them in their seminal studies—*Homo Ludens* (1938) and *Les Jeux et les hommes* (1958), respectively—apply to Nadja's game. It has all the basic elements of Roger Caillois' classification of play, namely, *alea*, *mimicry*, *agon*, and *ilinx*. Alea (chance) exists in that the two players meet by chance, and the game also begins in an aleatory manner, spontaneously and suddenly. What is more, the words come to Nadja at random. Mimicry is apparent in Nadja's game from the moment she starts her demonstration as to how her playmate should play, closing her eyes, pretending she is an actress. *Agon*, the competitive element, although not immediately apparent, is also present in Nadja's struggle to involve her fellow player in her game; she tries to win him over, while he stubbornly resists. The element of *ilinx* (vertigo) is also less apparent, but it could be seen to occur in the narrator's mind through the juxtaposition of the "two ... women ... wearing black ... in a park" that plunges him into the deepest perplexity—a kind of vertigo. This perplexity is evocative of the similar effect created in his mind by the reversal of the Greek myth of Theseus, in his crystal-like labyrinth with neither the Minotaur nor Ariadne's thread, in "L'introduction sur le discours sur le peu de réalité,"—a kind of personal myth for Breton. His prismatic, vertiginous view of the world around him might be similar to what Breton experiences when faced with the springboard to verbal freefall that Nadja's game is for him.

Turning to Huizinga, he claims that "play" cannot be fully defined, yet offers to identify its main characteristics. The first of these main characteristics is "that it is free, is in fact, freedom" (8). Its second characteristic is that "play is not 'ordinary' or 'real' life. It is rather a stepping out of 'real' life into a temporary sphere of activity with a disposition all of its own" (8) that only children can fully achieve. He then goes on to attempt the following definition:

> play is a voluntary activity or occupation executed within certain fixed limits of time and place, according to rules freely accepted but absolutely binding, having its aim in itself and accompanied by a feeling of tension, joy and the consciousness that it is "different" from "ordinary life" (28).

Thus, for Huizinga, "play" promotes the formation of social groups, which tend to surround themselves with secrecy and to stress their difference from the common world by disguise or other means. He also argues that play is irrational and enchanting, for it has all the elements of beauty: tension, balance, contrast, variation, solution, reduction, etc. "Play," in its higher activities, belongs to the sphere of festival and ritual, and lies outside the antithesis of wisdom and folly, and equally outside those of truth and falsehood, good and evil.

Nadja's game is without question a free activity that has no material gain, but certainly much immaterial gain. It proceeds within its own boundaries of time and space, according to rules "freely accepted but not necessarily absolutely binding." It unfolds in a taxi, itself a symbol of crossing both time and space, as the narrator makes his way home accompanied by Nadja, on the second day after their acquaintance (October 5, 1926). After a moment of silence, and therefore, of distance between the narrator and Nadja, a word game suddenly arises in all its spontaneity, bringing the two interlocutors closer as the use of the intimate "tu" in French indicates. Up to that point, Nadja, an "errant soul" as she calls herself, had used the more formal "vous" to address Breton, no matter how confessional her tone, when she spoke to her newly-acquainted friend about her lifelong adventures.[24] Once she joins the play-world—a convergence of Breton's text, theatre, and play—she immediately abandons this formula and liberates herself from the class constraints implied by the use of the formal pronoun "vous," and a special bond is achieved between the two players. As in a game, where all the players have equal status, Nadja now perceives her interlocutor as an equal, a play-mate. This simple game demonstrates how feasible the promise in fact is that Breton made in the *Manifesto of Surrealism* several years earlier (1924); that is, to give back to the dialogue its absolute truth, in the sense of liberating the two interlocutors from the obligations of politeness.

Nadja's game seems to have the elements most characteristic of surrealist thought: an unconventional dialogue that defies reason and finds its best expression in the language of children (and the insane), as well as a distinct image-building technique that, at first glance, looks like a cluster of incongruent images. Nadja's irrational, dialogic game acquires a new sense when seen as a form of surrealist language in the way Breton conceived it. Nadja truly does not aim to engage her interlocutor in a debate for intellectual satisfaction or to impose her views on him. Rather, she aims to lead him into a serendipitous moment of revelation, as she seems to have both a natural gift for making a surrealist use of language, coupled with an extraordinary lucidity in her communication style. She herself conceives of her role as one of "voyante," a medium who predicts at some point her interlocutor's future achievements: "André? André? … Tu écriras un roman sur moi. Je t'assure. Ne dis pas non" (*OC1* 707–8) [André? André? … You will write a novel about me. I'm sure you will. Don't say you won't (Howard 100)]. Nadja, the infant-woman, sees herself as a source of inspiration. When she starts her game, she acts like a child dealing with the "marvelous." She asks her playmate to play a game according to a fixed rule that consists in saying a word, any word that spontaneously comes to mind, such as a name or a number. She demonstrates that shutting one's eyes facilitates this game, as if this small gesture could take the participants to a magical yet concrete world, far from the world of reality and the constraints of reason. The nature of this world is captured in the following words by Louis Aragon, a close friend and collaborator of Breton's, in *Le Paysan de Paris*, a book also cited in *Nadja*: "Le fantastique, l'au-delà, le rêve, la survie, le paradis, l'enfer, la poésie, autant de mots pour signifier le concret. Il n'est d'amour que du concret" (251) [The fantastic, the beyond, dream, survival, paradise, hell, poetry, so many words signifying the concrete. There is no other love than that of the concrete" (Watson Taylor 217)]. Within this magical realm, Nadja effortlessly closes her eyes, showing how this game should be played, proceeding from words to action/acting, and then again back to words, establishing in this way a sense of ritual in her game. Breton himself much appreciated the element of ritual in Huizinga's play-model, in which he saw "a free activity par excellence," which "confirms in a permanent way and in the most highly elevated sense the supralogical character of our situation within the cosmos" ["affirme de façon permanente, et au sens le plus élevé, le caractère supralogique de notre situation dans le cosmos"] (quoted in Garrigues 218).

Meanwhile, Breton agrees with Huizinga's conclusion that it is necessary to "see in poetry the human realization of a ludic exigency at the heart of the community," and that "all that is getting recognized in poetry little by little as a conscious quality: beauty, sacred character, magic power, is inextricably found from the very beginning in the primary quality of play" (ibid.), one that is best exemplified in children's play. Breton valued children's play for its quality of free activity *par excellence*, which has nothing to do with any kind of play prescribed by adults, or confined by reason. In other words, in children's games there is something that is missing from adults' games; that is, the fusion of the real with the imaginary, in an entity exclusive to their "magnificent field of experience" (Breton, *OC2* 963). Nadja plays exactly like a child, except that she follows rules less stringently, guided only by the rule of free association. Like another Alice in Wonderland, she plays with words that form absurd stories, full of nonsense, which nevertheless lead her to the "other side of the mirror." In an essay on Lewis Caroll, Breton states:

> La complaisance envers l'absurde rouvre à l'homme le royaume mystérieux qu'habitent les enfants. Le jeu de l'enfance, comme moyen perdu de conciliation entre l'action et la rêverie en vue de la satisfaction organique, à commencer par le simple "jeu de mots," se trouve de la sorte réhabilité et dignifié (*OC2* 963).

> [Favoring the absurd reopens to mankind the mysterious kingdom that children inhabit. Children's play, as the lost medium of reconciling action and reverie for the sake of the organic satisfaction, starting with the simple "word game," is found somehow rehabilitated and dignified.]

Similarly, Nadja, starting with her simple word game, reconciles action and reverie. The first word Nadja utters, to offer an example to her interlocutor, is the number "two," alluding to its inherent dialectical potential: "Two, what?" Nadja further questions. "Two women," she answers herself, continuing her demonstration. This fragmented dialogue between Nadja and "Nadja-playing-the-other" continues until she brings to the fore the mysterious image of "two women ... wearing black." Nadja's game in her double role continues in a similar stichomythia to the point where a mosaic-like picture of these two women emerges out of this peculiar, fragmented dialogue-game,[25] where all these small segments find their place: "two ... women ... wearing black ... in a park." The absence of a finite verb in this static phrase-image reinforces the absence of action, graphically stressed in the text by the use of the suspension marks.

This gap in the image might be interpreted as a momentary blockage on Nadja's part, but given her proven ample imaginative skills, I do not believe this is a lapse in her memory. More likely, Nadja the "voyante" (who had already seen in her mind a few minutes earlier her interlocutor's wife sitting next to her dog and cat) stops deliberately at this point. She does so in order to force her interlocutor to engage in her little game by prolonging the perplexing "image" she has already created in his mind, one that is ready to be deciphered by him, or rather to lead him to another reality. Making use of this silent moment in a masterful way, Nadja resumes her game by asking "[B]ut what are they doing?", then continues like this: "Come on, it's so simple, why don't you want to play?" Thanks to this question, a clue is offered, not only about the narrator's reluctance to continue this game, despite Nadja's insistence, but also about Nadja's sense of meta-play. She steps out of the game for a moment to discuss its lack of progress and to question her interlocutor's resistance to being involved, despite the fact that she advertizes its consoling effects for her solitude. The narrator's reluctance to add a verb to the image of the two women that Nadja's game has created, or perhaps that Nadja's game has restored in his imagination, is worthy of speculation; we may well find a parallel between this resistance and Breton's overall attitude toward theatre.

The player's silence: Game over or the triumph of the game?

Several working hypotheses, not necessarily all mutually exclusive, are part of our investigation of the narrator's reluctance to be fully engaged in Nadja's game. All of these hypotheses take into consideration Breton's overall surrealist beliefs as stated throughout his prolific writings. I suggest the following three interpretive schemes:

a) The game is over because of the narrator/game spoiler.
b) The game is in question because it challenges the narrator/player, who resists surrendering to techniques of description that pertain to the realist tradition; at the same time, it reveals his preference for poetic rather than dramatic intensity.
c)   The effect of Nadja's game reaches its peak as it leads the narrator/player to a revelatory moment, or an experiencing of the "marvelous."

A) THE GAME IS OVER BECAUSE OF THE NARRATOR/GAME SPOILER

First, such reluctance on behalf of the narrator/player may represent a turning point for him, in that he finally becomes aware of how fundamentally different he is from Nadja. At this moment of suspension, he realizes that the game not only connects words among themselves, but also connects Nadja's two lives, in a make-believe world and in the real world. Yet he also comes to realize that this game cannot connect his own life with Nadja's, as he now understands how fundamentally different he is from her. For instance, while she so easily plays a double game of mirrors between play and life, he is unable to play this word game even in its initial phase. His unwillingness to give in further by making a suggestion to Nadja about what the two women wearing black in a park may be doing makes him a game-spoiler, all the while hinting at the realization to which Breton will soon come: the lack of attention paid one to the other, the lack of understanding, agreement, or even communication between the two of them: "J'avais, depuis assez longtemps, cessé de m'entendre avec Nadja. À vrai dire, peut-être ne nous sommes-nous jamais entendus, tant au moins sur la manière d'envisager les choses simples de l'existence" (*OC1* 735) [I had long since ceased to get along/agree with Nadja. To tell the truth, we had never perhaps reached a level of understanding/agreement between us, at least in the way of seeing the simple things of existence]. Or, as he later confesses: "Je n'ai peut-être pas été à la hauteur de ce qu'elle me proposait" (ibid. 736) [I have never perhaps reached the level of what she was suggesting to me]. In this sentence, Breton was referring to Nadja's unique "mad love," a love that had already started to take shape during her word-game and soon evolved into a game of seduction. Confronted by this seductive game, the narrator instinctively refuses to surrender to Nadja's magical power, as though he relies on a defense mechanism. Nadja's game becomes the proto-stage, in which a child is transformed into a seductress/actress who is able to lead her interlocutor to a marvelous world.

B) NADJA'S GAME AS A CHALLENGE TO THE NARRATOR/PLAYER

The narrator's reluctance to be wholly involved in Nadja's game is simply a result of his deliberate choice not to add anything that would disturb the tranquil tableau of these two mysterious women in a park. In this case, it is the effect of Nadja's game, rather than Nadja herself, that attracts the narrator. The image itself is intense enough for him to believe it would be demystified, or even become banal with the addition of a verb that specifies an action and creates with it a coherent sentence. Such an addition would spoil the inherent poetic intensity of the image, replacing it automatically with dramatic intensity. Breton is always clear, after all, about his preference for poetry, particularly in his *Manifesto of Surrealism*, overtly devoted to "poetic surrealism" (*OC1* 336). The image of "two … women … wearing black … in a park" keeps instead something of its poetic quality, a certain rhythm that follows a poetics of fragmentation. The addition of a verb quite simply runs the risk of creating the commonest of descriptions, reminiscent of the realist attitude, and best exemplified in those novels of the time that made an abuse of nature as a setting, represented here by the park. The refusal of the narrator to add this simple, yet powerfully prescriptive grammatical component is thus equivalent to a surrealist use of language, wanting nothing to do with the realist tradition, so faithful to futile descriptions, which Breton attacks in the *Manifesto of Surrealism*:

> Et les descriptions! Rien n'est comparable au néant de celles-ci; ce n'est que superpositions d'images de catalogue, l'auteur en prend de plus en plus à son aise, il saisit l'occasion de me glisser ses cartes postales, il cherche à me faire tomber d'accord avec lui des lieux communs (*OC1* 314).

> [And the descriptions! There is nothing to which their vacuity can be compared; they are nothing but so many superimposed images taken from some stock catalogue, which the author utilizes more and more whenever he chooses; he seizes the opportunity to slip me his postcards, he tries to make me agree with him about the clichés (Seaver and Lane 6).]

According to Breton, these descriptions, which he sees well exemplified in Dostoïevski's novel *Crime and Punishment*, are typical of the realist attitude that was responsible for the creation and dissemination of offensive plays. Such an attitude, inspired by positivism, Breton continues, was hostile towards any intellectual and moral source of inspiration:

Je l'ai (l'attitude réaliste) en horreur, car elle est faite de médiocrité, de haine et de plate suffisance. C'est elle qui engendre aujourd'hui ces livres ridicules, ces pièces insultantes. Elle se fortifie sans cesse dans les journaux et fait échec à la science, à l'art, en s'appliquant à flatter l'opinion dans ses goûts les plus bas; la clarté confinant à la sottise, la vie des chiens (*OC1* 313).

[I loathe it, for it is made up of mediocrity, hate, and dull conceit. It is this attitude which today gives birth to these ridiculous books, these insulting plays. It constantly feeds on and derives strength from the newspapers and stultifies both science and art by assiduously flattering the lowest of tastes; clarity bordering on stupidity, a dog's life (Seaver and Lane 7).]

In light of Breton's explicit hostility toward realism, it becomes evident that by refusing to add a verb to Nadja's fragmented phrase, the narrator expresses his determination not to serve the realist attitude that "suffocates" the receiver's imagination with its catalogue-like descriptions, whether they are meant for the page or the stage. It becomes evident now how, in Breton's eyes, the "paucity of reality" goes hand in hand with a very limited use of language. We can see how he envisions a new, pioneering use of language whose aesthetic qualities would spring from a deliberate disorder in the order of the words. Moreover, opting simply to gaze at the enigmatic duet of women in the park, the narrator aims to keep this image free of paraphernalia; he tests himself to see whether he can be led to a revelatory moment through this image evoked in his mind by Nadja's fragmented sentence.

c) Nadja's game as the path to the "marvelous"

Nadja's game opens the path to a revelatory moment, in the sense that the most common and banal image may be transformed to a source of the "marvelous" when approached by a non-linear, dream-like imagination. It is an imagination of this kind that is at work in the narrator's mind, transforming the utterly unremarkable image of the two women in a park to an enigmatic yet enchanting image. Breton now brings up another image of two women that left its mark on his mind, and resurfaces now on the occasion of its approximation to the sentence-image that Nadja's game has created. The result of latent dream-work—in the Freudian sense—triggered by the waking image, the arrival of this associated image is a good example of the way in which dream and wakefulness interact; something that has always fascinated Breton:

C'est que l'homme, quand il cesse de dormir, est avant tout le jouet de sa mémoire, et qu'à l'état normal celle-ci se plaît à lui retracer faiblement les circonstances du rêve, à priver ce dernier de toute conséquence actuelle, et à faire partir le seul déterminant du point où il croit, quelques heures plus tôt, l'avoir laissé: cet espoir ferme, ce souci. Il a l'illusion de continuer quelque chose qui en vaut la peine. Le rêve se trouve ainsi ramené à une parenthèse, comme la nuit. Et pas plus qu'elle, en général, il ne porte conseil (*OC1* 317).

[It is because man, when he ceases to sleep, is above all the plaything of his memory, and because in its normal state memory takes pleasure in weakly retracing for him the circumstances of the dream, in stripping it of any real importance, and in dismissing the only determinant from the point where he thinks he has left it a few hours before: this firm hope, this concern. He is under the impression of continuing something that is worthwhile.

Thus the dream finds itself reduced to a mere parenthesis, as is the night. And, like the night, dreams generally contribute little to furthering our understanding (Seaver and Lane 11).]

A similar process to that which renders a person a plaything of his/her memory is at work here in the narrator's mind, when he is confronted with Nadja's game. Between a state of dreaming and waking, he superimposes onto the image of the two women in the park that of Solange (a dance teacher) and her friend Mme Marthe Challens (the principal of a girl's institution), from Pierre Palau's play *Les Détraquées*, in the scene that shows them standing in front of a window leading to a park where girls play:[26]

La scène reste vide un long moment, puis par la baie, au fond, une femme paraît. Elle est jeune, mince, brune, le visage très pur; elle est vêtue de noir, sa tenue très simple mais élégante doit indiquer une très légère note masculine. Elle tient à la main une petite valise de cuir. Elle reste un moment à regarder le parc, du haut du perron, puis entre lentement, sans un geste, les yeux dans le vague, comme automatiquement. Elle pose son baggage sur le bureau et demeure appuyée, immobile. Un temps. Par la porte de gauche, Mme de Challens entre. Elle reste figée sur le seuil en apercevant Solange. Celle-ci n'a pas fait un mouvement (91–2).

[The stage remains empty for a long time, then by the bay window in the background a woman makes her appearance. She is young, thin, brunette, with a very pure face; she is dressed in black. Her dress, very simple yet elegant, must indicate a slightly masculine tone; she is holding a small leather bag in her hand. She remains still for a while looking at the park from the top of the porch steps; then she enters slowly, without any gesture, as though automatically, her stare unfocused. She puts her baggage on the desk and remains still, unmoving. A moment. From the left door, Ms. Challens enters. She remains still when she perceives Solange. The latter does not make any movement.]

The similarity between the two images of the two pairs of women erases a spatial and temporal distance in Breton's mind. Breton justifies this transference in the following passage from Nadja;

mais il est indiscutable, qu'à la transposition, qu'à l'intense fixation, qu'au passage autrement inexplicable d'une image de ce genre du plan de la remarque sans intérêt au plan émotif concourent au premier chef l'évocation de certaines épisodes des *Détraquées* et le retour à ces conjectures dont je parlais (*OC1* 675).

[but it is indisputable that the transposition, the intense fixation, the otherwise inexplicable passage of such an image from the level of a banal remark to the emotive level, necessarily includes a reference to certain episodes of *Les Détraquées* and the reversion to those conjectures I was speaking of (Seaver and Lane 51).]

In this passage, Breton stresses the amazing, yet inexplicable, capacity of the human mind to transform a run-of-the-mill image to a powerful one. The power of *metamorphosis*, so characteristic of dream in general, is evoked in the above passage, where Breton attempts to analyze a bizarre dream he had during his stay at the Manoir d'Ango, where he wrote *Nadja*. Breton was convinced that this dream was related to the play *Les Détraquées*, some scenes of which were stuck in his mind and never ceased to puzzle him: "Mais, pour moi, descendre vraiment dans les bas fonds de l'esprit, là où il n'est plus question que la nuit tombe et se relève (c'est donc le jour?), c'est revenir rue Fontaine, au 'Théâtre des Deux-Masques' qui depuis lors a fait place à un cabaret" (*OC1* 668–9) [But for me to descend into what is truly the mind's lower depths, where it is no longer a question of the night's falling and rising again (and is that the day?) means to follow the Rue Fontaine back to the Théâtre des Deux Masques, which has now been replaced by a cabaret (Howard 39–40)].

It is in this theatre that the strange Grand-Guignol play *Les Détraquées* was staged. A more detailed look at this play is necessary at this point, since this approximation is the main revelation that Nadja's game contributes, both for the narrator and us. Before this analysis, however, let me clarify the term "Grand-Guignol."[27] This theatrical genre is relevant to Breton's attitude towards the play *Les Détraquées* by Palau, a playwright whose work was featured quite often among the repertoire of the Théâtre du Grand-Guignol. The term "Grand-Guignol"—which literally means the "big puppet show"—took its name from the popular French puppet character Guignol, whose original incarnation was as an outspoken social commentator—a spokesperson for the canuts, or silk workers, of Lyon. Founded in 1897 by the French playwright Oscar Metenier, the Grand-Guignol theatre had the audacity to depict a milieu that had never before been seen on stage: "that of vagrants, street kids, prostitutes, criminals, and 'apaches,' as street loafers and con artists were called at the time—and moreover for allowing those characters to express themselves in their own language" (Pierron). Metenier was succeeded as director in 1898 by Max Maurey, who during the years 1898–1914 turned the Théâtre du Grand-Guignol into a house of horror, particularly under the influence of de Lorde (who collaborated on several plays with his therapist, the experimental psychologist Alfred Binet). Insanity became the Grand-Guignolesque theme par excellence. But "what carried the Grand-Guignol to its highest level were the boundaries and thresholds it crossed: the states of consciousness altered by drugs or hypnosis. Loss of consciousness, loss of control, panic: themes with which the theatre's audience could easily identify. The passage from one state to another was the crux of the genre" (ibid.). Maxa Camille Choisy directed the theatre from 1914 to 1930, and in 1917 he hired the actress Paula Maxa. During her career at the Grand-Guignol, Maxa, "the most assassinated woman in the world," was subjected to a range of tortures unique in theatrical history:

> she was shot with a rifle and with a revolver, scalped, strangled, disemboweled, raped, guillotined, hanged, quartered, burned, cut apart with surgical tools and lancets, cut into eighty-three pieces by an invisible Spanish dagger, stung by a scorpion, poisoned with arsenic, devoured by a puma, strangled by a pearl necklace, and whipped; she was also put to sleep by a bouquet of roses, kissed by a leper, and subjected to a very unusual metamorphosis, which was described by one theater critic: "Two hundred nights in a row, she simply decomposed on stage in front of an audience which wouldn't have exchanged its seats for all the gold in the Americas. The operation lasted a good two minutes during which the young woman transformed little by little into an abominable corpse" (ibid.).

Jack Jouvin directed the theatre from 1930 to 1937 and the repertoire shifted from gore to psychological drama, but it was the war that dealt the now struggling theatre a final death-blow. Reality overtook fiction, and attendance at post-war performances dwindled. In the spring of 1958, Anaïs Nin commented on its decline in her diary:

I surrendered myself to the Grand-Guignol, to its venerable filth which used to cause such shivers of horror, which used to petrify us with terror. All our nightmares of sadism and perversion were played out on that stage ... The theater was empty (quoted in Pierron).

In an interview conducted immediately after the Grand-Guignol closed in 1962, Charles Nonon, its last director, explained: "Before the war, everyone believed that what happened on stage was purely imaginary; now we know that these things—and worse—are possible" (ibid). In the narrator's eyes, Nadja's game functioned as a re-enactment of one such Grand-Guignol play, that is, of Palau's play *Les Détraquées*.

Nadja's game as a stage for *Les Détraquées*: From a banal image to an emotive image

In *Les Détraquées*, two insane, sadomasochistic, drug-addicted lesbian pedophiles, the principal of the institution for girls called "Les Fauvettes" ("Little Birds") and her friend Solange, a dance teacher, are responsible for the disappearance at the end of the school season of a girl called Lucienne. This is the second girl to disappear in two consecutive years under the same circumstances, so an investigation immediately begins and the girl's body is found in a cupboard in the principal's office. Lucienne's sudden disappearance from the stage (and life) is announced by her balloon that unexpectedly falls onto the stage,[28] the last trace of her once vivid life and a great source of mystery to both the female protagonists and, especially, for the narrator-reviewer of the spectacle. What happened next bemused Breton each time he saw or restaged this play in his imagination; to use his own words, "[l]e manque d'indices suffisants sur ce qui se passe après la chute du ballon, sur ce dont Solange et sa partenaire peuvent exactement être la proie pour devenir ces superbes bêtes de proie, demeure *par excellence* ce qui me confond" (*OC1* 673) [the lack of adequate indications as to what happens after the balloon falls and the ambiguity about precisely what Solange and her partner are prey to that transforms them into these magnificent predatory beasts is still what puzzles me *par excellence* (Howard 50)].

It was questions such as this about Palau's female duet as predatory beasts that led Breton to correlate it with a repugnant dream he had. In this nightmare, a moss-colored insect, about 20 inches long, is transformed into an old man who is just heading toward some kind of coin-fed machine, and has slipped one penny into the slot instead of two. Breton, the dreamer and dream-observer, feels this shortcoming is somehow unacceptable and he strikes the man/insect with a cane, only to feel two of its huge hairy legs on his throat. He is subsequently enveloped by a feeling of inexpressible disgust; the sensation of being suffocated. He stresses this dream's value as "symptomatic of the repercussion such recollections, provided one surrenders to them with a certain violence, may have on the course of one's thought" (Howard 50). Following this strand of thought, Breton also associates the suffocating effect of his dream to a recent, disturbing experience with a bird, as well as his recollection of specific scenes in Palau's play as *a double play of mirrors*. The real event to which he referred consisted in his observation of a bird, which was nesting in the ceiling of the loggia where Breton was writing, chirping and hopping around its nest in disgusting glee whenever it brought home its prey (Howard 50–51). For the Freudian Breton, there was no doubt that his dream about the moss-colored insect, with its two huge, hairy legs wrapping around his throat, represented the disturbing image of this bird playing with its prey, and the equally distressing acts of the female couple in *Les Détraquées*. This kind of over-determination thus clarifies the way in which the self is in-formed through the constant exchange of the real with the imaginary:

> La production des images de rêve dépendent toujours au moins de ce double jeu de glaces, il y a là l'indication du rôle très spécial, sans doute éminemment révélateur, au plus haut degré "surdéterminant" au sens freudien, que sont appelées à jouer certaines impressions très fortes, nullement contaminables de moralité, vraiment ressenties "par-delà le bien et le mal" dans le rêve et, par suite, dans ce qu'on lui oppose très sommairement sous le nom de réalité (*OC1* 675).

> [Since the production of dream images always depends on at least this double play of mirrors, there is, here, the indication of the highly special, supremely revealing, "super-determinant"—in the Freudian sense of the word—role which certain powerful impressions are made to play, in no way contaminable by morality, actually experienced "beyond good and evil" in the dream, and, subsequently, in what we quite arbitrarily oppose to dream under the name of reality (Howard 50).]

In such a framework, it would not be an exaggeration to suggest that the approximation of the sentence/image of the "two … women … wearing black … in a park," with the scene of Solange and Madame Challens seen at the window facing a park, is just such a product of over-determination, as defined by Sigmund Freud in *The Interpretation of Dreams*. Freud describes the transformation of latent dream-thoughts into a manifest content, in terms of the "condensation of multiple thoughts into one image or the displacement of one thought to another. The manifest content or image is thus 'over-determined' by the multiplicity of elements that become meaningful in their relation" (Taylor and Winquist 268). Likewise, the superimposition of the two pairs of women in Breton's case is the outcome of the passage from a banal image to an emotive one, due to a transformational process that has all the elements of over-determination. This inexplicable, dream-like passage can be seen as the source of the narrator's reluctance to participate in Nadja's game, as he does not want to spoil the mysterious sensations of being first caught by surprise (thanks to a new disposition of objects, embedded one into another, before his eyes), and then, being captivated by a sense of revelation.[29]

In our effort to explain Breton's fixation with Palau's play, it is important to keep in mind the similarities between *Les Détraquées* and Nadja's "play." Breton was without doubt fixated on *Les Détraquées*, if we consider that he revisited the play, publishing it in *Le Surréalisme même* in 1956, almost 30 years after his original detailed account of it in *Nadja*. In this account, Breton has unwittingly assumed the difficult role of a performance analyst who is in favor of Palau's play, four years after experiencing a range of intensely negative emotions while watching and re-watching this play on stage, and recalling the experience in his memory. We will follow Breton as he undertakes this task, drawing on

Patrice Pavis's model of performance analysis, the so-called "vectorization or semiotization of desire": "the desire of the body of the performance, as much as that of the spectator" (25). According to this semiotic model, developed in *Analyzing Performance* (2003), the goal of the performance analyst is to link networks of signs: "it consists of associating and connecting signs that form parts of networks, within which each sign only has meaning through the dynamic that relates to other signs" (17). Thus, we will follow Breton the performance analyst as he steps back and traces the contours and itineraries of the performance of Palau's play "from the perspective of the desiring, observing subject" (ibid. 20). Perhaps through this tactic we will retrace Breton's fixation with the notion of originality, in the surrealist sense of a "retrospective"—the necessity of always going back to the original.

The narrator's/player's past experience as a performance analyst: The acting style of Le Théâtre Moderne

This is not the first time that Breton undertook the role of performance analyst. He had already done so in his description of the Théâtre Moderne in *Nadja* at the end of the passage of the Opéra precisely where Breton meets Nadja. Breton had expressed his enthusiasm for the Théâtre and its new ludic acting techniques. Because they corresponded to his ideal for the stage, he overlooked the quality of plot of the plays staged there:

> *Le jeu dérisoire des acteurs*, ne tenant qu'un compte très relatif de leur rôle, ne se souciant qu'à peine les uns des autres et tout occupés à se créer des relations dans le public composé d'une quinzaine de personnes tout au plus, ne s'y fit jamais l'effet d'une toile de fond. Mais que retrouverai-je pour cette image la plus fugace et la plus alertée de moi-même, pour cette image dont je m'entretiens, qui vaille l'accueil de cette salle aux grandes glaces usées, décorées vers le bas de cygnes gris glissant dans des roseaux jaunes, aux loges grillagés, privées tout à fait d'air, de lumière, si peu rassurantes, de cette salle où durant le spectacle des rats furetaient, vous frôlant le pied, où l'on avait le choix, en arrivant, entre un fauteuil défoncé et un fauteuil renversable! Et du premier au second acte, car il était par trop complaisant d'attendre le troisième, que reverrai-je jamais de ces yeux qui l'ont vu le "bar" du premier étage, si sombre lui aussi, avec ses impénétrables tonnelles, "un salon au fond d'un lac", oui vraiment? (*OC1* 663–9; my emphasis).

> [*The ridiculous acting*[30] of the performers, who paid only the faintest attention to their parts, scarcely listening to each other and busy making dates with members of the audience, which consisted of perhaps fifteen people at the most, always reminded me of a canvas backdrop. But what could I find for the fleeting and so easily alarmed image of myself, that image I am talking about, which is worth the welcome of this hall, with its great, worn mirrors, decorated toward the base with gray swans gliding among yellow reeds, with its grillwork loges entirely without air or light, as suspicious-looking as the hall itself where during the performance rats crept about, running over your feet, where, once inside, you had your choice between a staved-in chair and one that might tip over at any moment! And between the first act and the second—for it was too preposterous to wait for the third— what would I ever see again with these eyes which have seen the "bar" upstairs, terribly dark too with its impenetrable bowers, "a living room at the bottom of a lake," yes really? (Howard 38).]

However challenging it might be to extract Breton's implicit dramatic theory from this highly eccentric account, it is important to point out here that the author is concerned with the fleeting and alarmed image of his "self" amidst a canvas-like backdrop that is composed of both the stage and the animated auditorium. In effect, what Breton looked for and expected from the stage becomes clear in the above passage; certainly, he did not look for something "serious" that would intellectually engage the spectators. Rather, he was looking for the quality of "a vector" that would connect the characters on stage with the audience—no matter how disconnected the actors might appear toward one another—and comply with the surrealist ideal of a dialogue that treats the interlocutors as enemies. These vectors or connections with an intimate audience are more easily formed through hilarious acting and the laughter that results from it. This kind of acting, judged by the standards of conventional theatre, clearly shows disrespect for the stage itself, where representation is traditionally conveyed through imitation. It also reveals a deliberate effort to abandon the "fourth wall" of the illusionist stage tradition that Breton hated so much.

This unconventional acting style—so appealing to Breton in his desire to defy seriousness on stage—coupled with the decadent ambiance that emanated from the ready-to-be-demolished theatrical space of the Modern Theatre, stresses the elements of entertainment, surprise, and revelation. All these elements suffice for Breton "the analyst" to live through an unusual experience, best exemplified in the mirror-like image of a "salon au fond d'un lac," an image situated on the borders of art and reality. The expression "un fauteuil défoncé et un fauteuil renversable," referring to the spectator's choice of seat, is also indicative of the magical power of the otherwise worthless space of the Modern Theatre. Within this strange theatrical space, surrounded by old, worn mirrors, their reflections bringing together the most incongruous images, the spectator's mode of seeing, perceiving, and imagining was reversed. This theatrical experiment might suggest that the marvelous can be contained in the most negligible elements of one's daily life. Thus, Breton's theatre is an "open door" that leads to obscure spaces, where free or illicit desires find their place, or where an unusual experience associated with love is offered to the spectator.[31] For the repertoire of this theatre was devoted exclusively to the subject matter of love, as Louis Aragon, who also describes the acting style practiced by the Modern Theatre in *Le Paysan de Paris*, states: "Ce théâtre qui n'a pour but et pour moyen que l'amour même, est sans doute le seul qui nous présente une dramaturgie sans truquage, et vraiment moderne" (131) [This type of theatre whose sole aim, whose sole means, is love itself, is without doubt the only one offering us a truly modern dramaturgy free of all fakery (Watson Taylor 120)].[32] Here, Aragon complements Breton's view in "L'Introduction sur le discours sur le peu de réalité" about the need for the stage to get rid of its fakery.

Both Breton and Aragon thus share the same view as far as the style of the Modern Theatre is concerned: its exclusive focus is on love. Aragon, for instance, states: "[L]a morale est celle de l'amour, l'amour la préoccupation unique: les problèmes sociaux ne sauraient y être effleurés que s'ils sont prétexte à exhibition. La troupe n'est pas payée et prend des libertés avec ses rôles, elle vit d'aventures" (133) [The moral is love; love is the sole preoccupation: social problems are never touched upon unless they provide the pretext for a display of nudity. The troupe is unpaid: the members take liberties with their roles, and they all exist on intrigues and love affairs (Watson Taylor 122)]. Irreverence towards money, as well as the amateurism of the actors of the Modern Theatre are things that Breton appreciates enormously; the equation of life with the stage, so desired by Breton, becomes a reality in the case of the Modern Theatre. Aragon goes on to specify in more detail the ambiance created by the natural communion of the audience with the stage, that retains something of a primitive spirit:

> L'esprit même du théâtre primitif y est sauvegardé par la communion naturelle de la salle et de la scène, dû au désir, ou à la provocation des femmes, ou à des conversations particulières que les rires grossiers de l'auditoire, ses commentaires, les engueulades des danseuses au public impoli, les rendez-vous donnés établissent fréquemment, ajoutant un charme spontané à un texte débité de façon monotone et souvent détonante, ou ânonné, ou soufflé, ou simplement lu au pied-levé, sans fard (133).

> [The very spirit of the primitive theatre is preserved here through a natural communion between audience and performers, arising out of desire on the one side and the girls' provocative behavior on the other, as well as out of the impromptu conversations frequently initiated by the audience's vulgar laughter, its comments, the tongue-lashings given by the dancers to rude individuals, the rendezvous exchanged across the footlights, conversations which add a spontaneous charm to a text delivered in a shouted or mumbled monotone, urged on by frequent prompting, or simply read straight from the script without any pretense (Watson Taylor 121).]

In the above passage, it is interesting how Aragon stresses the "primitive spirit of the Modern Theatre" that, at first glance, seems like an oxymoron. Yet, by this term, he stresses the sense of initiation, as opposed to representation, where the spectators cease to be spectators and become instead initiates. They want to feel an experience that is "marvelous," rather than to watch a spectacle; in other words, they expect to be personally transformed.

All these elements of the fragmented "poetics of theatre" of the Modern Theatre, pieced together on the basis of the accounts of its acting style that Breton and Aragon offer,[33] must be taken into consideration when one attempts to explain Breton's detailed focus on Les Détraquées, staged in the Theatre of the Two Masks.

From the aesthetics of the Théâtre Moderne to the aesthetics of the Théâtre de Deux Masques

Warren Motte briefly establishes the connection between the two theatres that drew Breton's attention, the Modern Theatre and the Theatre of the Two Masks, when he attempts to explain why Breton as narrator lingers so strangely over the description of Les Détraquées. For Motte, Breton does so because "it constitutes an aesthetic model for his own text, a model wherein the shocking marginality of the grand guignol is remotivated as innovative technique in a sustained attack on literary conventionalism" (47). The narrator's confession, that his desire to watch the aforementioned play was kindled by the harsh criticism it had received from established theatre critics, certainly supports Motte's point: "Bravant mon peu de goût pour les planches, j'y suis allé jadis, sur la foi que la pièce qu'on y jouait ne pouvait être mauvaise, tant la critique se montrait acharnée contre elle, allant jusqu'à en réclamer l'interdiction" (*OC1* 669)[34] [I once went there, though I have never been able to tolerate the theatre, supposing that the play being put on couldn't be bad, so harsh—to the point of demanding that the play be banned—had the criticism of it been (Howard 40)]. Nevertheless, Motte implies that Breton did not really see any value *per se* in Palau's play, other than the reactionary, shocking marginality of its characters. However, I believe that Breton did see something more than just this in the play, which became a fixation in his mind. Breton was truly fascinated yet troubled by *Les Détraquées*, in the same way that he was fascinated each time he entered the Modern Theatre. He must have become aware of how tangible his ideal personal esthetic of convulsive beauty could be. "Whether it be induced by a natural spectacle or by a work of art, the experience of authentic beauty is revealed when a shudder of a sudden feeling of inner disturbance (*un trouble*) occurs without warning" (Cauvin 23). In this light, I see Henri Béhar's explanation of Breton's account of Palau's play in *Nadja* as more accurate: "Neither his willed perversity, nor the desire to defend a work which had been disparaged, seemed to me to justify the detailed account of this play which he gives" ("The Passionate Attraction" 16). Judging from the mark that this play left on Breton, Béhar thought there was something else that attracted Breton to *Les Détraquées*: "More than five years after seeing the play the impression is still just as vivid, and the writer seems to relive his emotions as he transcribes only what floats to the surface" (ibid. 16). Béhar rightly states that "[w]ith *Les Détraquées* Breton's attention focuses on the stage. The play seems to him to be exclusively of the dramatic genre, in terms of its content as well as in the performance of the actors. And he has eyes only for the actress, whose expressions are for him the source of great mystery" (ibid. 18). For Béhar:

> [o]nly the atmosphere of the theatre, the staging, the acting, the intimate emotion of the spectator could have given rise to such admiration. Thinking of the definitive words pronounced by Breton to describe Blanche Derval, "the most admirable and without a doubt the only actress of our time," I [he] wanted to know more about this actress whose name I had never seen elsewhere … (ibid. 15).

Béhar indeed investigated the relationship between Breton and the actress Blanche Derval, and he discovered that Breton had sent her four letters. The first time he wrote, on January 29, 1922, was to solicit her collaboration for the Congress of Paris. He addressed her as follows: "It is to you and you alone that we made this request, because we know of no one other than you who incarnates the modern spirit in the theatre today" (ibid.).[35] Although this invitation never received an answer, "the actress was the only person, in the eyes of her admirer, *to incarnate modernity in the theatre*" (ibid. emphasis mine). This statement acquires its fuller sense when seen in the light of Breton's and Aragon's descriptions of the Modern Theatre. The two theatres now match perfectly. The two communicative spaces of the Modern Theatre—the stage and the auditorium—correspond exactly to the two masks of the homonymous theatre where *Les Détraquées* was staged.

In that space, Breton was able to experience something new which captured the spirit of modernity, and had nothing to do with the fake image of the self emanating from the mask of the eternal theatre of "L'Introduction sur le discours sur le peu de réalité." The Théâtre des Deux Masques, in other words, became in his eyes an ideal space that managed to put into practice the so-called "wireless" modern philosophy, first coined by Filippo Tommaso Marinetti, the leader of futurism. Marinetti had used this term in his *Manifeste technique de la littérature futuriste*, dated May 11, 1912: "Together we will invent the wireless imagination."[36] Making an explicit reference to Marinetti, Breton claims in "L'Introduction sur le discours sur le peu de réalité" that "wireless imagination" (a term modeled after "wireless telegraph," or "wireless telecommunications," and with which he opens the essay) is not only easily achieved, but also "permissible."[37] Coming from this perspective, he imagines himself as a new Theseus on the island of Crete, but with neither Ariadne's thread, nor the Minotaur; instead, he sees himself as one who is forever cloistered in his own labyrinth made of crystal, thrown in front of a constant *aporia*, both miraculous and wondrous in the face of modern invention.[38] For "[l]'invention, la découverte humaine, cette faculté qui, dans le temps, nous est si parcimonieusement accordée de connaître, de posséder ce dont on ne se faisait aucune idée avant nous, est faite pour nous jeter dans une immense perplexité" (Breton, *OC2* 265) [invention, human discovery, this faculty which we are hardly able to get to know through time, that is, to get to acquire that of which we had no clue before, is made in order to put us in an immense perplexity]. Breton seems to have made a similar invention when faced with both Nadja's game and Blanche Derval's acting as Solange, equivalent to a new experience in a place of existence, as Béhar rightly states: "[T]he stage was for this ideal spectator, on one certain occasion, the place of existence" ("The Passionate Attraction" 17). This is exactly the impact that Derval's portrayal of Solange has on the viewer/reviewer Breton; it makes him feel he is within a place where motion is suspended, a place of existence. For this he feels grateful to Blanche Derval:

> These photographs of *Les Détraquées* are far from giving me the extraordinary impression which certain episodes in the play left on me, and above all certain expressions which I saw you adopt during it. Such as they are, though, they are still infinitely moving, and I thank you for having given me the means of confronting my faithful and passionate memory of several evenings at the Two Masks with this all too fixed and objective a test (ibid. 16).[39]

Such a confession forms the link that pieces Nadja's game and Breton's experience together, first as a viewer and then again as a "reviewer" of Palau's play. More than the stage itself then, the transformational effect on the spectator's perception most interests Breton in that it owes its power precisely to the fact that there is no split between actress/character in the cases of both Nadja and Blanche Derval as Solange. What he so categorically denied in "Le Discours sur le peu de réalité" becomes possible in the cases of these two women, leaving him in a state of deep perplexity. Breton, as a witness to the spectacle of *Les Détraquées*, found a place of existence in the same way that Nadja did when she performed various imaginary roles and listened to herself as another auditor/spectator. Both "plays" (Nadja's word game and the staging of Palau's play) have the same perplexing effect upon the narrator/author as their goal. It is important to notice here that the effects of both kinds of play transform the narrator/author from a stupefied object to a newly-awakened subject, who finds a place of existence in a newly-discovered world—that of surreality.[40] Now we can see a new element that encompasses both Motte's and Béhar's explanations as to why Breton so highly praised an otherwise worthless play, devoting several pages of commentary to it.

My belief is that Breton, motivated by more than simply a desire to go against theatrical conventionalism, tests himself in terms of how intense his emotions remain through time. This test is congruous with his lifelong experiment with the interaction of the states of dreaming and waking, in an ultimate attempt to reach a state of absolute freedom. Portraying himself as a plaything of his memory, he embarks on a random juxtaposition of remarkable events in his life that, curiously enough, through the mechanisms of dream work, prove to have a latent coherence. In this light, then, the "wireless" connection of Nadja's game with Blanche Derval's portrayal of Solange becomes undeniable. Equally, a displacement mechanism, characteristic of the interaction between dream and waking, makes the identification of Nadja with Solange/Blanche Derval in the narrator's view. This triple identification, or over-determination, takes form in Breton's mind at the moment he first encounters Nadja's eyes, before even knowing her name. Her theatrical-looking, unfinished eye make-up immediately evokes Blanche Derval in the role of Solange in his mind:

> Il est intéressant de noter à ce propos, que Blanche Derval, dans le rôle de Solange, même vue de très près, ne paraissait en rien maquillée. Est-ce à dire que ce qui est très faiblement permis dans la rue mais est recommandé au théâtre ne vaut à mes yeux qu'autant qu'il est passé outre à ce qui est défendu dans un cas, ordonné dans l'autre? Peut-être (*OC1* 683–5).

> [It is interesting to note, in this regard, that Blanche Derval, as Solange, even when seen at close range, never seemed at all made up. Does this mean that what is only slightly permissible in the street but advisable in the theatre is important to me only insofar as it has defied what is forbidden in one case, decreed in the other? Perhaps (Howard 64).]

Nadja looks as though she is made-up for the stage and Derval is almost without its gaudy aid; this inversion of stage-like make-up immediately attracts Breton. Such an exchange between stage and reality could be considered a concrete image of the constant exchange of the two states of mind: dreaming and waking, imaginary and real. The composite of Nadja/Solange/Blanche is elevated to a symbol that reveals the possibility of the "marvelous" for this ideal spectator.[41] Finally, Breton created this triple identification, when he signed (with the puzzling initials G.L.) a four-page "plaquette," entitled "Nadja/Blanche," published in the 1980s, which contained four letters from Breton to Blanche Derval.[42]

The focus on the spectator is evident in both *plays* (that is, in Nadja's game and the staging of *Les Détraquées*). As if a transparent vector connects him with one of the stage protagonists, Solange, the spectator, experiences this connection as a magical moment and ignores the other character on the opposite edge of the stage. In fact, it may be possible that such wireless connection between the spectator and Solange goes even further back, to the time of *Poisson soluble* (*Soluble Fish*, 1924), where Breton talks about another Solange, who plays a love game with him that consists of multiple transformations and hide-and-seek games: "Quand il s'agit de Solange ... Huit jours durant nous avons habité une région plus délicate que l'impossibilité de se poser pour certaines hirondelles" (*OC1* 397) [When it's Solange ... For a week we lived in a region more delicate than the impossibility of alighting for certain swallows (Seaver and Lane 107)]. Thus, no matter how disconnected from each other the characters may seem on stage, this does not affect the spectator or his connection with one or more of them; we are reminded of Breton's statement in his first manifesto of Surrealism about dialogue as two simultaneous soliloquies.

My concern here has been to see how well the narrator carries out the task of the performance analyst. For, due to the passage of time, instead of being a mere viewer, he becomes rather a performance reviewer: Breton performs the function of a meticulous performance analyst, who is unconcerned by the absence of clear indicators in the plot. Instead, he relates the flow of dream-like images on stage to his own self-quest, a kind of a double play of mirrors between his states of dreaming and waking. From a novice, he becomes an initiate; from a player, he becomes a spectator of a continuously concatenated spectacle that foregrounds the same image. This image within an image that favors a new mode of seeing and perceiving announces another game that Surrealists have practiced since 1953, the famous game "l'un dans l'autre" (the one into another), which for some is equivalent to "the manifesto of the Surrealist games" (Garrigues 37).[43] Seen in terms of this game—almost an enigma to be solved by the viewers— Nadja's game becomes more coherent, offering clues about the impact on the narrator/author who is newly acquainted with it.

Conclusion

Breton is the "demain joueur," who lets himself become the plaything of memory during Nadja's game, a game that germinates both the "exquisite corpse" and the "one into another" games in which surrealist ludic activity culminate. This "player of tomorrow" has seen in Nadja's game a free activity *par excellence* that tests the limits of language and effortlessly fuses the real with the imaginary. As a participant on the margins of Nadja's peculiar game, despite his initial reluctance, he experienced a full range of irrational states of mind: surprise, confusion, bewilderment, challenge, resistance, fear, and a voyage to the "marvelous." As a playmate of Nadja's, Breton became at once a game-spoiler[44] and a game-validator. By surrendering to the evocative power of language, he was led on an inner journey back to what he thought were long-gone experiences in front of the stage. Nadja's game reawakened and reaffirmed the major themes at the heart of all surrealist imagery: the states of dreaming and waking, desire and mad love, sexuality, criminality, black humor (see Grand-Guignol), infancy-puerility, and myth reversal. In addition, the game featured all the major dream mechanisms that Freud discussed, such as condensation, displacement, consideration of figurability, and secondary revision. In short, her game was a microcosm of Breton's unstated dramatic theory.

It is now safe to argue that, for Breton, theatre should be like play, in the sense of *a free activity par excellence* aspiring to no material gain; this kind of play is related to the festival and the ritual, in the sense that it is *methectic* (initiative and participatory) rather than *mimetic*. Thus, there is no fourth wall present on this kind of stage. Furthermore, the stage is seen as an application of the concept of the surrealist dialogue that goes against conventional theatre. The subject matter of love is the exclusive focus of this kind of theatre. Nadja and her game had the power to force Breton to confront himself. She led him to re-create *ex nihilo* the image that had so much perplexed him as a spectator/analyst at his repeated attendance of *Les Détraquées*. Her game, resonating with the perplexing scene functioned as a stage on which it re-appeared, serving in some way as a model stage and a mirror for her playmate. More specifically, Nadja's game functioned for her playmate as follows: first, as an ideal stage, modeled after a children's play-world where Nadja acts like Alice in Wonderland. Second, Nadja's game is perceived through the eyes of Nadja-the-"voyante." Nadja's playmate feels the anxiety caused by the metamorphosis of a child transformed into a woman-enchantress. Finally, and most importantly, Nadja's game is a mirror-stage, in the sense of a particular case of the function of the *imago*—"the transformation that takes place in the subject when he assumes an image" (Sheridan 2). The receiver's "I" is transformed and is led to the "marvelous." How is this achieved?

The Lacanian model elucidates this process. The narrator/author's "I," prior to his encounter with Nadja's revealing *imagos* that issued from her game, felt "dismembered," in the sense of being suffocated by the "paucity of reality." Once the narrator/author's "I" encounters his own reflected image as Nadja's playmate—in a Gestalt form, that is, in its wholeness—he begins to assume this image, and thus he begins to be transformed. Such wholeness in his self is conveyed by Nadja's own wholeness, in sharp contrast to what he had thought in "Le Discours sur le peu de réalité," when he attempted to don a medieval soldier's armor. At that time, he felt fragmented, but after his encounter with Nadja's marvelous world, he became aware that such a passage from one persona to another is in fact possible, provided one allows a fusion of the real with the imaginary. He therefore reorients himself and starts anew within the world of surreality, which restores the magical power of words and images.

Any attempt to reconstruct Breton's theory should place the spectator at the center and take into consideration the play element that Nadja's game has activated. With her game, Nadja holds the promise, as her nickname in Russian suggests ("hope"), of a modern, inventive, "wireless," spectator-oriented stage. Such a theatre would comply with what Breton had expressed by means of automatic writing in his skit *S'il vous plaît*. This playlet reenacts a clash among the spectators in a theatre. One of them expresses his disappointment and indignation with regard to what he sees on the stage and leaves the theatre with his fist pointing out toward the scene, as if he wants to kill the actors:

Depuis quelque temps, sous prétexte d'originalité et d'indépendance, notre bel art est saboté par une bande d'individus dont le nombre grossit chaque jour et qui ne sont, pour la plupart, que des énergumènes, des paresseux ou des farceurs (*OC1* 153).

[For some time now, under the pretext of originality and independence, our fine art has been sabotaged by a gang of individuals whose number increases every day and who in their majority are fanatics, idles or farce makers.]

These words are quite telling, given the fact that they were the product of automatic writing. They reveal how deeply rooted in Breton's mind was the concern for the reaction of the public toward the new kind of theatre that he intended to implement. This new theatre was to stand in opposition to the conventional, well-made play, represented by the grand figures of French theatre such as Montaigne, Diderot, Voltaire, or Ernest Renan.

Breton became the model of a performance analyst in front of *Les Détraquées* and the Modern Theatre. His analysis was not one of a specialized critic, but one of a deeply troubled spectator guided by desire, just as Nadja was in her game. With it, she tested the limits of language in the same way that both the "exquisite corpse" and the "one into another" surrealist games did, both of which were somehow present in Nadja's game. The "paucity of reality" that Breton had perceived in the conventional use of language was challenged. He had already started to defy it when he and Philippe Soupault employed automatic writing to compose the series of poetic dialogues significantly entitled "Les Barrières" ("The Barriers," 1919). Breaking the barriers of limited reality, Nadja's verbal game serves as one of the means through which Surrealism became more valid, as it was defined in the *Manifesto of Surrealism*: "a psychic automatism in its pure state by which one proposes to express—verbally, by means of the written word or in any other manner—the actual functioning of thought" (Seaver and Lane 26). Such a psychic automatism is directly dictated by thought, in the absence of any control exercised by reason. To use Matthew's words, "to the surrealist, language is not the faithful record of previously formulated thought, logically expressed so as to appeal to 'desiccated reason'" (*Theatre* 277–8). Nadja's game is situated in accord with Surrealism's belief "in the disinterested play of thought" (Seaver and Lane 26). Through free association, dream work, and the imagination's free play, the Surrealists tested the limits of language, with a use that was equal to:

an enrichment of the active vocabulary of poetry, a release from verbal inhibitions, a selection of word association beyond the barriers set up by logic, a new metaphor built upon these incongruous word groupings, and the images resulting from the association of the metaphor with another—which one might call the square of the metaphor (Balakian, *The Road* 135).

Nadja's game stands as an imaginary stage for Breton's ludic dramatic theory, as it discloses the relation between conscious and unconscious and leads to a derangement of all senses. Like the "one into another" surrealist game, Nadja's playground forms the fluid dream-like stage, which is magically transformed to interchangeable similar stages. Nadja herself melts into at least two other female characters (Solange/Blanche Derval) presenting thus the ultimate challenge for her playmate-observer: her game debunks Breton's fantasy of a unified "total" personality, leading him back to the unconscious depths of language as the play of multiple meanings, which subverts all ego-formation. Whereas she has come to terms with the otherness of the self, the narrator/author Breton finds it impossible to reconcile himself with such an idea. His fixation with the imaginary makes him resist Nadja's game as if it were a case of counter-transference. Rather than accepting her multiplicity of selves, he abandons her in order to elevate her to a permanent symbol of the eternal feminine, who strangely blends beauty with sexuality and mystery. Yet, one fact remains undeniable: through her game, Nadja has irreparably transformed her playmate. She makes him clearly see the reversibility of the realm of reality with that of the stage. What he so stubbornly denied in the latter—that is, the identification with the other—he experienced himself in Nadja's game. Nadja became an iconic figure of the function of the theatre as an endless play of meanings far from a fixed idealized meaning. She became the *demain jouer* herself, the deferred player of tomorrow, always to remain unattainable and forever desired. This is indeed the ideal stage of which Breton had been dreaming, as an ideal successor of the Romantics; it was a stage that had inherent in it the ludic element. Such a stage was too fluid, too cinematic, too playful, and too dependent on the spectator's imagination to be put into practice at Breton's time, when stage techniques were not developed enough. Such a theatre is not impossible in today's world, however, with the advanced use of light and space on stage as well as the presence of intermediality—that is, the incorporation of various media. Breton's supposed hostility towards the theatre may simply have been his awareness of the impossibility of putting into practice at the time the ludic element he held to be the ideal. The ever-elusive and fluid nature of *play*—more akin to the cinematic form—that so attracted Breton was quite simply incompatible with the more static nature of the stage as he had experienced it. The very element, which so fascinated the leader of Surrealism in the element of play was ironically the main impediment to its practical realization on stage.

The following chapters explore the major techniques and themes that Nadja's game encapsulated and revealed (with a particular focus on desire culminating in "mad love") in a variety of surrealist and post-surrealist plays. What Breton himself refused to put into practice, for fear of failing to reproduce the authenticity of the ludic element inherent in surrealist language, was ironically attempted in the name of Surrealism by two ex-members of the surrealist group. I refer to Roger Vitrac and Antonin Artaud, founders of the Théâtre Alfred Jarry, who made the first attempt at putting Breton's implicit ludic dramatic theory into practice when they produced *The Mysteries of Love: A Surrealist Drama* in 1927. Their experiment was repeated more systematically three decades later, by the Greek playwright Nanos Valaoritis. How all these attempts to "play" with Breton's ludic dramatic theory transpired will be the subject matter in the next chapter.

Notes

1   See Breton, *Nadja*, trans. Richard Howard, 74. Hereafter, I will refer to this translation of *Nadja*. Unless otherwise indicated, all translations are mine. In each case, I offer the original quotation along with my translation, when no other translation is available; I wish the reader to have access to both texts and the chance thus to evaluate my choice of translation. The original is based on the first volume of the latest Gallimard edition of Breton's *Œuvres complètes* edited under the direction of Marguerite Bonnet, in collaboration with Philippe Bernier, Étienne-Alain Hubert, and José Pierre (1988).

2   It is interesting to note that, in an effort to clarify the expression "the extreme limit of the Surrealist aspiration," Breton's footnote is accompanied by yet another footnote in the 1988 Gallimard edition. I refer to footnote n. 4 on page 690, which is developed on page 1544. The entire footnote in the original reads: "Aspiration à la conquête de la liberté par la disponibilité, l'errance, l'attente (voir n. 3, p. 681) et la puissance de l'imaginaire. Mais notons qu'il s'agit ici de cette aspiration à son *extrême*, 'à sa plus forte *idée limite'*. Un des problèmes majeurs de Breton et du surréalisme consiste à aller au plus loin dans cette quête, mais sans basculer au-delà de la *limite*, en cheminant sur la crête étroite qui domine le précipice. Périlleux équilibre, qui ne fut pas accordé à tous" (*OC1* 1544). [Aspiration to conquer freedom by the availability, wandering, waiting (see n. 3, p. 681) and the power of the imagination. But note that this is the aspiration to its *extreme*, 'to its highest *idea-limit'.* One major problem of Breton and Surrealism is to go further in this quest, but without tipping beyond the limit, walking along the narrow ridge overlooking the precipice. Perilous balance, which was not granted to everyone.]

3   More specifically, the first three acts of *S'il vous plaît* premiered during the Dada evening that took place in the Théâtre de l'Œuvre on March 27, 1920, with Breton and Soupault being among the cast of actors, along with Miss Doyon, Paul and Gala Eluard, Théodore Fraenkel, Henri Cliquennois, and Georges Ribemont-Dessaignes. These three acts also appeared in issue number 16 of the revue *Littérature* in September–October 1920. As far as *Vous m'oublierez* is concerned, its two first acts appeared in the first issue of *Cannibale*, on April 25, 1920, while the entire text appeared in the fourth issue of the new series of *Littérature* on September 1, 1922. It was also staged in the Dada "happening" in the Gaveau room on May 27, 1920 with the following cast: Breton, playing the role of un umbrella; Philippe Soupault in the role of a bathrobe; Paul Eluard in the role of a sewing machine; and Theodore Fraenkel playing an unknown person.

4   Pierre Brunel chronicles the clash between Breton's surrealist circle and Antonin Artaud over the staging of Strindberg's *Dream Play*. See Brunel, "Strindberg et Artaud."

5   For more details, see Béhar, "The Passionate Attraction."

6   The reference in question is: "I have myself shown in the social dialectic that structures human knowledge as paranoiac why human knowledge has greater autonomy than animal knowledge in relation to the field of force of desire, but also why human knowledge is determined in that 'little reality' ([ce peu de réalité]), which the Surrealists, in their restless way, saw as its limitation" (Sheridan 3–4). For more details, see Lacan, *Écrits: A Selection*, trans. Alan Sheridan.

7   Marguerite Bonnet notes that this epithet was attached to Breton on several occasions as a posthumous homage to him. For example, Maurice Blanchot published a text entitled "Le Demain joueur" in the special issue of the journal *Nouvelle revue française*, dedicated to Breton, on April 1, 1967. Also, an internal resolution, entitled "Pour un demain joueur," was undertaken by the editorial board of the literary review *Archibras* on May 10, 1967. See endnote 3, Breton, *OC1* 1608.

8   Warren Motte devotes to *Nadja* the second chapter of his book *Playtexts*, 31–47.

9   Motte borrows Breton's term "beauté convulsive" ("convulsive beauty") with which he closes *Nadja*: "La beauté sera CONVULSIVE ou ne sera pas" (*OC1* 753) [beauty will be CONVULSIVE or will not be at all (Howard 160)]. Breton employs again the same term in *Amour fou* (*Mad Love*) and enhances it. More specifically, he closes the first chapter of this work with this sentence: "La beauté convulsive sera érotique-voilée, explosante-fixe, magique-circonstantielle ou ne sera pas" (*OC2* 687) [Convulsive beauty will be veiled-erotic, fixed-explosive, magic-circumstantial, or it will not be (Caws 19)]. Its first appearance, however, was in an autograph by Breton, dated April 15, 1934, and

its first publication was in the surrealist revue *Minotaure* (May 12, 1934, 9–16). Cauvin argues that this phrase resumes Breton's concept of esthetic emotion, characterized by unpredictability and surprise. "Convulsive beauty," he states, "is defined by Breton not as motion but as 'l'expiration exacte de ce mouvement,' that is, motion in suspension" (23).

10   Béhar, *André Breton* 198. The affair between Nadja and Breton was ephemeral. This is how Henri Béhar sums up Nadja's fate: "Due to a crisis of hallucinations in her hotel, she was led to the asylum on March 21, 1927, then at the St. Anne's and later on at the Perray-Vaucluse asylum in the Department of the Seine. At her parents' request she was transferred next year to the North. Nadja will remain interned in a psychiatric institution until her death in 1941." Marguerite Bonnet offers more details about the tumultuous relationship of Nadja and Breton in her notes to *Nadja* included in *OC1* 1502.

11   At least Marguerite Bonnet, the editor of André Breton's *Œuvres complètes* does not leave any doubt about this: "Nadja est incontestablement un récit autobiographique où tout s'efforce non seulement à la vérité, mais à l'exactitude, malgré la place essentielle qu'y tient le non-dit, les rétractions de l'écriture, le halo des silences dont, néanmoins, la réverbération secrète projette sur le texte une sorte de lumière incertaine" (*OC1* 1496). [Nadja is undoubtedly an autobiographical narrative in which everything is forced not only toward truth, but also to exactitude, despite the essential place that the non-expressed takes there, along with the retractions of writing, the aura of the silences the secret reverberation of which at least projects on the text a kind of uncertain light.]

12   According to Claude Maillard-Chary, in her article "Melusine entre Sphinx et Sirène, ou la 'queue préhensile' du désir rattrapé" [Melusina between Sphinx and Siren, or the "Tail Able to Seize" the Regained Desire], Melusina is the ending and the key to the surrealist quest. In her, "tout interdit levé, toute transcendance désavouée et reniée, l'amour passionnel rejoint l'humour léger, l'humour 'sublime' et 'libérateur', celui des jeux de mots ensorcelants ..." (228) [every raised interdiction, every disavowed and renounced transcendence, the passionate love rejoin the light humor, the "sublime" and "liberating" humor, one of the enchanting word games ...]. For more details, see Maillard-Chary, "Melusine entre Sphinx et Sirène, ou la 'queue préhensile' du désir rattrapé."

13   See André Breton, *OC1*, 646 and 1516. This is how André Breton thinks of *Nadja*, thereby stressing its anti-literary character.

14   In this first writing sample Breton's voice is fused with Philippe Soupault's voice thanks to the use of automatic writing. The most characteristic example of this dialogue-monologue type bears the interestingly liminal title "Les Barrièrres" ("The Barriers").

15   See Breton, *Manifestoes of Surrealism*, trans. Richard Seaver and Helen R. Lane, 123–4.

16   For more details on this game, see Garrigues, *Les Jeux surréalistes* 29–30 and 69–70. This is the fifth volume of the Surrealist Archives. Here, Garrigues quotes the following definition of this game offered in *Le Dictionnaire abrégé du surréalisme*, which served as a catalogue in the Exposition de 1938: "Jeu de papier plié qui consiste à faire composer une phrase ou un dessin par plusieurs personnes, sans qu' aucune d'elles puisse tenir compte de la collaboration ou des collaborations précédentes" (31) [Game of a folded paper consisting of a phrase or a drawing made by many people being unaware of the previous collaborations]. See also Cauvin, "Literary Games of Chance." Cauvin describes this parlor game as follows: "Cadavre exquis ('exquisite corpse') is the surrealist version of a parlor game in which various players add to a sentence or drawing without seeing the preceding entries, the latter being concealed from view by a folding of the sheet. The first sentence so composed gave the game its name" (18).

17   This game first appeared in *Medium*, n. 2 (February 1954) and n. 3 (May 1954). It started one evening in the café of the place Blanche in which Breton, referring to the power of analogy, argued that a lion could be well described as the flame of a match he had lit.

Philippe Audoin describes this game as follows: [Striking a match, Breton recognized a lion. Why indeed couldn't a lion be an inflamed match? The game begins there. One of the players leaves the room and identifies himself secretly with some object, a chocolate bar, for example. During his absence the other players decide that he is a boar. The bar of chocolate is going to describe itself in the language of a boar until it is discovered. "I am"—it will say—"a boar of very small dimensions that lives in a copse with a brilliant metallic look, surrounded by rather dangerous foliage. My dentition is exterior to me: it is made up of millions of teeth ready to sink into me"] (quoted in Orenstein Feman 28–9). For more details see Garrigues, *Les Jeux surréalistes* 38.

18   The following examples are characteristic of the dialogue in the sense that Breton defined it, taking place between a doctor and a patient in certain pathological states of mind: "Q. 'How old are you? A. You,' (Echolalia) Q. 'What is your name? A. 'Forty-five houses' (Ganser syndrome, or beside-the-point-replies)" (Seaver and Lane 34). Obviously, in both examples there is a clear lack of logical coherence; however, there is a newly-emerged logic, that of the image-building technique.

19   Michael Riffaterre's contribution to the process of metaphor formation in surrealist poetry is also illuminating/ instructive: "Ce qu'on appelle métaphore filée est en fait une série de métaphores reliées les unes aux autres par la syntaxe—elles font partie de la même phrase ou d'une même structure narrative ou descriptive—et par le sens: chacune exprime un aspect particulier d'un tout, chose ou concept, que représente la première métaphore de la série" (*Text Production* 47) [What we call web-metaphor is in fact a series of metaphors linked among themselves through syntax—they make part of the same phrase of the same narrative or descriptive structure—and by means of the content: each one expresses a particular aspect of a whole, thing or concept that the first metaphor of the series represents].

20   This expression is an explicit reference to the aforementioned significant text "Introduction sur le discours sur le peu de réalité" ("Introduction to the Discourse on the Paucity of Reality"), written by André Breton in September 1924.

21   It is not only the relevance of the seminal Lacanian essay "The Mirror Stage" to some of Breton's surrealist beliefs about language that makes indispensable the co-examination of these two leading French figures. Basing their statement on Anna Balakian's findings, Muller and Richardson also assert that "Lacan was one of his [Breton's] numerous well-known friends, and he apparently had a significant influence on Lacan's thought and style" (316–17). Likewise, Stamos Metzidakis leaves no doubt about Breton's impact upon Lacan's thought. For more details, see his article "Breton's Structuralism."

22   Muller and Richardson expand on this issue in the following passage: "In any case, the image is a form that in-forms the subject and makes possible the process of identification with it. Identification with a constellation of images leads to a behavioral pattern that reflects the social structures within which those images first emerged. It is through the complex that images are established in the psychic organization that influence the broadest unities of behavior: images with which the subject identifies completely in order to play out, as the sole actor, the drama of conflicts between them" (28).

23   Freud's "La Question de l'analyse par les non-médecins" was cited in the issue 9–10 of *La Révolution surréaliste* on October 1, 1927.

24   Nadja—whose real name, according to Marguerite Bonnet, was Leona-Camille-Ghislaine—was born in the region of Lille on May 23, 1902 (*OC1* 1509). During her first meeting with Breton on October 4, 1926, among other things, she talked about her father and her mother, her friends, and her wanderings in the streets of Paris in search of small jobs. She also learned about Breton's marital status and saw Breton's wife as a star towards whom her interlocutor was directed.

25   In fact, Nadja introduces in the text of *Nadja* what a year later would become the official game of the surrealist circle, led by Breton, and called "The Dialogue in 1928."

26   The term "détraquées" has multiple meanings revolving around insanity. According to the dictionary *Le Robert quotidien* (ed. 1996), it means "dérangées" (deranged), "troublées" (troubled), "déréglées" (unruled), "désaxées" (unaxed), "abîmées" (destroyed), "déséquilibrées" (unbalanced), "fous" (mad), "détériorées" (deteriorated). According to *Harrap's New Standard French and English Dictionary* (rev. ed. 1972), the term means: "broken in health, broken down, shattered in mind and body." It is in the latter sense that the playwright himself, Pierre Palau, means the term "détraquées," while admitting the adventure of the title before its finality. Inspired by some incidents that happened in a girl's institution in the Parisian area, he asked Paul Thiery's help because he would deal in his play with a case of periodical and circular insanity and therefore needed a doctor's expertise to advise him on the scientific aspects of his work. This expertise was offered to him by the preeminent Joseph Babinsky, Breton's own professor when he was a medical student at the Salpetrière Hospital. The initial title he had chosen for his play was "Mademoiselle Solange, professeur de danse et de maintien," but the director of the theatre in which it was agreed to be staged objected and suggested instead the title "Les Vicieuses." Palau, in turn, completely disagreed with this title because, in his view, the case of insanity with which he was dealing had nothing to do with any kind of vice. Finally, they came to an agreement with the title *Les Détraquées*. All the above information is given in a note signed by Pierre Palau that accompanies the publication of this play in the first volume of *Le Surréalisme même* (third trimester of 1956), 121.

27   Information gathered from Pierron "House of Horrors."

28   One wonders here whether Breton's attention to the balloon on stage is not also associated, at some latent level, with another similar scene in the famous play by Guillaume Apollinaire that Breton overtly admired. I refer to the play *Les Mamelles de Tirésias* (*The Breasts of Tiresias*). The term "surrealist" appears for the first time in this play's prologue, which Breton borrowed to use in a different manner. There the balloons symbolize Thérèse's breasts, which she releases at the end of the play along with other balls to serve the audience both for feeding and playing. It's interesting also to note the last line of the play: "Luck is a game win or lose/just keep your eye on the play" (91).

29   Breton admired the feeling of surprise expressed in the work of the surrealist painter Giorgio De Chirico. In *Nadja*, he writes: "De Chirico a reconnu alors qu'il ne pouvait peindre que surpris (surpris le premier) par certaines dispositions d'objects et que toute l'énigme de la révélation tenait pour lui dans ce mot: surpris" (*OC1* 649). [De Chirico understood then that he would not be able to paint but while being surprised (surprised the first) by certain dispositions of objects and that every enigma of revelation was comprised for him in this word: surprised].

30   Howard's translation here leaves out the ludic element of the performers' acting. "Le jeu dérisoire des acteurs" literally translates as: "the ridiculous game of the actors."

31   Louis Aragon, in his own detailed description of the Modern Theatre with which he closes the first part of *Paysan de Paris* (1926)—a text which is also cited in *Nadja*—locates these illicit desires in the audience's voyeuristic wish to see the nude "skin" of the actresses (131).

32   Aragon, *Paris Peasant*, trans. Simon Watson Taylor, 120.

33   There is no doubt about the influence of one on the other in their work. Breton himself quotes *Le Paysan de Paris* in *Nadja*, while they are both living in the same area in 1927 when Breton is composing *Nadja* and Aragon the *Traité du style*. Marguerite Bonnet informs us that during this period the two friends see each other on a daily basis and exchange views to the point that they comment on each other's different writing styles.

Thus, Breton talks about Aragon's playful style of writing: "comme en se jouant, moi d'autant plus difficilement que la narration n'a jamais été mon fort" [as if playing, while for me it was much more difficult since narration has never been my strength]. He continues: "Il me disait, il est vrai, l'autre jour qu'il avait par rapport à moi l'impression, lui, d'écrire d'une manière si creuse" [he was telling me, it is true, the other day, that he had the impression in regard to myself that he was writing in an empty manner] (*OC1* 1503).

34   Palau's account of the controversial reception of his play is interesting: "La répétition générale eut lieu le samedi 19 février 1921. Ce fut un scandale sans précédent. L'indignation de ces messieurs-dames de la Critique atteignit à son paroxysme. Je fus littéralement accablé sous les injures; entre autres, une certaine dame qui devait par la suite s'illustrer dans la littérature, après avoir été elle-même quelque peu malmenée sur la scène du Moulin Rouge, hurlait plus fort que les aboyeurs accrédités, au point de s'attirer ce rappel cinglant de Fernand Nozière: 'Ah non! ... surtout ... pas vous!' En compensation, *Les Détraquées* se jouèrent 278 fois de suite devant des salles pleines, et reprises par la suite déjà trois fois, toujours avec la même fortune et même, curieux retour des choses d'ici-bas, avec les louanges de la presse ... Parmi ces louanges, l'une m'a toujours été au cœur, et je la reçus d'André Breton, qui a bien voulu consacrer à ma pièce un chapitre enthousiaste dans son livre *Nadja*" (121). [The dress rehearsal took place on Saturday the February 19, 1921. It was a scandal without precedent. The indignation of those ladies and gentlemen of the Critique reached its paroxysm. I was literally harmed by these injuries; in addition, a certain lady who would soon be portrayed in literature, after having been somehow ill-brought to the stage of Moulin-Rouge, hurled more than the most renown dogs to the point that she recalled this rappel of Fernand Nozière: "Ah no! ... certainly ... not you!" In recompense, *Les Détraquées* was put on stage 278 consecutive times in front of full audiences and staged again later on three occasions, always having the same chance and even, a curious return of events happening here on earth, with the appraisals of the press ... Amidst those appraisals, one which I always cherish, I received from André Breton, who also wanted to devote to my play a chapter in his book *Nadja*.]

35   It is interesting to point out that Nadja is also explicitly associated with the modern spirit in *Nadja*, when Breton implies that Nadja had cut the pages entitled "L'esprit nouveau" from his book *Le pas perdus* given to her the previous day. The following quotation from *Nadja* describes the relevant passage of *Les pas perdus* where Breton and his friends Louis Aragon and André Derain came across an irresistible sphinx, in the form of a charming young lady, "allant d'un trottoir à l'autre interroger les passants, ce sphinx qui nous avait épargnés l'un l'autre et, à sa recherche, de courir le long de toutes les lignes qui, même très capricieusement, peuvent relier ces points-le manque de résultats de cette poursuite que le temps écoulé eût dû rendre sans espoir, c'est à cela qu'est allée tout de suite Nadja" (*OC1* 691).

36   According to Marguerite Bonnet, Breton started writing this text immediately after he completed the *Manifesto of Surrealism*, but he finished it only in January 1925 and published it in March 1925, in the winter 1924 issue of the journal *Commerce*. For more details see *OC2* 1438–46.

37   It is also interesting that Breton closes *Nadja* with a broken message transmitted through a threadless telegraphy about a lost plane in the area of l'Ile de Sable. The message begins thus, "Il y a quelque chose qui ne va pas" (*OC1* 753), to be followed by this famous phrase, which closes *Nadja*: "La beauté sera convulsive ou ne sera pas" (*OC1* 753).

38   See André Breton, *OC2* 265. This reference to Greek mythology acquires a greater significance once one recalls that this is the only myth cherished by the Surrealists from Greek mythology, an otherwise neglected mythology in their circle.

39   The play in question was *Les Détraquées*, performed by Le Théâtre des Deux Masques in February 1921. In a letter dated September 26, 1927, Breton thanks Derval for giving him permission to use her photographs in *Nadja* by explaining to her: "Yours, first, Madame, because I have admired you more than any artist in the world, which I state with unmistakable clarity in my book, and then one of a scene from the play as well, because my memories of it will never fade" (Béhar, "Passionate Attraction" 16). Breton's following words, also addressed to the actress Blanche Derval in a letter, dated September 14, 1927, are characteristic: "I am about to publish, as I briefly told you, a work which is, properly speaking, neither an essay nor a novel, in the course of which I evoke among other significant and decisive episodes of my life, two or three evenings which I once spent at the Two Masks, and I speak of you, and you alone, in this connection" (16).

40   This issue is evidently related to the explicit question that operates in *Nadja*, namely, "Qui suis-je?" [Who am I?] or [Whom am I following?].

41   A fourth persona could also merge into this triple female identification in this ideal spectator's case. I refer to Jeanne Duval, Baudelaire's muse whose name sounds similar to Derval's, a connection further supported by the general affinities between Baudelaire and Breton. In any case, both Derval and Duval function as muses.

42   Marguerite Bonnet offers more details on this issue in Breton, *OC1* 1536.

43   See note 8, above.

44   One could also justify the narrator as a game-spoiler if he/she sees him as a tentative psychoanalyst who has to remain silent in order to censure the cure of his/her patient, who in this case is Nadja herself.

2

Staging "mad love" in the Théâtre Alfred Jarry: Breton's ludic dramatic theory in practice

Si le théâtre est un jeu, trop de graves problèmes nous sollicitent pour que nous puissions distraire, au profit, de quelque chose d'aussi aléatoire que ce jeu, la moindre parcelle de notre attention. *Si le théâtre n'est pas un jeu*, s'il est une réalité véritable, par quels moyens lui rendre ce rang de réalité, faire de chaque spectacle une sorte d'événement, tel est le problème que nous avons à resoudre (Artaud, *OC2* 11; my emphasis).

[*If the theatre is a game*, so many serious problems require that we be able to distract, to our advantage, the smallest part of our attention by something so aleatory as this game. *If the theatre is not a game*, if it is a true reality, by which means we should give it back this rank of reality and make of each spectacle a kind of event—this is the problem we have to solve.]

Introduction

André Breton may have been too cautious to practice his own notion of surrealist theatre for fear of compromising its ludic nature and, thereby, its free and aleatory character, particularly after he made several minor attempts when he was still under the influence of Dada.[1] After these attempts, he became convinced that no stage director would ever accept any surrealist play; a conviction that allowed him to pursue, unhindered by the issue of any potential staging, his quest for absolute freedom when writing his theatrical pieces. His collaborator Philippe Soupault is very explicit in this regard. In his letter to Tristan Tzara, of January 14, 1920, as Marguerite Bonnet informs us, he writes: "Écrire une pièce de théâtre était une entreprise qui n'était qu'un défi. Nous savions qu'une pièce 'surréaliste' … ne serait jamais 'reçue' par aucun directeur de théâtre. Cette conviction nous permettait d'écrire en toute liberté" (quoted in Breton, *OC1* 1174) [Writing a theatrical piece was an undertaking, which was nothing but a challenge. We knew that a "surrealist" play would never be "accepted" by any stage director. Such a conviction allowed us to write in absolute freedom].

However, two ex-members of the surrealist movement—Roger Vitrac (1848–1948) and the well-known Antonin Artaud (1899–1952), who was himself a stage director—dared for the first time to give "flesh and bones" to Breton's latent ludic dramatic theory, two years before *Nadja*'s publication. In an attempt to infuse the stage with "surreality," ironically enough immediately after their excommunication from the surrealist group by Breton, they founded the Théâtre Alfred Jarry in Paris in November 1926 along with Robert Aron.[2] Together they announced a theatre that would break with the strict conventions of an illusionistic theatrical tradition and would instead function as a game—but a serious one. If the kind of theatre they envisioned was a game, Béhar remarks, they wanted to play it out within their own being, as well as the spectator's. They hoped, Béhar adds, that a spectator would "give himself/herself to a veritable operation in which not only his/her spirit but also his/her senses and flesh participate in this game" (*Un réprouvé* 136). Vitrac and Artaud thus transformed the Théâtre Alfred Jarry into a playground, where they played with and risked their own inner lives and those of the spectators. Treating play as a serious thing complies with the Surrealists' desire to obliterate all antinomies. As they claim rather characteristically in the program of the 1926–1927 season of the Théâtre Alfred Jarry, "the spectator and we personally cannot take ourselves seriously if we do not have a very clear impression that a part of our inner life is at stake in this action that has as a frame the stage. Comic or tragic, our game will be one of those games during which we laugh heartily" (Artaud, *OC2* 15).

Drawing on the revolutionary spirit of Alfred Jarry, the creator of *Ubu-roi*, after whom their theatre was named, Vitrac and Artaud set out to enact the well-assimilated notion of the surrealist dialogue (as defined in the previous chapter), and to test its validity on stage in its quintessential theme of "mad love." In 1927, they staged *Les Mystères de l'amour: drame surréaliste* (*The Mysteries of Love: A Surrealist Drama*), labeling their play quite overtly as surrealist. According to Philip Auslander, this play represents the culmination of Vitrac's experimentation with surrealist drama, utterly justifying its subtitle (362). In it, "the author combines tendencies shown in his short plays of 1922 into a drama that attempts to unite life and theatre through the medium of dreams" (ibid.). Written by Vitrac at approximately the same time as the *Manifesto of Surrealism* appeared (1924), *Les Mystères de l'amour* was included in the first bill of the Théâtre Alfred Jarry in 1927[3] under Artaud's direction. Nanos Valaoritis,[4] the "last Greek Surrealist" and a member of Breton's surrealist circle during the 1950s, resumed Artaud and Vitrac's experiment with Surrealism and the stage in his play *L'Hôtel de la nuit qui tombe* (*The Nightfall Hotel*, 1957), premiered on April 27, 1959, in Paris.

The present chapter will demonstrate how Breton's implicit ludic surrealist dramatic theory was gradually put into practice over a span of 30 years, in the form of staged "mad love." We will look at how it took flesh for the first time in the Théâtre Alfred Jarry and how it reached its peak in Valaoritis's self-conscious experimentation with the surrealist games, after he joined the surrealist group in its last phase, before its "official" expiration in 1969.[5] Vitrac's *The Mysteries of Love* and Valaoritis's *The Nightfall Hotel*, quite apart from their thematic similarity that culminates in the treatment of "mad love," are examined here jointly because of their shared modeling of Breton's concept of the surrealist dialogue-game. Through a comparative study of these two plays, I shall show that surrealist ludics brings the subject of language into play even when applied to the stage. I argue that surrealist theatre remains faithful to the basic tenet of Surrealism: it functions entirely within the surrealist concept of language, which seeks to change one's perception of reality. Therefore, this theatre can indeed exist and be fruitful despite Breton's doubts and consequent reluctance to put into practice his dramatic principles.

With a focus on the theme of "mad love" in these plays, we will revisit some of Breton's surrealist credo, as well as some seminal theoretical texts, heavily influenced by Breton's ideas, signed by both Vitrac and Artaud and published during the period 1927–30. Among these, emphasis is given to the seminal text "Le Théâtre Alfred Jarry et l'hostilité publique" ("The Alfred Jarry Theatre and Public Hostility"), written in 1930 by Vitrac, after the staging of *The Mysteries of Love*, but published, interestingly, under Artaud's name.[6] Finally, several theoretical excerpts about Surrealism from Valaoritis's books—*Για μια θεωρία της Γραφής* (*For a Theory of Writing*) (1990) and *Για μια θεωρία της Γραφής Β* (*For a Theory of Writing B*) (2006)—are also examined here to illustrate better the development of the reception of Breton's ludic ideas.

The Mysteries of Love: A Surrealist Drama as a serious playground

The Mysteries of Love: A Surrealist Drama premiered on June 1, 1927, at the Théâtre de Grenelle under Artaud's direction, with his beloved Génica Athanasiou playing the female lead, Leah. Based on the first three of the play's five tableaus, this production revolved around the multitudinous games in which "mad love" appeared, Surrealism's hallmark theme. In it, Leah and Patrick experience love in the way Breton conceived of it in his *Manifesto of Surrealism* (much earlier than in either *Nadja* or *Mad Love*, his more exclusive treatises on love and insanity); that is, they experience "an exceptional situation" to which normal man is no longer equal and in which all games are permissible (4). The love felt by Patrick and Leah is a perfect illustration of the Surrealists' proclamation "amour fou, amour unique" [mad love, unique love]. Maurice Nadeau explains:

> *fou* in that it broke down all barriers within which society wanted to imprison it, in that it takes all the licenses compatible with its nature; unique in that it makes the beloved, the "other" into the epitomized and living world which it is henceforth permissible to possess, in which it is henceforth possible to lose oneself (223).

Vitrac borrows "mad love" from Surrealism and presents it in a way that reflects its disjointed complexity. To use Benjamin Crémieux's words, "Mr. Vitrac put in all the images that the word 'love' can connote, without linking them through any plot at all" (quoted in Artaud, *OC* 52). No plot exists in the Aristotelian sense. The whole plot, in fact, consists of one single tableau: the depiction of the tumultuous relationship between Leah and Patrick through a series of smaller tableaus that capture all possible aspects of this relationship. Annette Levitt summarizes the plot as follows: "a young couple, Leah and Patrick, moves from courtship through marriage, unhappiness, separation, and finally reconciliation" (250).

Vitrac then enriches and polishes the theme of surrealist love by incorporating the element of the absurd that he found in Jarry's *Amour absolu*, which expresses Jarry's belief in absolute love. "Jarry used to say: I believe in absolute love because it is absurd, like believing in God" (Andreoli 374). This echoes Vitrac's belief in an absolute theatre in the sense of a theatre devoted to absolute freedom. In a collection of press releases on Le Théâtre Alfred Jarry, dated from around December 15, 1926, and paraphrased by Béhar, it was written:

> Un groupe de jeunes écrivains réunis pour ressusciter l'idée d'un théâtre absolu va fonder, sous le nom du Théâtre Alfred Jarry une companie théâtrale nouvelle. Leur effort vise à créer un théâtre qui se développera dans le sens d'une entière liberté et qui n'aura d'autre but que de satisfaire aux exigences les plus extrêmes de l'imagination et de l'esprit" (*Un Réprouvé* 135).

> [A group of young authors, united to revive the idea of an absolute theatre, will found under the name of Théâtre Alfred Jarry a new theatrical company. Their effort aims at the creation of a theatre that will develop in the sense of an entire freedom and which will not have other aims but to satisfy the most extreme needs of the imagination and of the spirit.]

Vitrac admired Jarry's *Amour absolu*, because it placed poetry in the foreground in a unique way: "God, Family, Logic, Intelligence, Thought, Language intermingle, dissolve, and reemerge in the form of startling constructions. Everything here is set under doubt. Only poetry remains intact" (quoted in Andreoli 374). Vitrac named such an absurdity of love "mysteries of love," in his homonymous play *The Mysteries of Love*, where he illustrates an interplay of shadows that is love: "Surrealism perceived a duality of love in the way lovers can both adore and despise the object of their passion" (Auslander 364). In this dual relationship of love and hatred, "the mysterious feelings of love transcend all possible communication via language" (Orenstein Feman 107). The ludic principle of transformation presides and materializes "mad love." Love "is not just courtship, marriage, and children, but also the sometimes violent disruption of these patterns and the revelation of deeper, often painful fears and desires which may lead to fuller understanding" (Levitt 269). An understanding of this kind lies in the unrestricted release of emotions, particularly as they are released by the transformational play/ acting concept in the minds of both characters and the audience. During such transformational play/acting, the most contradictory feelings give way to each other, accompanied by the most puzzling and contradictory transformations of the characters on stage, ranging at times from the animate to the inanimate, a typical device in Vitrac's work. This transformational game was well shown, for instance, in Génica Athanasiou's acting, in which she was able to transform herself multiple times "from a butcher to become at once docile, enchantress, passionate esthete" (Artaud, *Messages* 67). A revue on the Théâtre Alfred Jarry, observes:

> Well, such a spectacle is the ideal theatre. This anxiety, this feeling of guilt, this victory, this comfort at once describe the tone and the state of mind in which the spectator must leave our theatre. He will be disturbed and terrified by the inner dynamism of the spectacle that

unfolds in front of his eyes. And this dynamism will be related to the anxieties and concerns of his entire life (Artaud, *OC2* 13).

Exploding "in violent action and startling scenic effects," the tension develops in this play-spectacle, "in keeping with surrealist methods, by the juxtaposition of startling images or stage effects against one another, rather than from the interaction of the characters or ideas contained within the play" (Bennison 130–31). In *The Mysteries of Love*, surreality infuses the stage, in effect, through the workings of the surrealist ludic techniques that engage the imagination of both the actors and the audience. At the same time, these techniques expose their own role in creating the fictive unity of the human subject. The "one into another" surrealist game, in particular, that was detected in Nadja's game and was refined in the 1950s within Breton's surrealist circle, seems to have a significant role *avant la lettre*, in various avatars in *The Mysteries of Love*. This technique is vividly demonstrated in the 12-minute animated film *Dimensions of Dialogue* by the Czech surrealist Jan Švankmejer, included in the film *Jan Švankmejer, Alchemist of the Surreal* (1990). *Dimensions of Dialogue* illustrates Breton's concept of dialogue in a captivating way, as two thoughts treat each other as enemies. These two thoughts are illustrated by two mouths, composed of all kinds of things, such as kitchen or bathroom materials. Each time one of them devours the other it acquires a new form, only to be restored to its prior form after throwing out the devoured things. In this way, one is quite literally in and into another, and the game goes on endlessly—a game of jeopardy between the two mouths that at the same time devour each other and renew each other (both in terms of eating and of speaking, and thus, exposing each other's fragile fictive unity). If we imagine Patrick and Leah in *The Mysteries of Love* as two Švankmejer-esque mouths, we can uncover the ever-elusive identities formed from their linguistic exchanges, particularly through a version of "the one into another" game, all of which can be summed up in a multifaceted love–hate game with all its power-driven implications. Understanding Leah and Patrick's mad love as a new dimension of dialogue in Švankmejer's terms puts their love's inherent concept of Breton's dialogue-game at the foreground, and helps the reader/viewer find coherence in this otherwise obscure and, at the time, controversially received play.[7] In the following pages, I highlight the way in which the game "one into another" appears in *The Mysteries of Love*. Vitrac's approach to "mad love" reflects his understanding of the game in one of its earlier versions, an understanding acquired during several years' involvement in Breton's circle.[8]

The Surrealists' favorite ludic strategy of transformation permeates both the script and the production of *The Mysteries of Love* in the pivotal role of the lovers' relationship. As Martin John Bennison explains, "innumerable possibilities abound in the play for the juxtaposition of the central relationship to persons, places, and events without regard to logic or course" (124). Almost all relationships are interchangeable and can assume multiple roles at once, except in the case of Leah, even though the traditional role of the character is minimized here: "characters tend to be skeletal at best. Complex psychological portraits of a specific nature do not occur in surrealist drama. Usually, motivations are totally lacking in any of the characters' actions" (Bennison 197–8). Similarly, places are interchangeable. Thus, in this play one place can be at once a railway station, a dining car, the seashore, a hotel room, a draper's shop, or a public street. Such successive transformation of the place echoes Arthur Rimbaud's letter to Paul Demeny of May 15, 1871, known as *La lettre du voyant*. There, Rimbaud argues for a *dérèglement de tous les sens* [a disorientation of all senses], explicitly embraced by Breton himself: "Car je est un autre. Si le cuivre s'éveille clairon, il n'y a rien de sa faute" (*OC* 254) [For I is another. If the copper wakes up as a trumpet, it is not at all its fault]. The unusual transformational scenic requirements of surrealist drama, Bennison explains, "indicate an awareness, on the part of the writers involved, of the possibilities for picturing on stage the surrealist dimension of reality—the magical or super-real" (108).

Of course, one might wonder how much the theatre can sustain this endless spatial transformation, as it stands on the limit of possible presentation. Antle wonders, for example, if Vitrac's sketches are in fact impossible to present. She suggests that the use of film or video screen would be a solution, but for Vitrac "film was never the equal for theater" ("Towards Re-Presentation" 24). The novelty of Vitrac's sketches, she concludes, "resides in the fact that they are addressed to the reader as much as to the spectator, since they require an imaginary stage" (ibid.). In other words, the scenic space in Vitrac's work is a virtual space in which virtual images unfold. It is an imaginary stage or off-stage and "calls for a poetics of space, constantly questioning the concept of traditional presentation," while leading the way to modern theatre, as it is "the meeting point of all arts: performance (theatre/dance) as well as non-figurative painting" (ibid. 25). In the next section of this chapter, I focus on several forms of "one into another" ludic surrealist techniques, including one artistic medium into another artistic medium (for example, painting within a play, cinema within a play, play within a play), dream into reality and its reverse, as well as character into another character, or space into another space.

The "one into another" game-dialogue: From one artistic medium into another

The short prologue of *The Mysteries of Love*, which has not received much attention to date, introduces the spectator to the surrealist principles that guide the play. The most obvious and immediate example is its version of the "one into another" ludic technique, implemented here through the incorporation of a painting into the play—one artistic medium into another. The play opens onto a striking portrait of a woman, hung on the wall of a house in a public square that forms the stage's background. This portrait—with a full-lipped, smiling or smirking lip-stick-darkened mouth; black, lash-like, mascara-heavy markings; and a fiery, single eye, rising vertically from the forehead, bizarrely staring out alongside the woman's hair—brings the audience face to face with the "eternal feminine," with all the sensuality and terror this evokes. This mixture of feelings is further emphasized by the disproportionate hair of the woman in the portrait, composed of 10 sinuous lines in all shades of black; framed by two strong, thick black lines, one of which seems to be the brow to her "third" eye; and finally, with the vertical eye balanced on the other side by something that resembles the blade of a large knife, or a pen, or even a finger nail—the open top of which is marked by a finger-print-like constellation of fine dots. Anyone familiar with surrealist paintings immediately understands that this portrait, with its startling dis-placement of elements, belongs to their group. The most startling image, both in its arbitrariness and in its aggressive overtones, is the knife, which becomes a recurring image in the play. The surrealist artist's technique of the picture does double duty by also embodying the surrealist game "one into another." But this version of the game—this one artistic medium into another—does not stop with the portrait, but interlocks further with the stage and the action of the prologue.

The action of the play opens with Patrick on his knees, drawing lines in the mud. Soon a policeman enters and asks him in an authoritative voice what he is doing. Patrick calmly responds: "Vous le voyez, monsieur, je termine sa chevelure. *Il sort en traçant une ligne sinuesque. Le rideau tombe lentement*" (13) [As you see, Sir, I'm finishing off her hair. *He leaves, tracing a sinuous line. The curtain slowly falls* (Gladstone 229)].[9] At first glance, such a response seems nonsensical, but in the context of the portrait on the wall, Patrick's line of thought is easy to follow. He simply continues woman's hair.[10] But what does his gesture mean? Perhaps Patrick is consoling himself in some way, as Nadja did in playing her word-game. Or perhaps, by playing a similar game to Nadja's in which fantasy and reality are blurred, Patrick is bringing a lifeless female creature to life. Through this gesture of Patrick's, Vitrac illustrates in the most natural way the basic surrealist principle of the unity of the opposites. Placing Patrick at the opening of the play, drawing strokes of hair in the mud, immediately establishes his refusal to distinguish life from art or dream from reality. Like another Pygmalion, who carved his ideal woman, Galatea, from a piece of ivory that was then brought to life, Patrick attempts to bring to life his own ideal woman. At the same time, his response to the policeman, who represents here the rule of reason, indicates his determination to ignore any kind of censorship. Also, by transforming the mud that is represented reality into art, he shows his will to transform an ugly reality into something marvelous, part of his endeavor to give life to this woman (who hangs lifeless on the wall of the public square). As Breton himself defines it, "the marvelous is the element of surprise with which man greets each of his discoveries of new facets of reality" (quoted in Balakian, "André Breton as Philosopher" 40). It is as if Patrick wanted to withdraw her from the public place where she hangs as a decorative object of art, and make her part of his own life.[11] Or, he expresses his desire to possess this woman so as to give vitality to his own life. Love, as the absolute means of redemption and truth, is something that Breton will also stress in his *Second Manifesto of Surrealism* (180). For him, woman—particularly the child-woman—is the key to the beyond. As Simone de Beauvoir states:

> [t]here is in Breton the same esoteric naturalism as was in the Gnostics who saw in Sophia the principle of Redemption and even of the creation, as was in Dante choosing Beatrice for his guide and in Petrarch enkindled by the love of Laura. And that is why the being who is most firmly anchored in nature, who is closest to the ground, is also the key to the beyond. Truth, Beauty, Poetry—she is All: once more all under the form of the Other, All except herself (237).

Patrick, then, becomes the mythical creator who attempts to give life to his first creature from the clay, and thereby gain his own redemption. In one gesture, Vitrac introduces his audience to both a real and mythical world, where reality, dreamland, fantasy, and imagination coexist just as they do in surrealist poetry and painting.

As soon as Leah is introduced in the following scene, this initial painting (on the wall and in the dirt) makes more and more sense. Thus, a surrealist aura infuses the stage through the unified female portrait(s) and prepares the audience for a highly emotional effect. In essence, with the incorporation of painting in his theatre, Vitrac embraces the surrealist tenet of the prevalence of image, even on stage, and his intent to produce a theatre of creation, in which man's innermost desires are visually externalized. This "surrealist beam" (in Béhar's words; also "a denial of realism" or "a poetic dimension") forms one of surrealist theatre's main features, along with "the extraordinary place it gives to man and his problems" (quoted in Baranska 35). Both of these elements are present in *The Mysteries of Love* from its very beginning. The importance of the visual component introduced by the painting soon becomes more dramatically expressive. More precisely, a chaotic *mise-en-scène* will triumph, where a surrealist dialogue evoking violent images will assault the audience's sensibility. In this *mise-en-scène*, visual and auditory elements, along with dream and its mechanisms, take priority to create a kind of magical theatre, such as Vitrac envisioned in his 1921 article "The Alchemist," in which he calls for a sacred and ritual character of scenic (re)presentation.

Such is the case, for instance, in the following tableau from the first act, where a play within a play takes place between an old man with a long, dirty beard trailing on the ground and his son, a young man. The latter seems to be a magician, as he pulls a bird out of his pocket, while predicting his own death:

> LE JEUNE HOMME (*tirant un oiseau de sa poche*). Papa, tu as devant toi celui qui va mourir" (23).

> [THE YOUNG MAN (*pulling a bird out of his pocket*). Dad, you have before you one who is about to die (238).]

This scene is the product of automatic writing that brings to the stage an echo of Jesus' talk with his Father before his crucifixion. This "brief symbolist drama, in which the characters are less people than abstractions representing the stages of man's life" (Levitt 262) is a foreshadowing of what will soon happen between Patrick and his newborn son, who will die because his father deliberately lets him fall down. Such a controversial act is not the only one in *The Mysteries of Love*. Rather, it is a typical feature of the play. The disjunction of diction and action in the play's dialogue constitutes the most blatant evidence of Breton's new concept of dialogue as one in which the interlocutors treat each other as enemies.

Applying Breton's dialogue-game: Action against diction

The audience is constantly caught by surprise during *The Mysteries of Love*. In fact, the play is a tour-de-force of surprise due to "the uninhibited use of space and the auditorium" (Bennison 122). The first act, for example, does not take place on stage but in a lodge in front of the stage in the audience, generating confusion vis-à-vis its traditional role, one might even say threatening it. But more than that, the incompatibility of words and gestures that the characters demonstrate throughout the play surprises the audience to such a degree that its members are actively involved and give voice to their feelings of frustration and protest:

> UNE VOIX (*dans la salle*). Mais, pourquoi? Juste ciel! Pourquoi? Êtes-vous malades? (18).

> [A VOICE (*in the audience*). But why? Merciful heavens! Why? Are you both ill? (233).]

This is the scripted reaction of a member of the internal audience to Leah's opening vow to the audience:

> LÉA (*à la salle*). J'aime Patrice. Ah! J'aime ses tripes. Ah! j'aime ce pitre. Ah! j'aime ce pitre. Sous toutes ses faces, sur toutes ses coutures, sous toutes ses formes. Regarde-les, Patrice. Écoute-les. Ah! ah! ah! ... (*Elle rit aux éclats.*) (18).

> [LEAH (*to the audience*). I love Patrick. Oh! I love his guts. Oh! I love the clown. Oh, I love the clown. From every viewpoint, from every seam, from every form. Look at them, Patrick. Listen to them. Oh! Oh! Oh! ... (*She bursts into laughter.*) (233).]

This confession, culminating in Leah's laughter, puzzles the audience. In fact, Leah's laughter echoes ideas by Vitrac and Artaud about the primacy of laughter on stage. Interestingly, the flyer "Le Théâtre Alfred Jarry and Public Hostility" (1930) sets extreme laughter as its final goal: "Basically, we propose as theme: *current events* in all directions; as medium: humor in all its forms; and as our goal: extreme laughter, laughter that goes from conspicuous immobility to bursting into tears" (Béhar, *Théâtre ouvert* 191). Perhaps Leah's laughter would not have surprised the audience, if they had not witnessed another surprising disjunction earlier, when Patrick slapped Leah in the face at the very moment he offered her a bouquet of flowers:

> LÉA. Patrice! Que faites-vous?
> PATRICE (*toujours agenouillé*). Mais rien, Léa, rien. Vous le voyez; je me promène. Ah! mais à la fin, voulez-vous avouer?
> LÉA. Non.
> PATRICE. Acceptez ces quelques fleurs. (*Il la gifle.*) (14).

> [LEAH. Patrick! What are you doing?
> PATRICK (*still kneeling*). Why, nothing, Leah, nothing. You can see: I'm out for a walk. Ah! But will you confess now?
> LEAH. No.
> PATRICK. Then do accept these few flowers. (*He slaps her.*) (230).]

Far from any logic, it is the physical language that is more telling here than the verbal, which seems inadequate to express the characters' inner feelings. The characters' gestures contradict their verbal language or, rather, their actions treat their words as an enemy as they act out the opposite of what their verbal language indicates. In other words, physical language reacts against the communicative value of verbal language and transforms it purely into a bearer of emotion, devoid of meaning yet full of feeling. This is one of many examples in this play that clearly demonstrate how "surrealist aspirations impose the inversion of established modes of communication through language" (Matthews, *Theatre* 279). The inversion of theatrical tradition in this particular episode is coupled with the inversion of the traditional courtesy code. Like a new Romeo, Patrick kneels in front of Leah, not to confess his love to her as one would expect but, on the contrary, to extract with force her confession of love. Seen in this light, the slap Patrick gives Leah is not so paradoxical. It is less paradoxical still, if one considers that he acts like a clown in front of an audience; his duty is to make the audience burst into laughter. Or perhaps, this act simply confirms Patrick and Leah's mad love for one another, a love that masochistically flatters her instead of making her feel abused by him.

A similar incompatibility between words and actions is shown in the relationship between Leah and her ex-lover, Dovic, Patrick's double. Leah continues to be mistreated, this time by Dovic, who claims that he still loves her:

> DOVIC. Ah! non. Pas de scandale ici, n'est-ce pas? Je proteste Léa. (*Il la gifle.*) Je t'ai toujours aimée. (*Il la pince.*) Je t'aime encore. (*Il la mord.*) Il faut me rendre cette justice. (*Il lui tiraille ses oreilles.*) Avais-je des sueurs froides? (*Il lui crache au visage.*) Je te caressais les seins et les joues. (*Il lui donne des coups de pied.*) Il n'y en avait que pour toi. (*Il fait mine de l'étrangler.*) Tu es partie. (*Il la secoue violemment.*) T'en ai-je voulu? (*Il lui donne des coups de poing.*) Je suis bon. (*Il la jette à terre.*) Je t'ai déjà pardonné. (*Il la traîne par les cheveux autour de la loge. Patrice se lève.*) (21).

> [DOVIC. Oh, no! No scandal here, right? I protest, Leah. (*Slapping her.*) I've always loved you. (*Pinching her.*) I still love you. (*Biting her.*) Give me credit for that? (*Pulling her ears.*) Did I have cold sweats? (*Spitting in her face.*) I caressed your breasts and your cheeks. (*Kicking her.*) Everything I had was yours. (*Making as though to strangle her.*) You left me. (*Shaking her violently.*) Did I hold it against you? (*Striking her with his fist.*) I am good-natured. (*Throwing her on the ground.*) I have already forgiven you. (*He drags her around the box by the hair. Patrick rises.*) (236).]

This word/action incompatibility reaches its peak in this sadomasochist episode, when Leah subsequently presents Dovic to Patrick as "a real gentleman" (236). When the latter asks the former what interests him in life, Dovic replies that love in the form of Leah interests him, incarnating the Surrealist's fusion of an abstract idea with a concrete image: Leah is Love, a love that is threatening, not only to Leah, but also to the audience. This assault on the audience is for Vitrac and Artaud one of the explicit goals of the Théâtre Alfred Jarry:

> The spectator who comes to us knows that he/she will agree to undergo a true operation, where not only his spirit, but also his/her flesh will be endangered. From now on he/she will go to the theatre as he/she is going to the surgeon or the dentist. In the same state of mind with the thought that obviously he/she will not come out intact from there (Artaud, *OC2* 14).

This sense of personal physical threat culminates in the following scene from the first tableau, reminiscent of Alfred Jarry's *Ubu-roi*. In this tableau, the house lights go off and the box alone is half-lit; Patrick behaves in a totalitarian way, as if he were another King Ubu performing his provocative "trap scene," only in this instance with Leah's consent, which stands in sharp contrast to Mother Ubu's objections to her husband's acts of massacre. I refer to the following scene from *Ubu-roi*, in which Père Ubu throws all the nobles in a pit:

> NOBLE. Count of Vitepsk.
> PÈRE UBU. What's your income?
> NOBLE. Three million six-dollars.
> PÈRE UBU. Condemned! (*He grabs him with the hook and passes him to the pit.*) What beastly savagery! Second Noble, who are you? Are you going to answer, buffoon?
> NOBLE. Grand Duke of Posen.
> PÈRE UBU. Excellent! Excellent! That's all I want to know. Down the trap door. Third Noble, who are you? You've got an ugly mug.
> NOBLE. Duke of Cousland, of the towns of Riga of Revel, and of Mitau.
> PÈRE UBU. Good! Fine! Is that all?
> NOBLE. That's all!
> PÈRE UBU. Down the trap door, then! (64–5).

The scene from *The Mysteries of Love* that echoes the above trap scene is the following:

> PATRICE. Tais-toi. Et maintenant, monsieur le Préfet, enchaînez-moi tout ce joli monde.
> UNE VOIX (*dans la salle*). Monsieur Patrice, vous êtes un criminel (19).
>
> [PATRICK. Shut up. And now, Commissioner, please chain all these fine people up for me
> A VOICE (*in the audience*). Mr. Patrick, you are a criminal. (234–5).]

In an absurd way, Patrick immediately denies the accusation of being a criminal by shouting that he loves Leah, as if this declaration alone could render groundless all kinds of accusations. Then he accuses the audience member by stating:

> PATRICE. Moi, monsieur? Non, monsieur. Êtes-vous sourd? J'aime Léa. Il fallait crier que vous aimiez Julie, Marie, Thérèse, Michelle ou Esther et Léa serait dans le tas (19).
>
> [PATRICK. I, Sir? No, Sir. Are you deaf? I love Leah. You should have shouted out that you love Julie, Marie, Theresa, Michelle, or Ester, and Leah would naturally have been among them (235).]

Patrick then addresses Leah and tells her that a lot of people are signaling to them. They return friendly gestures to the audience while the house lights come on. The lights go off again for violence to occur (a stage device reminiscent of French neo-classical tragedy) and Leah shoots a spectator, confirming the danger that comes with this new kind of theatre—a theatre that is inseparable from real life and where all barriers have been taken down, the traditional barrier between stage and audience, as well as that between reality and dream. Indeed, dream and reality in this play are inseparable, appearing in a constant interplay; for theatre in Vitrac's view is "the meeting point of all artistic media of expression," as "a true alchemy of dream and reality" (Antle, *Théâtre* 87).

"Dream into reality," "reality into dream": "One into another" again

The Mysteries of Love unfolds in a series of five tableaus divided into three acts, defined by a transformational, dream-like quality, which betrays affinities with cinema. Annette Levitt makes a distinction between "reality" and "dream" scenes; according to her, "the opening scenes of each of its three acts develop the prosaic plot" (250). The "reality" scenes, she continues, "are offered with minimal set directions, while the dream scenes appear in the context of extremely detailed and realistic, believable settings" (251). The interplay between "reality" and "dream" scenes unfolds at a frenetic pace, more appropriate to the cinema. The game-like, frenetic rhythm of cinematic images is particularly appealing to Vitrac, who vividly describes the cinematic image in an article on surrealist cinema:

> The image enters the movement. It neighs, it becomes impatient. It embarks on agitated tours throughout the world. Everything becomes a gallop, disheveled pursuit, frenzy. The engine starts moving rapidly. The mystery is automatic. *It is a game* (quoted in Antle, *Théâtre* 76; my emphasis).

In the dizzying, cinematic game of *The Mysteries of Love*, Vitrac expressly emphasizes the role of dreams. After its performance he describes it as "an ironical work which renders concrete on stage the disquiet, double solitude, dissembled criminal thoughts and eroticism of lovers. For the first time, a *real dream* was realized on stage" (Artaud, *OC2* 38). Also, in the preface of his completed works, he offers the following comment on the mysteries of love that the young couple, 22-year-old Patrick and 18-year-old Leah, experience: "'To live as dreaming.' 'To dream as living'" (9).[12]

Once again, the mingling of dream and reality in this play that deals with love and its unconscious ramifications "blurs the barriers between reality and dream, extending to the ones between the auditorium and the stage. These barriers have fallen apart, and there lies its difficulty and attractiveness at once for the spectator" (Auslander 364). To borrow Matthews' words, Vitrac "has given up establishing boundaries between the true and the false, the fanciful and the factual because, apparently, such boundaries no longer have any validity in his estimation" (quoted in Cardullo and Knopf 331). While many reviewers were critical of this fluidity of boundaries, some critics, nevertheless, saw originality in this technique and claimed that Artaud and Vitrac had quite simply found their "new language." Fortunat Strowski, for example, finds "freshness, authenticity, diversity and sometimes an original profundity" in the Théâtre Alfred Jarry (quoted in Artaud, *OC* 54). Part of this originality, however, is that the spectator has to come to terms with the unprecedented violence of this play, as it "seeks to depict the sadomasochism of love, the violence inherent in the human subconscious" by "condensing the ambiguous experience of love into a short narrative" (Auslander 366). Indeed, as Stamos Metzidakis argues, bizarrely violent images are a common feature of many modern literary quests for originality (*Difference Unbound* 128). Below are some scenes from each tableau characteristic of the strange interplay between often harsh or brutal reality and dream.

The first tableau opens with Patrick and Leah arguing in the presence of Leah's mother, Mme Morin. Patrick is shouting at Leah: "Au nom du ciel! avouez, Léa" (14) [In the name of God, confess, Leah]. The two of them look like children playing a love scene in front of Mme Morin. Patrick in particular behaves in a childish way, provoking Leah's mother with insulting questions and comments, which she calmly disregards:

> PATRICE (*même jeu*). C'est vous, le bœuf?
> MME MORIN. Et toi, l'aimes-tu?
> LÉA. Comme de juste.
> PATRICE (*même jeu*). Mouchez le homard votre père. Fillette!
> MME MORIN. Il grandira peut-être, ma chérie (13).

> [PATRICK (*still shouting*). Are you the ox?
> MRS MORIN. And you, do you love him?
> LEAH. Why, naturally.
> PATRICK (*still shouting*). Go blow that lobster your father's nose, Girlie!
> MRS. MORIN. Perhaps he will grow up, dear (231).]

Patrick's insistence on continuing his own game, in spite of Mme Morin's refusal to be drawn in, indicates his stubborn and rebellious nature. Leah then anxiously asks him about her face, to which he cynically replies:

> PATRICE. Allons bon! Tu me rappelles un coup de couteau. Une blessure (20).

> [PATRICK. Come now! You remind me of a slashing knife. A wound (235).]

This response is pivotal, shedding further light on the relationship between Leah and the portrait of a woman that Patrick tried to modify at the start of the play. Leah's ambiguously perceived, virtual facial wound is identical to that of the painting. It is the first sinister hint of what is to come, the unfolding throughout the play of a nightmare both virtual and real. This interplay between reality and dream, conscious and subconscious is conveyed through the concrete stage device of an on-off light effect and the curtain's repeated rise and fall. Patrick's indifference to Leah's past, despite her insistence that he ask her about it, only serves to increase Leah's inner wounds:

> LÉA. Dis? Tu ne me demanderas rien de ma vie, mon Patrice?
> PATRICE. Non (23).

> [LEAH. Tell me: You won't ask me anything about my past life, Patrick?
> PATRICK. No (238).]

Patrick simply replies "No." At this moment a woman in a nightgown enters, whose presence torments Leah, who believes the woman is having an affair with Patrick. When she asks him who she is, ironically Patrick replies that she is the Virgin. This scene is obviously not part of reality, but rather one of the scenes that Leah's mind creates. The first tableau ends with the theatre manager appearing and informing the audience that the play is over and that its author, Théophile Mouchet, has just killed himself. The author then appears on stage, according to the following stage directions:

> *Le rideau se relève. L'auteur apparaît. Il est en bras de chemise. Son visage et ses vêtements sont couverts de sang. Il rit. Il rit aux éclats. Il rit de toutes ses forces en se tenant les côtes. Les deux rideaux tombent brusquement* (24).

> [*The curtain rises again. The Author appears. He is in his shirt-sleeves. His face and clothing are covered with blood. He laughs. He laughs heartily. He laughs with all his might holding his sides. Both curtains suddenly fall* (239).]

This episode that suggests great violence remains a mystery as it throws the internal and external audience into great confusion. Who is this author? Is he the author of the drama enacted by Leah and Patrick? The author of the play within the play, that took place between the Old Man and the Young Man? Or, is he the author of his own drama, his attempted suicide? And then, in what state does he appear? Is his auto-sarcastic laughter the result of an unsuccessful suicide attempt? Is he in a ghost, or simply another actor who tests the audience's tolerance for violence and for the inexplicable shifting of realms with his hideous appearance on stage? All these questions blur the boundaries between reality and illusion, while the laughing, blood-covered author creates a shock effect in the audience, similar to the laughter of Ionesco's *Tueur sans gages* and Jean Paul Sartre's *Huis Clos*. We can see a meta-theatrical element inserted here at random by Vitrac to test the audience's limits, by introducing a "twilight zone where horror and laughter commingle ... and where the dead and the living converse" (Cardullo and Knopf 330).

The second tableau continues in the same kind of twilight zone, but the dead and the living coexist in an increasingly intense rhythm. The stage is divided into three sets, all visible at the same time. Bert Cardullo offers a concise summary of the scene:

> On the Quai des Grands-Augustins in Paris, Patrick is seen as a lieutenant of Dragoons. Leah is carrying a doll. She says it is his child, but Patrick drops the baby in the Seine anyway. In his bedroom Lloyd George (played by Dovic, he looks like a certain British prime minister) lifts the sheets on a bed, showing Leah, who recognizes it with horror, the head of a little girl resting on the pillow. When he pulls the sheets right back to uncover the child, "It is naturally only a bust of flesh sawn off at the shoulder level." In the presence of Leah and Patrick, Lloyd George proceeds to demonstrate his skill by sawing off the head of a young boy he has carried in under his arm (330).

Lloyd George, played by Dovic, is a new character. He makes his appearance advising Leah on how to make the necessary arrangements to conceal that a crime has taken place, while her father continues telling this story: "However, that evening the sea was rough. Sardines were being taken by the netful. But the night, the thunder, the lighting, and especially, the Negroes in the boiler room, not to mention the leopard ..." (242). This story uses typical surrealist poetic imagery, the product of automatic writing—in this case, that of a thunderous night—full of revelations and intimations, such as Breton imagined in his image of "la nuit des éclairs."[13] The reference to a leopard is striking here, alluding as it does to Dante's *Inferno*; a reference made all the more convincing by being uttered by the dead Mr Morin. In *The Inferno*, the leopard appears at the very beginning of Dante's journey through the wilderness. It constitutes the first of his numerous dreadful encounters. Here, this key reference prepares the next scene, in which the subconscious, insanity, and a released dream all intermingle in Leah's mind immediately after Mr Morin's interlude. Lloyd George agrees that Leah is mad, for she walks with her mother toward the bed, where "two arms are being raised which resemble two dead branches, but whereon are flowering two enormous, very white hands" (243). In spite of her mother's warning ("Ah! My child! Don't go near. She has leprosy"), "Léa kneels by the bed, recognizes the victim's resemblance to herself, and concludes, 'You really must agree that one doesn't die of love'" (Matthews, *Theatre* 123). The scene is easily understood as a nightmare of Leah's, as Matthews explains, since "she has the last word, and we see her lying in bed as the next tableau opens the second act" (ibid. 123). In her nightmare, Leah's beloved ones are all present: to judge her (like the Lloyd George Dovic), to protect her (like her mother), to draw her attention (like her dead father), and in each case, to draw her away from her doomed love for Patrick. When she sees a figure like herself lying in the bed and being distorted by leprosy (a mirror image of herself? her child with Patrick? Patrick himself?), she faces reality and accepts it as a sacrifice for love's sake. After all, no one dies of love, she concludes, keeping in her mind the image of the two dead branches in blossom.

Leah's unconditional love for Patrick is shown again in the third tableau, which opens the second act. It takes place in a hotel room, showing Leah stretched out on the bed next to Patrick. After a coded conversation that shows Patrick's visions, Leah asks him to kiss her hands. When he does so, he is burned by smoke rising from her hands. Leah then goes toward the washstand and plunges her hands into the water. This surrealist scene, so vividly and concretely illustrating Leah's burning passion for Patrick, reminds us of Vitrac's idea of the "théâtre de l'incendie" ("incendiary theatre"), as the author wished to call the plays he wrote during the period of the Théâtre Alfred Jarry, including *The Mysteries of Love*.[14] Leah's passion for Patrick stumbles, however, due to his stubborn, visionary character. Leah falls into despair:

PATRICE. À l'avenir occupe-toi donc de tes yeux et laisse les miens tranquilles.
Léa pleure
PATRICE. Ce n'est pas une raison pour pleurer.
LÉA. Le monde m'ennuie.
PATRICE. Où est-il, le monde?
LÉA. Je suis là, mon Patrice, je suis là.
PATRICE. Pardon, Léa. Le monde s'il te plaît.
Léa s'allonge sur le lit.
LÉA. Viens, Patrice. (31–2)

[PATRICK. So in the future take care of your eyes, and leave mine alone.
Leah weeps.
PATRICK. That's no reason to cry.
LEAH. The world bores me.
PATRICK. Where is this world?

LEAH. Here I am, Patrick; here I am.
PATRICK. Pardon Leah. The world, if you please.
Leah stretches out on the bed.
LEAH. Come, Patrick (245).]

Patrick remains indifferent to Leah's invitation. Both characters are self-absorbed, making it impossible for them to understand each other. It is as if they are engaged in an antagonistic game, as was exactly the case between Breton and Nadja. Likewise, the audience cannot grasp the above dialogue according to any rational standards. If we read it as a surrealist dialogue, however, in which one thought treats the other as enemy, upsetting the interlocutors' innermost emotions, their exchange becomes meaningful: when Leah associates the world with herself and provokes Patrick's reaction, we now have a harbinger of her mental and emotional deterioration. More than that, Leah's desperate desire to reach Patrick creates tension. When she says that the world bores her, she means it, since Patrick is still reluctant to be connected with her. And when she tells him "here I am," her thought has already jumped to another one: that she herself is the world. This equation (cosmos=Leah) seems an exaggeration to Patrick, but not to Leah, of course. Leah's feelings and desires transcend language, or rather *transform* language into a state of feelings. Leah expresses her unhappiness again after a dark episode with a butcher, who arrives to collect a parcel tied with string and then complains that the parcel is too little. Patrick questions Leah about him in these terms:

PATRICE. Toi, c'est la bouche qui t'éclaire. Elle est comme une carrière de sang.
LÉA. Et allez donc! La poésie.
PATRICE (*la giflant*). Attrape!
LÉA. Je ne suis pas heureuse avec toi.
PATRICE (*la giflant*). Et cette fois?
LÉA. Je suis malheureuse!
PATRICE (*la traînant par les cheveux*). Je serais curieux de savoir si je serai toute ma vie une pendule. Ou plutôt le pendule d'une pendule, ou mieux le pendu d'une pendule.
LÉA. Grâce, Patrice, grâce! Je ne recommencerai plus, je serai toujours heureuse (34–5).

[PATRICK. You, it's the mouth that lights your way. It's like a quarry of blood.
LEAH. What nonsense! What about poetry?
PATRICK (*slaps her*). Take that!
LEAH. I'm not happy with you.
PATRICK (*slaps her again*). And now?
LEAH. I'm unhappy.
PATRICK (*dragging her around by the hair*). I'd be interested to know if I'll be a clock all my life. Or rather a clock's pendulum, or even a pendant from a clock.
LEAH. Have mercy, Patrick; have mercy! I won't start up again. I'll always be happy (248).]

Patrick's violence toward Leah extends now to himself. He expresses the idea of committing suicide, something that forces Leah to lie again and insist that she is happy with him, although he is completely cut out from Leah's world, abandoned to his own imagination:

LÉA. Tu te fais des idées.
PATRICE. Je ne fais plus rien. Je suis la machine à tourner dans le vide. Il y a le cerveau, dis-tu? Il est empoisonné par le travail. Il est à l'état tétanique. Gentil animal celui-là. Hier encore, je pouvais manger. Aujourd'hui c'est bien fini, Léa. Le cerveau est dans le ventre. ... Ma pauvre cervelle, cette pâte divine, se plie à toutes les besognes (32).

[LEAH. You're imagining things.
PATRICK. I'm not doing anything any more. I am the machine that is to turn in a vacuum. That's the brain, you say? It's poisoned by work. It's at the stage of tetanus. A nice animal that one. Only yesterday I could still eat. Today, Leah, it's all over. My brain is in the belly ... My poor brain, that divine dough, bends under any yoke (246).]

Patrick's unpredictable behavior, coupled with his defying of reason, continues when he strikes down both Mme Morin and Dovic, whom he had summoned, while Leah was giving birth to a boy offstage. Meanwhile, a conversation takes place between him and the author:

AUTEUR. Écoutez, mon garçon, votre cas ne m'intéresse guère. Il n'intéresse guère le public non plus.
PATRICE. Croyez-vous? (38)

[THE AUTHOR. Listen, my boy, your case doesn't interest me very much. It doesn't interest the public very much, either.
PATRICK. You don't think so? (251)]

This strange interference by the author at this point, who seems, moreover, no longer to be the Théophile Mouchet of the earlier tableau, could simply be an allusion to Vitrac himself; like Breton, who had expressed concern about the reception of his playlet *S'il vous plaît*, Vitrac was also anxious that his creation would not meet the public's expectations. The third tableau finally closes with the death of Leah and Patrick's son, after Patrick attempted to set the child on a pedestal over the fireplace, from which he could (and did) easily fall. When an officer shows up once again to examine the case, Leah simply tells him that her son fell and caught scarlet fever. Leah deliberately lies again, holding all her sadness within herself to save Patrick. But Patrick had deliberately killed his son, who, he admitted, "infinitely disturbed him" (249). Thus, by end of this tableau, Patrick has committed infanticide (in killing his child); matricide (in killing his mother-in-law); and fratricide (when he kills his double, Dovic, whom Mme Morin called also called son-in-law). It is as if Vitrac, by including here in one scene all the crimes that inflamed Greek tragedy, wanted to parody the kind of drama upon which the entire Western dramatic tradition was founded, thus aligning himself once more with Breton, in this instance with his overall attitude toward the Greek legacy.[15] Parody, that both criticizes and generates laughter, is indeed an intrinsic part of the Théâtre Alfred Jarry.

It was at this point—with Patrick having committed a triple murder—that the staged play ended. The following tableau, according to Matthews, lacks the inventiveness of the previous ones and, not surprisingly in his opinion, was omitted in performance in the Théâtre Alfred Jarry. Nevertheless, I consider the unperformed scenes from the play to be vital to our understanding of this surrealist drama. Matthews offers the following summary:

the fourth tableau shows us Patrick as Mussolini and Madame Morin as a stranger in mourning. Madame Morin disappears as soon as she has entrusted her two dogs and child to someone she does not know—Leah, who finds the little boy looks like "the one I have at home, like my Patrice." Unable to get rid of the child she gives us a chance to observe that, as she remarks, "A love is always a big nuisance" (*Theatre* 125).

In contrast to Matthews, I believe this tableau is key to the drama and that its omission from the staged play could lie not in any inherent defect, but in practical considerations, whether financial restrictions, time restrictions, or problems with the physical staging of the play. For here, more than anywhere else, we see Leah's gradual slipping into madness. We see her desire for motherhood. She is fond of the child she is given and takes good care of him, as if she has found a substitute for her dead child. She buys a pair of blue booties for the boy, although they do not fit him. Mussolini, her interlocutor, remarks: "Well! It's obvious you've never had a child before. You're running like a madwoman, running as though you were alone, and you're dragging the brat on the floor" (256). The bizarre choice of Mussolini as a character here adds the weight of his extreme authority to his judgment about Leah. After he makes his statement, Leah runs around the stage like a true madwoman, holding the child in her hand while stating:

> LÉA. Oh! C'est vrai. Maintenant il court aussi vite que moi, il court aussi vite que moi, il court aussi vite que moi.
> *Elle s'arrête et prend l'enfant dans ses bras.*
> LEA. Mon petit, mon petit, maintenant nous ne nous quitterons plus. Tu n'auras plus de perruque. Et pour qu'on ne te reconnaisse pas, je te teindrai les cheveux en noir (45).

> [LEAH. Oh! It's true! Now he runs as fast as I, he runs as fast as I, he runs as fast as I. (*She stops and takes the child into her arms.*) My little one, my little one, now we will never part again. You will have no more wigs. And so that you may pass unrecognized I will dye your hair black) (256).]

No more wigs for her and no more disguise; only madness and death. Leah exits, followed by the dogs, while Mussolini holds his head in his hands, confirming his belief in her madness.

The fifth tableau, which introduces the third and final act of the written play, seals Leah's madness as a fact that leads her to another reality, where communication with Patrick is finally, miraculously achieved on the plane of surreality, and where words regain their magical power. In this tableau, Leah goes down in a hotel elevator and stands between two policemen, her hands bloody, and her white dress in shreds. We learn, Matthews summarizes, that she has broken the mirror-wardrobe, demolished the dressing table, set fire to the drapes of her room, and strangled the goldfish. She has done all this, it appears, because Patrick did not keep a few impossible promises, such as taking her to the North Pole and giving her stars of his own fabrication. "In the vestibule Léa shows strange faculties, giving testimony to the magic power of words. She announces that a door will open of its own accord; it does so" (Matthews, *Theatre* 125–6). Then, she intones the word "Patrick" like an incantation and Patrick appears in front of her, justifying what Artaud believed of Vitrac—that he granted words unprecedented freedom of action.[16] Leah and Patrick then kiss each other and thunder sounds, as if to acknowledge their bond, and the two of them finally agree that "today is Corpus Christi day" (260), a moment of ultimate salvation for both. At this point, three children enter and have a strange conversation with them. But more strange than their conversation is their disparate identities: one of them is the son of the bakery's horse, another is the offspring of his mother's sewing machine, and the third is the father of a colonel of Zouaves, but he will always be the son of love, Patrick's son. When one of the children shoots the other two, Leah and Patrick express their exasperation with them all, and Patrick tells Leah a story about the harvesting of factory smokestacks. The author then enters and asks Patrick if he needs him. Although the latter replies negatively, the author hands him a revolver, assuring him that it will be of use to him. Patrick tries to shoot the author, but the bullets cannot penetrate him. When Patrick then returns the revolver to him, the author replies: "Please. If you won't do it for me, then do it for the sake of the drama you are enacting. I assure you that a shot at the end of the play is absolutely necessary for the development of the plot" (264). These words echo the unprinted and unperformed fourth act of Breton's and Soupault's *If You Please* in which, according to Alain Jouffroy, "one of the authors picked at random must shoot himself on stage by means of a shot of a revolver" (quoted in Breton, *OC1* 1173). A fatal shot does indeed come at the end of the play, not from Patrick, but from Leah, to whom the author had previously given another revolver at her request. Her revolver is aimed at the internal audience and a spectator is killed. Does Leah make a bad shot? Did she mean to shoot Patrick instead of the spectator? Does she simply relieve her pain this way, in order not to harm Patrick for whom she has waited so long? Whatever her motive, this final shot confirms not only her descent into madness, but also the denouement of the drama that she and Patrick have enacted—the mysteries of their peculiar love. Auslander offers an interesting approach to the play's depiction of Leah's madness:

> True to the plays' origins, its meaning can only be assessed by comparison between the emotions it evokes and the viewer's or reader's own emotional life. Vitrac's rendering of love is altogether poetic, both in its language and its visual aspects, but largely unromantic. It is love as seen by Léa, who chooses Patrice over Dovic only to be abandoned by him, only to be fettered with symbols of domesticity (children and dogs) only finally to go mad alone in a hotel, awaiting the return of her beloved. The play charts Léa's descent into madness and the cynicism she acquires from it while implying that her madness is not madness at all, but simply the intensity of emotional experience that is love (366).

Such an idea of love, which encompasses pain, kindness, forgiveness, and death, gives meaning to the final dialogue between Leah and Patrick, just before Leah's fatal gunshot embodies Breton's definition of "the simplest Surrealist act" (quoted in Levitt 268):

> LÉA. Il y a la mort.
> PATRICE. Oui, la mort. Mais la mort comme le pardon. Comme la neige sur la montagne. Le pardon, comme le feu que l'on coupe au couteau. Le pardon, comme l'eau dont on fait les maisons. Le pardon, comme l'assassin dont on fait d'autres crimes. Le pardon, comme les vivants dont on fait d'autres morts … Le pardon, comme moi, dont je fais un coupable.

Le pardon, comme toi, dont je fais le vitriol. Le cœur est déjà rouge. Coule, Léa. Les mains sur le cuivre des ombres. Le cœur est déjà rouge jusqu'au fond du théâtre où quelqu'un va mourir.
LÉA. Assez, Patrice (*Elle tire un coup de feu*) (58).

[LEAH. There is death.
PATRICK. Yes, death. But death like forgiveness. Like snow on the mountain. Forgiveness, like fire you slice with a knife. Forgiveness like the water houses are made of. Forgiveness, like the murderer other crimes are made of. Forgiveness, like the living other dead are made of .... Forgiveness, like me, whom I am making criminal of. Forgiveness, like you whom I am making a deadly acid of. The heart is red already. Flow, Leah. Hands on the copper of shadows. The heart is red already as far as the end of the theatre where someone is about to die.
LEAH. Enough Patrick! (*She fires a shot*) (267).]

"The heart is red," Patrick claims; his own heart, Leah's, and the audience's as well. Everyone present has undergone a real, alchemic transmutation due to the mysteries of love. For love "is the site of ideal occultation of all thought" (Seaver and Lane 181). Its revitalizing force gives credit to Vitrac's idea of incendiary theatre that is able to reconcile man with both life and pain.

This close reading of *The Mysteries of Love* reveals, I believe, not only Vitrac's attempt to create a "théâtre de l'incendie," but also his faithful use of surrealist ludic strategies, exemplified in the free interplay between reality and dream, between the various artistic media, as well as the fluidity of the characters (except in the case of Leah). Characters and theatrical spaces continuously flow "one into another" on both the page and the stage. It portrays a fascinating game of sameness and otherness that catches the spectator by surprise, and creates, *avant la lettre*, the "one into another" surrealist game. One element of this dialogue game is especially well exemplified in the hostile disjunction of the words and actions of the characters. At first glance, there is no common element between the inimical terms that are brought together. But soon, this hidden common element. Patrick's declaration of love to Leah, for instance, as we have seen in the opening tableau, is accompanied by his offering her a bouquet of flowers and a subsequent slap in her face. These verbal and physical languages are brought together here in a most strange and incompatible fashion that overturns all logic and decorum.

However, for the reader or the spectator of this act, a new logic is established—one that could be summed up in this formulation: "Patrick to Leah: I love you like I hate you," modeled after the "one into another" surrealist game. Furthermore, in this reformulated logic, the spectator sees the common element that links love and hatred together, particularly when Leah, at some point, refuses to declare her love to Patrick; something he then attempts to get from her through violence. We see in this example Vitrac's attempt to illustrate the surrealist ludic use of language—both verbal and non-verbal—as if he wanted to reveal its hidden, magical potential. This treatment of language transposes the core dramatic element of conflict from the level of action to that of diction, which is now identical to action.

A similar dialogue-game was employed 30 years later by Nanos Valaoritis in his play *The Nightfall Hotel* (1957)—the focus of the next section of this chapter. The main difference between Vitrac and Valaoritis is that the younger playwright's game used the concept of the surrealist dialogue in a self-conscious manner, making use of the entire gamut of surrealist games mastered during his association with the Surrealists. Where Vitrac's play proved the error of Breton's skepticism (about the possibility of there being a truly surrealist theatre), through an intuitive embracing of Surrealism and Breton's basic tenets, Valaoritis set about a systematic disproving of Breton's claims, using the surrealist leader's very own ludic techniques.

The ludic techniques of *The Nightfall Hotel*

Nanos Valaoritis wrote *The Nightfall Hotel* in French in 1957 when, as a member of Breton's surrealist circle, he actively participated in its last phase of surrealist ludic activity.[17] Valaoritis was a true disciple of Breton and Surrealism; as Valaoritis himself states, "With André Breton, I met in 1954, and until 1960 we kept a quite close relationship, often on a daily basis" (*For a Theory of Writing B* 47). Emmanuel Garrigues, when he examines the famous surrealist game of analogies that took place during the excursion at the Saint-Cirq-La Popie, cites Valaoritis's name, along with the answers he gave during the game.[18] *The Nightfall Hotel* is the first of Valaoritis's plays that was staged outside Greece. The International Art Studio staged it on April 27, 1959, for four consecutive evenings, in the Theater of the American Artist's and Student's Center under Marc O's direction. In the main roles were Georges Vander and Marpessa Dawn, already well known from Marcel Camus's film *Orfeu Negro* (*Black Orfeus*). The 18-year-old Filipino-American actress-dancer magnetized the audience and captured the attention of almost all theatre critics, particularly as she would be a special guest at the then Cannes Film Festival.

Despite the prominent celebrity of the case, this play did not receive great reviews. It would be easy to claim that Valaoritis was simply not familiar with the rules of playwriting, in the sense of the "well-made" play, where action is the secret of success. Yet, this is not the case. Valaoritis is simply envisioning a new way of "writing for the stage" and this is why he stubbornly dares to keep writing plays where all action is transposed to the level of "talking" as opposed to "acting." He has faith in the so-called "speech-act" that one performs simply by making an utterance. His faith stems from his belief in the "alchemy of the word," a transmutation of the word that constitutes one of the surrealist principles. This transformation draws on Arthur Rimbaud's own "alchimie du verbe," according to which words emerge in all their sonority and imagistic majesty.[19] It is essentially a poetic use of language *par excellence*, where the uttering of words is an attempt to reveal the magical power of those words. In many cases this happens by eliminating the distance between a metaphorical use of a word and its literal meaning. Such a deep concern with the effects of the words in people's lives fascinated Valaoritis, and is deeply rooted in the surrealist use of the language. His initiation into the liberating language of Surrealism came about through a series of encounters: in his youth, his friends Odysseas Elytis and Nikos Gatsos in Greece first introduced him to this world; later, during his stay in England, he associated with Toni Del Renzio and the gallery-owner Mesens, who hosted surrealist exhibitions, through both of whom he met Nicolas Calas, a major theoretician of Surrealism. After this, Valaoritis was already eager to adhere to Breton's spirit of Surrealism when the opportunity came in 1954 in Paris. There, he followed Breton's entire itinerary and choices "with the attention of a novice" (*For a Theory of Writing B* 171). "Without this six-year internship with the Parisian group," Valaoritis admits,

> it would have been impossible for me to complete my knowledge on the most secret and invisible and most personal aspects, since I met there so many other people, such as Alain Jouffroy, Victor Brauner, Wilfredo Lam, Maurice Henry, Matta, Marcel Jean, and of course Calas. Surrealism at that time seemed to have been erupted and its fragments were dispersed everywhere, like a newly-appeared constellation and not only under Breton's control, Peret's and of the group of the younger members (*For a Theory of Writing B* 171).

The Nightfall Hotel is a curious blend of loyal discipleship to Breton and Surrealism, and a desire in Valaoritis to prove his emancipation from this relationship, using the very tools acquired from his association with the movement to strike at its ideas. Yet, most reviewers at the time saw this play simply as a new version of *Romeo and Juliet*[20] and thus, few of them paid attention to its ludic structure. Stéphane Vallaire, in *Les Lettres françaises* of May 7, 1959, stated negatively: "C'est un jeu. Celui de l'histoire improvisée à plusieurs" [It is a game. That of improvised collective history]. Also, Marcelle Capron of the newspaper *Le Combat* noticed the "strange game" that was played on stage by the young duet, and confessed that she was "un peu agacée par ce jeu obscur" [somewhat annoyed by this obscure game] and by the inundation of words and endless talk. But, when this chatter is finally transformed into barks and growls, the same critic concluded that the young couple was playing dog ["ils jouent au chien"] precisely in order to put an end to the empty talk. Capron admits that Georges Vander plays the loyal dog of Marpessa Dawn very well, and concedes that Dawn also delivers an astonishing monologue.

The scene is indeed the acme of this play—it alone would suffice to give the play a surrealist aura. Nevertheless, I would argue that what best identifies this play as surrealist is its self-conscious experimentation with surrealist games throughout. In these games, Valaoritis discovered the surrealist dialogue *par excellence*, as in the text "Barriers," by Breton and Soupault. This is, at least, what Valaoritis himself, in one of his interviews, claims for this play, as well as for the still unpublished 40-odd plays he wrote between 1954 and 1960, the period of his interaction with Breton's circle in Paris. In this interview, he also states that he was deeply influenced by Roger Vitrac's work; indeed, it was to Vitrac's *Mysteries of Love* that he turned to find the support he needed in his first attempt at creating a surrealist theatrical work meant not only to be read, but also staged. It is no accident, then, that Martha and Yves, the couple in *The Nightfall Hotel*, suggest a reincarnation of Patrick and Leah rather than of Romeo and Juliet, as several French critics pointed out when they initially reviewed the play. In light of Valaoritis's own admission, it is imperative to read *The Nightfall Hotel* in conjunction with Vitrac's play, since they are both organized on the same ludic surrealist principles.

The Nightfall Hotel is in effect a guessing game about the players' identities that the young couple agrees to play in a competitive spirit. As in the "one into another" game, the game/play is guided by some logic-bound rules that aim to shed light on a hidden point, namely, each players' true identity. For example, the couple guesses the motivation behind their meeting in the room of a soon-to-be-demolished hotel. This game immediately involves the members of the audience, as the element of suspense is dominant. At the beginning of the play, we get the impression that the audience is the real opponent in this game of "identification" that Martha and Yves play against them. However, as the play unfolds, we realize that both Martha and Yves are desperately trying to find the truth out about each other's identity, since they do not have any clue about each other's past. Thus, instead of opponents of the pair, the spectators gradually become co-players, free to choose sides. The ever-changing character of this game owes much to Nadja's game of questions and answers that we examined in the previous chapter; Martha and Yves's game is founded on the same principle of appeal to the listener's imagination in an attempt to unearth poeticism. One poses a question and the other makes up a story using free association. Then, the other person starts or continues his own version of the story by picking up the narrative thread each time the other player stops. The only difference here with Nadja's game is that both players are eager to play the game. They both throw themselves into it, into a frantic game of story-telling and guessing that cancels each previous version, as if they were trying to prove Breton's point about the interlocutor as the enemy. It behooves us here to follow step-by-step the various versions of the game that Martha and Yves begin immediately after their stage entrance. Their labyrinth-like game forms the plot of the play and unfolds in a total of 14 scenes, modeled after Vitrac's tableaus or snapshots. Interestingly, in Valaoritis's manuscript, eight variants are offered for the third scene, two variants for the seventh scene, and another two for the twelfth scene, indicating the inherently ludic character of this play from a structural as well as a thematic point of view.

The first scene is a banal, realistic scene. It introduces the couple as they are having a conversation with the hotel owner, who explains to them that they could not find a better room for the price offered, despite its darkness, its lack of windows and hot water, and its similarity to a medieval crypt. The couple takes the room while they and the hotel owner repeat these two key phrases: "et pour ce prix-là" [and for this price here] and "et puis?" [and then?], as in the following example:

JEUNNE HOMME. Nous avons un plancher pour ce prix-là …
JEUNNE FILLE. Et un toit pour ce prix-là!
JEUNNE HOMME. Et deux chaises pour ce prix-là!
JEUNNE FILLE. Et un lit pour ce prix-là!
JEUNNE HOMME. Et de l'air pour ce prix-là!
JEUNNE FILLE. Et du silence pour ce prix-là!
HÔTELIER. Et puis?
JEUNNE HOMME (*menaçant*). Et puis?
HÔTELIER (*déconcerté*). Et puis?
JEUNNE HOMME (*plus menaçant*). Et puis? Allons!
HÔTELIER (*faible*). Et puis …

JEUNNE HOMME. Vous hésitez; vous renoncez à nous dire pour ce prix là …
HÔTELIER. Il n'y a plus rien! (1)

[YOUNG MAN. We have a floor for this price here …
YOUNG GIRL. And a roof for this price here!
YOUNG MAN. And two chairs for this price here!
YOUNG GIRL. And a bed for this price here!
YOUNG MAN. And air for this price here!
YOUNG GIRL. And silence for this price here!
HOTEL OWNER. And then …
YOUNG MAN (*threatening*). And then?
HOTEL OWNER (*uneasy*). And then?
YOUNG MAN (*more threatening*). And then? Come on!
HOTEL OWNER (*weak*). And then?
YOUNG MAN. You hesitate; you renounce telling us for this price here …
HOTEL OWNER. There is nothing left!]

Several conclusions can be drawn from this child-like conversation between the couple and the hotel owner, marked by repetition (there are 10 occurrences of the conjunction "and"; seven of the phrase "for this price here"; five of the segment "and then?"; and seven exclamation points). First of all, this elementary dialogue shows the young couple's excitement, mixed with self-irony, as they enumerate the objects they get for the unknown "price here." These objects are both concrete and abstract, brought together in accordance with the favorite surrealist tenet of the approximation of dissimilar objects. The dialogue also betrays the young man's ill-tempered character as he threatens the hotel owner twice while addressing him with the question "and then?" Perhaps this elliptical question, however enigmatic, is a hint of the young man's frustration at the hotel owner's limited use of language, a linguistic narrowness that perhaps goes hand-in-hand with the limited worldview of the bourgeois hotel owner. The lack of imagination in his language bores the young man, who threatens him into coming up with something different. And this happens immediately afterwards, when the hotel owner is suddenly transformed into a more eloquent user of language with poetic qualities:

HÔTELIER (*malin*). Et puis, et puis, et puis, n'en parlons plus. Ce sont des vieilles histoires sans importance. Elles vous tracassent la nuit. Et puis un beau dimanche bleu, tout disparaît, la terre disparaît, le ciel disparaît, les fleurs disparaissent, les fruits disparaissent des marchés. Les vendeurs disparaissent, les boutiques disparaissent, les poteaux télégraphiques disparaissent, la lune disparaît, le soleil disparaît, l'océan disparaît. Et puis … (2–3).

[HOTEL OWNER (*sneaky*). And then, and then, and then, let's not talk about this anymore. They are old stories without importance. They torment you at night. And then a nice blue Sunday, everything disappears, the earth disappears, the sky disappears, the flowers disappear, the fruits disappear from the markets. The sellers disappear, the stores disappear, the telegraph poles disappear, the moon disappears, the sun disappears, the ocean disappears. And then ….]

The hotel owner suddenly becomes talkative and philosophic, although his speech remains repetitive. The young couple remains mostly silent, while he continues to talk about disasters, as if he wanted to justify his prior reluctance to use language more completely. While this "conversation" ensues, the hotel owner tries to lock the young couple in the room while the cracks in the hotel's walls become more and more pronounced, completing the ambiance of a suffocating room. Whether the hotel owner is just a bad person or simply executes the order given to him by the young man is not clear at this point. All we know is that, in such a claustrophobic atmosphere, the only way to get out is through playing a game or dreaming or a combination of both. Thus, their game now functions as escape. This, at least, is what the young man claims in the second scene, when asked by the young girl whether they are locked in or not: "Comme on est enfermé dans un rêve. On n'à qu'à se réveiller pour en sortir" (4) [As if we were locked in a dream. We have but to wake up in order to get out of it].

The second scene begins with the story-making game of "Who am I?" which corresponds to the surrealist game "The Dialogue in 1928."[21] The basic rule of this game is as follows: each player has to improvise as quickly as possible in response to a question posed at the beginning of the game such as, "What part of the female body do you like the most?" or "Is suicide a solution?" or "Would you open the door if Freud visited you at night?" (see Garrigues, *Les Jeux surrealistes*, for a compilation). Each question lies at the heart of Surrealism's concerns and aims to disclose the players' innermost desires and fears, provided they comply with another general rule of the game, namely, that they dare to tell the truth, uninhibited by any constraint. To help eliminate the possibility of constraint, each player must give his answer as quickly as possible, supported by free improvisation. The sum of the players' input, despite their fragmentary production, creates a new form of dialogue on the subject matter introduced by the initial question. Thus, the young couple's game in *The Nightfall Hotel* is similar, with similar rules. The only difference is that instead of many players, there are only two, although they are in a sense multiplied through the diverse identifications that emerge from each player's improvised story-telling in response to the opening question of "Who am I?" Thus, the young man tells the young girl (we still do not know their names) that she likes being noticed and that this is why she once walked naked through the crowds. The young girl replies indignantly that this is nonsense, since he just met her in a railway station and told her when he first approached her that, in case she were asked by anybody, she should pretend that he had an appointment with her, that his name was Alain Champeret, that he was 22 years old, and that he was an acrobat. She was also to pretend to have met him the previous night. All these made-up stories would save him from being condemned for either an illegal act or perhaps a putsch against the state. Or, perhaps this was simply a farce. But she pretends that none of them was the case. Rather, it was love at first sight that made her follow him. This declaration of hers is soon turned upside down when the young man shows some jewelry from his pocket:

JEUNNE HOMME. Tu vois que tu as tout changé de notre histoire. Ça ne s'est pas passé comme ça du tout. Voyons! Moi, je suis venu à côté de toi. Je t'ai passé un paquet en te disant: "Ne me demandez rien. Gardez ça pour une minute. Et je reviens! Ne bougez pas. Vous ne me connaissez pas. À tout à l'heure." Quand je suis revenue, je t'ai remercié pour le risque que tu avais accepté de courir pour moi. J'ai repris mon paquet, et alors ... (5).

[YOUNG MAN. You see that you changed everything in our story. This has not happened like this at all. Look! I myself came to your side. I handed you a package while saying to you: "Don't ask me anything. Keep this for a minute. And I'll be right back. Don't move. You don't know me. Later." When I came back, I thanked you for having taken the risk for me. I took back my package and then ....]

The young girl laughs at this version and says that it is her turn now to tell her own version of their relations. Taking an imitative tone she changes her voice and pleads with an unknown gentleman in the railway station to protect her from somebody suspicious who is following her, since it is too dangerous for a woman to wander in a big city. The young man admits that this is a nice story and they kiss each other. At this point the spectators might suspect that they are watching an anonymous young couple playing a game of inventing and re-inventing their own identity. Like Nadja, who in her game invented innumerable stories about herself, the young couple does the same. They get involved in the game, not necessarily as a means of escape from boredom, locked as they are in the hotel room, but rather as an attempt to know each other better, regardless of how feasible this might be.

In the third scene, their imaginative game takes as its point of departure a hole in one of the walls of their room. They start inventing stories about the occupant of the next room, whom they imagine to be a naked woman. The "hole" and the "naked woman" function as marker-words for the two players to play a game that I like to call "parallel stories," similar to several of the Surrealists' games. Within this game, they are bound by the rules to incorporate some marker-words into their stories, as "each player independently writes the 'automatic' account of an identical event, one which they all could have witnessed" (Gooding 148). As they give free rein to their fantasies, they end up by acting out eight different versions of their game of parallel stories, reminiscent of the surrealist "game of variants." Both these games resemble the parlor game "telephone" or "Chinese whispers," where "the first player whispers a sentence to his neighbour, who whispers the same sentence to the next player, and so on. The first and last sentences are then compared" (ibid. 32). All of their eight versions are an organic part of the play, and are not options the author gives the stage director to decide upon for inclusion into the final stage production. Interestingly, among these variants, one is a reenactment of the moment in the taxi between Nadja and Breton, when she first introduced her game to him; Valaoritis purposely alludes to Nadja's game with his own variant of the taxi ride. Finally, it is worth mentioning that, in this frantic exchange of made-up stories between the young man and the young woman, whose name—Martha—is finally revealed in one of these eight versions, there may be some elements that are part of their real lives. Mingling reality with fantasy, all these invented stories that the young couple acts out blur the boundaries between truth and falsehood and give illusion its literal meaning, that is, "in play" (from *inlusion*, *illudere* or *inludere*), as Huizinga points out (11).

The fourth scene is another example of illusion. The young man tells a made-up story about the jewelry that he holds in his hands, the outcome of a robbery. In his story, he entered an apartment and, as he was picking up the jewelry from a dresser, he felt as though somebody was watching him. That somebody turned out to be a naked woman with thick hair, lying on a red sofa. He thought all this was a dream and yet also felt that the woman had invited him. But, at that moment, everything disappeared. The next day he awoke with a terrible headache and found that he was holding in his hands the jewelry soaked in tears or dew. This detailed description is, of course, a typically surrealist event that evokes Breton's following excerpt from *Nadja*:

> J'ai toujours incroyablement souhaité de rencontrer la nuit, dans un bois, une femme belle et nue, ou plutôt, un tel souhait une fois exprimé ne signifiait plus rien, je regrette incroyablement de ne pas l'avoir rencontrée (*OC1* 668).

> [I have always, beyond belief, hoped to meet, at night and in the woods, a beautiful naked woman or rather, since such a wish once expressed means nothing, I regret, beyond belief, not having met her (Howard 39).]

Martha reacts to the above story with no surprise, so the young man teases her that she has ruined everything. Meanwhile, her reaction leaves some hints that the couple is perhaps like another Bonnie and Clyde, or they at least imagine themselves to be. Martha's statement that they are imprisoned in the desert of love reinforces this idea. In the next scene they try to recite a poem together while performing a kind of chorus on a very pessimistic theme.

In the sixth scene, their multi-faceted linguistic game, modeled after Nadja's game, becomes unbearable for Martha as she complains that she is the loser and is not playing anymore: "Arrête, arrête! Je suis battue. Tu as gagné. Je ne joue plus. (*Elle se bouche les oreilles*) (11) [Stop it! Stop it! I am beaten. I'm not playing anymore. (*She shuts her ears*)]. These words constitute the first explicit sign that the audience is witnessing a verbal and mimetic game. Martha utters them after being scared by two consecutive cracks occurring in the building walls, but even more, by the words she hears coming out of Yves's mouth. His words depict the rotten hotel, with its horrifying termites and crumbling walls, and their starvation imprisoned in the room. Yves continues to describe these terrible images, which he calls "marvelous," while Martha stops her ears. Meanwhile, Yves refers to himself for the first time by his name and mentions his father, whom he has not yet forgiven for an unknown reason. Martha seems now after all to re-enter the game, which now takes the form of a guessing game where she is required to keep her ears closed. She keeps teasing Yves by repeating this sentence "Ton père est un réchaud, et ta mère est une pantoufle" (12) [Your father is a utensil and your mother a shoe]. Yves remains calm, however, as he continues their game by replying with nonsensical sentences in the same way that Patrick did to Leah's questions in *The Mysteries of Love*. Appearing unconquerable, Yves switches to another game, the "If/When" surrealist game, part of the "Dialogue in 1928," according to which one writes a conditional clause, while another writes a principal clause without knowing the content of the conditional clause. Here, however, Yves undertakes the job for both players:

> JEUNNE HOMME. Et si je te bandais les yeux aussi?
> Comme ça tu serais aveugle.
> Et si je te remplissais la bouche avec un mouchoir?
> Tu deviendrais muette.
> Et si je t'attachais les pieds et les mains?

Tu serais alors une aveugle, sourde, muette.
Enchaînée.
N'est-ce pas? C'est pas mal! (13).

[YOUNG MAN. And if I stripped your eyes as well?
You would be blind in this way.
And if I filled your mouth with a handkerchief?
You would become speechless.
And if I chained your hands and your feet?
You would then be blind, speechless, voiceless
In chains.
Right? It's not bad!]

At this point, the "if" game has become sadistic, nevertheless Martha challenges him to put it into practice. Yves claims to be too tired for this.

In the next scene and the next game, also given in two versions, Martha, keeping her ears closed as another way to elicit the power of imagination, has the leading role. Her goal is to create a reaction in Yves when she accuses him of "being afraid" in a series of short strophes of free verses such as this: "Tu as peur de connaître le goût sucré et amer de tous les jours. Tu as peur des cérémonies creuses de la naissance, des mariages et de la mort. Peur de m'embrasser trop souvent! (13). [You are afraid of knowing the bitter-sweet taste of everyday. You are afraid of the hollow ceremonies of birth, wedding, and death. Afraid of kissing me too often!]. Yves replies in a nonsensical, yet confessional tone. Both of them seem to have achieved a deeper understanding now, since they pay close attention to each other in their new stories, despite Martha's covered ears. These new stories, like a Greek tragedy, seem to evoke mostly past traumatic experiences of the couple, including Martha's experience as a lover of her mother's lover that follows her like a shadow all her life. After the release of their stories, Martha removes her hands from her ears while Yves now ties a handkerchief around her head to cover her eyes.

Next comes a hide-and-seek game that unfolds in the eighth scene. This is not a regular hide-and-seek game, as Yves takes a knife out of his pocket, reminding us of the knife in *The Mysteries of Love*. He challenges Martha to find him, as Nadja once challenged Breton to find her and, through her, to find himself: "Regarde-moi bien. Tu me vois? Qui suis-je? Où suis-je? Cherche. Trouves-moi!" (15) [Look at me well. Do you see me? Who am I? Where am I? Look for me. Find me!]. After a while, Martha manages to get Yves's knife and throws it at the wall. Yves takes off her blindfold to bring their game to an end, without wanting to admit that he is the loser. They continue the game by quoting verses to impress each other until they hear some steps outside their room. They blow the candle out and rush toward the hole in the wall, while Martha puts on the jewelry.

After an intermezzo, the ninth scene begins in the form of yet another game, the goal of which is to describe the hole and what it reveals on the other side of the wall, a device typical of many surrealist films. The tenth scene then reaches its climactic moment in the description of the hole that overtly uses surrealist symbols, such as the ones that haunted Breton all his life: long white gloves, a hut, a beam of light and of obscurity, like in *la camera obscura*, an early form of cinema. The "one into another" game is also applied here quite literally, as Yves reveals to Martha what lies behind each object he sees in the hole and what is contained in each object he sees. Thus, there is an open window that gives way to another open window, behind which there is a long, empty hut, lying on a bed of roses along with a pair of gorgeous hands and a shadow that caresses the curtain in a mild wind. There is also the sky and another shadow on a wall that resembles a face smiling like the falling night. The dark smile seems familiar to both of them. This series of interlocking descriptions constitutes the culmination of the couple's "one into another" game and ends with the personification of the falling night that appears in the title of the play. This interwoven "one into another" game finally unlocks all the mysterious layers of the marvelous yet terrifying encounters of the young couple, who finally feel more comfortable with each other. This endless game ultimately offers them a sense of acquiring an identity, as the last scene clearly illustrates: to Yves's question of exactly what she wants from him she replies:

> MARTHE. Une identité. Une espèce de réalité qui dépasse l'ordinaire. Cesse d'être un fantôme et deviens toi-même. Explique-moi exactement ce que tu as ressenti en me voyant. Me désires-tu vraiment ou pas? Je suis capable de disparaître à l'instant sans laisser aucune trace (18).

> [MARTHA. An identity. A kind of reality that surpasses the everyday. Cease being a phantom and become yourself. Explain to me exactly what you felt when you first saw me. Do you really desire me or not? I am capable of instantly disappearing without leaving any trace.]

Martha has finally become another Nadja, who shows her capacity to live another life. But most of all, she has the power to redirect Yves and bring him face to face with his desire. Their game has come full circle, as if this were its goal from the very beginning; or it is like a hall of mirrors, another image from *Nadja*. Treating each other like enemies for much of this labyrinth-like game, Martha and Yves finally come to realize that they are destined to be "one into another." This explains why they both decide to continue their strange game, ignoring the imminent demolition of the hotel where they are staying. This is what Valaoritis intended to convey, by insisting on the recalcitrant young couple's game. In the program of the play's première, Valaoritis wrote:

> Un couple dans une chambre d'hôtel recrée le passé, vrai ou imaginaire, et tente de vivre le présent, du paradis à l'enfer. ... En dépit des fréquents avertissements, les jeunes gens ignorent avec persistance que le monde autour d'eux est en train de s'écrouler, et continuent leur jeu étrange" (quoted in Vallaire).

> [A couple in a hotel room recreates the past, true or imaginary, and tries to live the present, from paradise to hell. ... Despite the frequent warnings, the young couple persistently ignores that the world around them is in the process of crashing, and they continue their strange game.]

Waiting for their tragic end while playing a game is the most audacious act of faith in their mutual mad love. In this way, perhaps their approaching night, captured in the title of the play, may become for them another "nuit des éclairs," such as the one at which Breton marveled: "C'est la plus belle des nuits, la nuit des éclairs: le jour, auprès d'elle, est la nuit" (*OC1* 338) [It's the most beautiful night, a night full of lightning: the day, compared to it, is night]. Here, in the night of lightning, Valaoritis discerns a similar game between life and death from which "an enthusiastic experience of death" emerges, which writes itself (*For a Theory of Writing* 314). Therefore, rather than a pessimistic tone that would come closer to that of the Theatre of the Absurd or the Existential Theatre of the time, one discerns in Valaoritis's work a more optimistic surrealist tone and aspiration conveyed through his emulation of Breton. Thus, he pays tribute to the surrealist leader. As I have pointed before, this tribute at the same time constitutes an act of rebellion: the Greek playwright chooses the theatrical form, Breton's least favorite artistic form, and succeeds with it. Our next chapter will further clarify this issue.

Conclusion

"One into another" is the ludic principle that guides both *The Mysteries of Love* and *The Nightfall Hotel*. In between them stands Nadja's own "one into another" game. All converge in a version of the game that can be called "mad love," which consists of "madness in love" and "love in madness." All of them magically encapsulate the lovers' unified yet fictive selves: "Leah in Patrick" or "Patrick in Leah"; "Martha in Yves" or "Yves in Martha"; "Nadja in André" or "André in Nadja"—ludic avatars that are responsible for each character's new state of being. Likewise, this interlocking game may take another form, such as we first encountered in Palau's play *Les Détraquées*: "Solange in Blanche Derval in Nadja in Leah in Martha," a chain that embeds the highly valued surrealist image of the "mad woman." Each one of these female characters is at once unique and multiple, exactly as Surrealism wished. "One into another" is the ludic process that allows each player to acquire a sense of a unified self, through endless identifications, similar to the ones that can be generated by a chain of mirrors in a crystal palace—Breton's obsessive image. In *Nadja*, for instance, Breton claims:

> Pour moi, je continuerai à habiter ma maison de verre, où l'on peut voir à toute heure qui vient me rendre visite, où tout ce qui est suspendu aux plafonds et aux murs tient comme par enchantement, où je repose la nuit sur un lit de verre aux draps de verre, où *qui je suis* m'apparaîtra tôt ou tard gravé au diamant (*OC1* 651).

> [I myself shall continue living in my glass house where you can always see who comes to call; where everything hanging from the ceiling and on the walls stays where it is as if by magic, where I sleep nights in a glass bed, under glass sheets, where *who I am* will sooner or later appear etched by a diamond (Howard 18).]

In Breton's infamous "maison inhabitable de sel gemme" [residence made of a gem of salt],[22] one's own identity will be crystal-clear, carved by a diamond, since in such a place,

> l'inanimé touche ici de si près l'animé que *l'imagination est libre de se jouer à l'infini sur ses formes d'apparence toute minérale*, de reproduire à leur sujet la démarche qui consiste à reconnaître un nid, une grappe retirés d'une fontaine pétrifiante (Breton, *OC2* 681; my emphasis).

[the inanimate touches here so closely the animate to the point that *the imagination is free to play with itself endlessly on the level of its apparently totally mineral forms*, to reproduce on their account the process consisting of recognizing a nest, a vine withdrawn from a petrifying fountain.]

Thanks to this infinite play of imagination that vividly transforms one image into another, the player stands amazed by his/her newly revealed sense of identity. Likewise, the spectator becomes aware of the transformational power of this game of imagination to which he/she willingly succumbs, as Breton himself did as Nadja's "playmate."

This is the kind of theatre that Artaud and Vitrac attempted to activate in the playground of the Théâtre Alfred Jarry. Initially puzzled about the nature of theatre, whether it is in fact a game or not, Vitrac and Artaud found the solution they sought in the practice of the "one into another" surrealist formula, prior to its official establishment. From that moment on, theatre for them ceased to be a matter of a "game or not" and became rather a matter of "a game in life" and of "life in game." In other words, it became intertwined with their outside experience. That way, they guaranteed at once the aleatory nature and the non-mimetic character of their new, experimental theatre, in which referentiality "loses its fixity to assume a mobility" (Antle, "Towards Re-Presentation" 19).

The Théâtre Alfred Jarry thus became a first-class avant-garde theatrical endeavor of the inter-war period, particularly during the years 1927–30. It was transformed into a realm of genuine collaboration between these two exiles of Surrealism to the point that they have been considered the only figures who are "associated with a serious effort at the creation of a surrealist theatre" (Auslander 357). Vitrac and Artaud had no other choice, indeed, than to found their own theatre, as theatre was an inseparable part of their lives. In doing so, they did not lack in the revolutionary spirit, which Breton so much admired. Naming their theatre after their fabulous precursor, the creator of the anarchic and grotesque *Ubu-roi* and author of the text "L'Amour absolu" ("Absolute Love")—both of which texts were very influential on them—bears the best proof of their revolutionary spirit.[23] In their revolutionary statements of intention concerning the Théâtre Alfred Jarry that "come close to being manifestoes for a surrealist theatre" (Auslander 357), both Artaud and Vitrac show the same zeal as Breton for changing the ossified theatre of their time that was bound to the realist principle of the stage as a mirror of reality. Together they joined their efforts to overturn realism in theatre by applying the surrealist principles they had assimilated when they were active members of the surrealist movement, particularly when they were practicing so-called surrealist games. What they learned from their mingling with Breton and his circle was that "verisimilitude and consistency in character, consideration of time and space relationships, and a concern for logic" should play no role in the organization of their theatrical works (Bennison 124). Instead, reliance on the mechanisms of games that had the potential to unearth the mechanisms of dreams would be the surest road to their new concept of theatre. And through these games, they ensured one more thing: humor and laughter, to the point that laughter commingles violence and offense. "Laughter in violence" and "violence in laughter" is itself a revolutionary act that defies logic, or at least destroys clear-cut binaries, and constitutes the best homage to their precursor, Alfred Jarry, and of course, to Breton himself, who was deeply influenced by Freud in this regard. He quotes the following words from Freud in "Le discours sur le peu de réalité": "Humour is not resigned, it is rebellious … The humorous attitude … refuses to undergo suffering, asseverates the invincibility of one's ego against the real world and victoriously upholds the pleasure principle" (quoted in Suleiman 2). "One into another," a free activity *par excellence*, rises to the level of a magnificent ludic tool for surrealist theatre, because it can take all possible directions and thus amplify language. Therefore, it introduces new forms of life. This is what Vitrac and Artaud, as well as Valaoritis, achieved when they staged "mad love." They brought to life a new state of being, which functioned as a springboard for the audience's imagination, and, through this new form of life, they challenged language itself.

Vitrac and Artaud continued to challenge language within the Théâtre Alfred Jarry more explicitly still when, in 1928, they staged *Victor ou les enfants au pouvoir* (*Victor or Children in Power*), in which other ludic experiments took place, the most significant being children's puns targeting the life of adults. This play and its ludic techniques are the focus of the next chapter, where I compare Vitrac's *Victor ou les enfants au pouvoir* with Nanos Valaoritis's *The Round Tables* and *Henriette où est-elle passée* (*Where Did Henriette Go?*), a deliberately loose adaptation of the former, which was also influenced by Palau's *Les Détraquées*. *The Round Tables* epitomizes his self-conscious experimentation with the surrealist games. Through this play, I explore a new function of surrealist ludics, namely its ironic, irresistible criticism of bourgeois values. Such criticism is most effective when it is the product of children's games. Children's "childlike" use of language is at the heart of the next chapter and it reveals without question that surrealist theatre never committed the "sin" of conformism, that Breton considered inevitable on the stage.

Notes

1   See note 3 in Chapter 1.

2   Henri Béhar informs us that Vitrac was excluded from Surrealism by Breton in September 1926, while Artaud's exclusion took place a month later (*Étude* 227–8). As far as Robert Aron is concerned, he had never officially adhered to Surrealism, but was surrounded by surrealist friends. As to the reasons for which Breton dismissed them, the views vary. Vitrac and Artaud "were on sufficiently friendly terms to spend the summer of 1925 together, returning from a holiday to discover that Vitrac had been excommunicated from Surrealism by André Breton. Artaud was excluded later in the year" (Auslander 357). Artaud's exclusion from the group was publicly announced in the pamphlet *Au grand jour* (1927), signed by Aragon, Breton, Eluard, Péret, and Unik. Artaud "countered with *La Grande Nuit ou le Bluff Surréaliste*, deriding this particular group as a 'grotesque sham,' and a 'masquerade.' The final break came after he had contributed to the 1928 issue of *La Révolution Surréaliste*" (Knapp 88). The expulsion of Vitrac and Artaud from the movement reached full-blown hostility where Breton's *Second Manifesto of Surrealism* (1930) is concerned. The arguments and counter-arguments in this debate which culminated in the scandal following the representation of Strindberg's *Dream Play* by the Théâtre Alfred Jarry, and which signified the definitive break of Artaud and Vitrac with the surrealist group, have been largely discussed. I align myself with Henri Béhar

who summarizes the three reasons for which Breton rejected Vitrac from the surrealist movement (and, which equally apply to Artaud) (*Théâtre ouvert* 22). First, because he pursued "literary" ends; secondly, because he refused to be politically engaged, that is, to comply with the communist ideology; and finally, because he opted for the dramatic genre. Among these reasons the last seems to be the strongest reason for Breton to exclude them from the movement, as any involvement with the theatrical world inevitably entails a degree of commercialization, something that was incompatible with the spirit of absolute freedom and revolution that Surrealism advocated.

3   The same bill also included Artaud's *Le Jet de sang* (*The Spurt of Blood*), published in his collection *L'Ombilic des limbes* in 1925. This concise play, apart from its premiere, remained practically unstaged until Peter Brook discovered it and included it in his 1964 London Theatre of Cruelty production with much success. Christopher Innes offers some details about this production (128–9). *The Spurt of Blood* will be further discussed in the next chapter in relation to its ludic techniques.

4   See Levi, "The Last Greek Surrealist."

5   After Breton's death on September 28, 1966 in Paris, according to Gérard Durozoi, "the question of whether to pursue a collective surrealist activity would become more and more crucial, until in October 1969, Jean Schuster [the appointed leader of Surrealism after Breton's death] publicly announced that it would be impossible" (635). See Durozoi, *History of the Surrealist Movement*, trans. Alison Anderson.

6   See Béhar, *Un réprouvé* 137.

7   Benjamin Crémieux, for instance, dismissed the play, judging it from a realist perspective: "Let's stay in the domain of theatre. In the theatre there must be a continuous flow. However, the fragmentation of visions that Mr. Vitrac suggests here lacks such a continuity of flow, intrigue or ambiance" (quoted in Artaud, *OC* 54). There is no doubt that this play is an "obscure" play, as Vitrac himself characterizes it in the preface of the 1948 Gallimard edition of his completed works, where he also explains that he hesitated to publish it along with his other non-surrealist plays. Finally, he published it complying with Apollinaire's advice that "one must publish everything."

8   Emmanuel Garrigues, for instance, mentions his name among the names of the participants in the surrealist game "Quelques préférences de ..." (Some preferences of ...) that was published in the second series of *Littérature* on April 1, 1922. For more details, see Garrigues, *Les Jeux surrealists* 53–7. It is also interesting to note here the close relationship that had developed between André Breton and Roger Vitrac. Vitrac had been with the surrealist movement from its beginnings when it emerged from the French Dada movement (1920), and he participated in the practice of surrealist games. In 1923 he contributed to the journal *Le Journal du peuple*, in which he declared that "he shared almost absolutely Breton's ideas," while in 1924 he was assigned to edit, along with Paul Eluard and Jacques-André Boiffard, the first number of the monthly review *La Révolution surréaliste* (Hubert 11). Breton himself acknowledges him in his first manifesto among those who practice Absolute Surrealism. In fact, Vitrac almost deified Breton at one point; meeting with Breton, he wrote in *Le Journal du peuple* on January 5, 1924, was for him "a grace that he wished for everyone" (ibid. 12). In 1924, he met Artaud who also joined the Surrealists at the end of the same year. Soon Artaud "took over the management of the bureau and planned the virulent third issue of *La Révolution surréaliste*" (Durozoi 651).

9   Hereafter I will refer to this translation of *The Mysteries of Love* by Ralph J. Gladstone and included in Benedikt and Wellwarth, *The Avant-garde, Dada, and Surrealism* 227–67.

10   Vitrac may have had as a model for this scene Melisande's long black hair from Maurice Maeterlink's play *Péleas and Melisande* (1892).

11   Judging from an autobiographical perspective, such an interpretation complies with Vitrac's dedication of the play to his partner at the time, Suzanne, to whom he addresses the following lines from Jarry's work "L'Amour absolu": "The women who love us / renew the true Sabbath" (Benedikt 227). The word 'Sabbath' empowers the portrayed woman with a religious aspect, who then becomes a redeemer for Patrick, who is perhaps Vitrac's alter ego. Vitrac indeed "believed in woman's redeeming character and that man could only attain an absolute knowledge through a total love" (Béhar, *Théâtre ouvert* 18).

12   These lines echo on the one hand, Calderòn's *La vida es sueño* (1635) and on the other hand, Hamlet's relevant scene from Shakespeare's *Hamlet*.

13   For more details see Breton, *OC1* 338.

14   Henri Béhar devotes an entire chapter on Vitrac's project to create his *Théâtre de l'incendie*. For more details, see *Un réprouvé* 159–204.

15   Characteristic of Breton's attitude towards the Greek legacy is the following anecdote that Henri Béhar mentions: in the spring of 1957, when Elisa Breton was in Greece, Breton was asked by Loleh Bellon, the companion of the critic Claude Roy, why he did not join her on her trip. Breton replied: "My dear Loleh, would you go for tourism to Germany during occupation?" Loleh did not understand this reply so Breton added: "Since for more than 2,000 years we have been occupied by the Greco-Romans, therefore, I will never put my feet either in Greece or in Italy!" (Béhar, *Le Grand indésirable* 425).

16   Interestingly, this episode anticipates the similar episode that will occur in Breton's *Nadja* (1928), as Béhar reminds us. See *Un réprouvé* 177.

17   Information released in a personal interview he gave me on May 21 in his home at Oakland, California. Valaoritis, born in Lausanne, Switzerland in 1921, represents a rare case of a multi-lingual avant-garde writer who experiments with all genres in three languages—namely, English and his two mother tongues, Greek and French. Author of about 13 books of poetry and fiction and more than 50 mostly unpublished plays and skits, Valaoritis received numerous awards in Greece, France and the United States. Part of his work is now archived at Princeton University.

18   For more details about the close relationship between Valaoritis and Breton and the unforgettable days he spent with him and his wife Eliza and their circle of friends in Saint-Cirq la Popie, see Valaoritis, *For a Theory of Writing B* 45–7.

19   See Arthur Rimbaud's "Delires II, Alchimie du verhe" from *Une Saison en enfer* and a single letter of Rimbaud's, dated May 15, 1871, to his friend Paul Demeny in which the French poet develops his theories that he described later as the "alchimie du verbe."

20   Marcelle Capron, for instance in *Le Combat* of April 29, 1959, names the two protagonists of *The Nightfall Hotel* "nos Roméo et Juliette 1959" (our 1959 Romeo and Juliet), while *France-Soir* in the column of spectacles printed the following title: "Marpessa Dawn et Georges Vander dans le 'Roméo et Juliette' moderne, intitulé *L'Hôtel de la Nuit qui Tombe*."

21   For more information see Emmanuel Garrigues, *Les Jeux surréalistes* 58–63. Antonin Artaud was one of the participants in this game.

22   This comes from Breton's *L'Amour fou* (*Mad Love*, 1937).

23   Another important originator of Surrealism to whom the Théâtre Alfred Jarry renders homage is Guillaume Apollinaire. He coined the term "Surrealism," yet in another sense, he opposed naturalism, in an attempt to stress the need for a new mode of dramatic expression. In the preface he added in 1917 to his famous play *Les Mamelles de Tirésias* (*The Breasts of Tiresias*, 1903), a play about the need for love and fertility, Apollinaire inserted the adjective "surrealist" to express his ideas against the concept of the stage

as mirror to reality. With Breton's reemployment of the term, "Surrealism" acquired a new meaning, while Vitrac and Artaud illustrated this new meaning on stage within the Théâtre Alfred Jarry.

3

STAGING CHILD'S PLAY IN ROGER VITRAC'S *VICTOR OR CHILDREN IN POWER*: BETWEEN *PAIDIA* AND *LUDUS*[1]

> The sight of the masked figure … carries us back to the world of the savage, the child and the poet, which is the world of play (Huizinga 26).

> And this child is the child not of Christ but of Heraclitus. It is the innocent power as eternity, beginning its game of creation and destruction each time anew, without remorse, in blissful self-forgetfulness (Nietzsche, quoted in Sutton Smith 113).

Rationalistic thought "seems to have dominated most of Western thinking about play," both in terms of play itself being seen as rationally guided, and in terms of using a rationalist approach to interpreting play (Sutton Smith 81). However, many great thinkers, such as Friedrich Nietzsche, saw children's play "as a kind of irrational power" (ibid. 112). Likewise, Huizinga, in this chapter's opening quotation, overtly equates the world of play in general with the world of the primitive, the child, and the poet, hinting at their common lack of reason. André Breton also aligned himself with this approach to play, seeing it as irrational and ritualistic,[2] heralding play's basic indeterminism, chaos, irrationality or even absurdity:

> La complaisance envers l'absurde rouvre à l'homme le royaume mystérieux qu'habitent les enfants. Le jeu de l'enfance, comme moyen perdu de conciliation entre l'action et la rêverie en vue de la satisfaction organique, à commencer par le simple "jeu de mots," se trouve de la sorte rehabilité et dignifié (Breton, *OC2* 963).

> [Favoring the absurd reopens the mysterious kingdom that children inhabit to mankind. Children's play, as the lost medium of reconciling action with reverie for the sake of organic satisfaction, starting with simple "word games," consequently becomes rehabilitated and dignified.]

For the leader of Surrealism, children's play constitutes a "magnificent field of experience" (*OC2* 963), a road to the marvelous, which, in Anna Balakian's words, is "the sacred both sublime and terrifying" that opens the path to the supreme category of "surreality" (quoted in Orenstein Feman xiv). In the realm of surreality, the real is fused with the imaginary in exactly the same way they are fused in the field of play. For the deliberately anti-literary Surrealists, playing a wide variety of games—especially dialogue games—guaranteed the marvelous, as they combined the most arbitrary images that might fascinate an audience. These games "could serve to elicit *le merveilleux* and so fill bleak reality with suggestive revelation" (Gershman 54.) They used language that evoked unexpected visual images to describe a character or an event. Breton referred to the mysterious effects and the particular pleasures derived from such images as the effects of "the opium" that enraptured people (*Manifestoes* 36). Furthermore, for Breton, surrealist games supported Johan Huizinga's conclusion in *Homo Ludens* about the "supra-logical (supralogique) character of our situation within the world" (quoted in Garrigues 218). Starting from a simple pun, word games can become a powerful means of revelation, and initiation to the marvelous. Indeed this was the goal of the Surrealists when they started performing their ludic activities in a systematic fashion. As Mel Gooding notes, "[m]ost specially and remarkably, it was through games, play, techniques of surprise and methodologies of the fantastic that they (Surrealists) subverted academic modes of enquiry, and undermined the complacent certainties of the reasonable and respectable" (12).

In this chapter, I argue that surrealist theatre ingeniously places the inherent logic of games in the service of the irrational, in order to become a tool for the subversion of social order. This idea came to me when I interviewed Nanos Valaoritis,[3] and he commented that many surrealist dialogues were generated by surrealist games. The games have rules, so the seeming "incoherence" of surrealist texts was, in fact, a function of so-called rational standards. The idea of a dialogue that advocates incoherence according to standards of rationality fascinated Valaoritis, particularly when he contrasted surrealist dialogues with Plato's dialogues, which displayed a coherent logic. In surrealist dialogue he felt a pleasure derived from the feeling of surprise and disorientation, rather than from a successful communication as in the case of Platonic dialogues. Surrealist dialogue satisfies the audience, not with the logical transferal of meaning, but because it reveals the most audacious clusters of arbitrary images resulting from free improvisation and the release of the subconscious.

In contrast to another giant of ancient Greek thought, Valaoritis argued that dialogue, rather than plot—as Aristotle thought—is the essence of drama. Indeed, he fully embraced the belief of the Surrealists that, to the extent that plot would count at all in surrealist theatre, "it would tend to function mainly as a support for dialogue—while the dialogue itself would be allowed to push forward on a level of exchange where common sense and normal sequence surrender their claim to attention" (Melzer Henkin, *Latest Rage* 166). Such a belief called for a reversal of dramatic conventions. In other words, poetry was liberated through this kind of dialogue, at the expense of drama. Intrigued by the apparent incoherence of surrealist dialogues, the contemporary Greek playwright admitted that he had used surrealist games to write plays. He added that an audience might enjoy his plays more if it had a grasp of the game rules he had used in this process. The same precondition, I believe, applies to all surrealist texts, including the theatrical ones. Seemingly incoherent contradictions, both in surrealist texts and, especially, in surrealist images, are in fact rule-generated, and it is the understanding of these latent yet prescriptive rules that makes surrealist texts truly interesting.

Knowing that rules underlie an apparently chaotic surface actually blurs the boundaries between reason and non-reason. On the one hand, it becomes clear that reason is fragile; on the other, what was considered nonsense is, in fact, founded on reason. Furthermore, the latent structure of Surrealism created the condition for looking at surrealist texts more seriously, while it made clear that meaning is contingent upon context and circumstances. As Michael Riffaterre notices, "in the reality of the text" surrealist images "are arbitrary only in relation to our habitual logic and utilitarian attitude toward reality and language" (*Text Production* 202). More specifically, Riffaterre argues, within the microcosm of a text, "a logic of words comes to be, a logic that has nothing to do with normal linguistic communication. This verbal logic creates a special code, a dialect within language, causing the reader to undergo the disorientation of the senses that the Surrealists saw as the essence of the poetic experience" (ibid.). Therefore, it was evident that such surrealist texts were meaning-bearing and not simply nonsense. Nonsense, Elizabeth Sewell claims,

> is not merely the denial of sense, a random reversal of ordinary experience and an escape from the limitations of everyday life into a haphazard infinity, but is on the contrary a carefully limited world, controlled and directed by reason, a construction subject to its own laws (5).[4]

Likewise, children's games form their own carefully limited world, answering and answerable to their own laws alone. By embracing this world of children's games, surrealist games have the potential to subvert the social order because of their "inherent capacity to innovate and transform its rules" (Goldman 17). This idea of the potential for subversion has been known, of course, since Plato: "[c]hild play is the biggest menace that can ever afflict a state" (*Laws* 1.798). In this chapter, I explore the ways in which both children's games and surrealist games are incorporated in surrealist theatrical output to become a tool of social disruptiveness.

In the following discussion, I use the same classification of games that I used for Nadja's game in the opening chapter—that introduced by the mid-twentieth-century French sociologist and one-time member of the surrealist circle,[5] Roger Caillois, in his seminal study *Man, Play and Games* (1958). According to Caillois, games may be classified as *agon* (competitive games), *alea* (games of chance), *mimicry* (simulacrum and mimesis devoted to make-believe games), and *ilinx* (vertigo, such as carnival rides or roller coasters) (12). All of these types of games could appear alone or in combination with one another. Moreover, Caillois argues that games in any of these categories stretch along "a continuum between two attitudinal poles: *paidia* or infancy, characterized by free improvisation and fantasy, and *ludus*, characterized by constraint, arbitrary rules, and effort" (Motte 7). These two poles are evident in each of the surrealist plays that constitute the focus of this chapter, although there is a common tendency to move from *ludus* to *paidia*, that is, from logic towards improvisation and free association, more than the reverse. By consciously experimenting with games, the surrealist writers materialized the path from a rule-bound, and thus limited, reality to a more free-spirited reality, where rules are looser and unrestricting. The works that will be discussed in this chapter are Roger Vitrac's *Victor ou les enfants au pouvoir* (*Victor or Children in Power*) (1927) and two of Nanos Valaoritis's plays—*Henriette où est-elle passée* (*Henriette Where Did She Go?*) (1957)[6] and *Les Tables rondes* (*The Round Tables*) (1957)[7]—both modeled after Vitrac's piece. Valaoritis wrote these plays during the last phase of ludic activities by André Breton's surrealist group in Paris, from 1954 to 1960.[8] In the following pages, I examine closely how ludics is specifically employed in these three plays and what its effect is in each play, starting with the model piece, *Victor or Children in Power*. To clarify, the term ludics[9] in this chapter is now expanded to include the dialogue produced through children's games, in addition to the surrealist games of Motte's original use of the term.

Victor or Children in Power: The triumph of children's games

Written in 1927, this play premiered on December 24, 1928, in the Théâtre Alfred Jarry under Antonin Artaud's direction. Although it follows the conventions of a bourgeois drama, this play in three acts is imbued with a spirit of anarchism and represents the peak of Surrealism. As Marie-Claude Hubert states, "*Victor ou les enfants au pouvoir* est considéré, à juste titre, comme le chef-d'œuvre du théâtre surréaliste" (8) [*Victor or Children in Power* is considered, for legitimate reasons, the masterpiece of surrealist theatre]. Also, in March 1973, the drama critic Philippe Sénart declared that *Victor* should be recognized a masterpiece: "Comment ne s'est-on-pas aperçu en 1928, lorsque le Théâtre Alfred Jarry présenta *Victor ou les enfants au pouvoir*, que cette pièce était un chef-d'œuvre?" (quoted in Beachler Severs 141) [How did we not realize in 1928, when the Théâtre Alfred Jarry presented *Victor or Children in Power*, that this play was a masterpiece?]. *Victor*'s success lies in the fact that children's ludic activity explicitly becomes the organizing principle of the play. If in *The Mysteries of Love*, as we have seen in the previous chapter, ludic activity plays an important role in terms of the underlying structure of the play, in *Victor or Children in Power*, this activity is all-encompassing: everything starts as a child's game that affects everyone. In the end, the game itself emerges as the only master of the play. Concerned with the revelatory power of words, these games anticipate Breton's statement from his *Second Manifesto of Surrealism* (1929), that Surrealism's goal was to deal with the more general problem of:

> human expression in all its forms. Whoever speaks of expression speaks of language first and foremost. It should therefore come as no surprise to anyone to see Surrealism almost exclusively concerned with the question of language at first (Seaver and Lane 151).

In *Victor or Children in Power*, language indeed triumphs through the mouths of two children at play, Victor and Esther, who reveal all the hypocrisy that governs the lives of their otherwise respectable bourgeois families. Both children, naturally endowed with poetic skills, mimic the language of adults in a context of games, giving unprecedented power to their language. Their mimicry and linguistic play outlines the fact that human expression is, in fact, the key for understanding all the other problems that torment the family members in the play.

Victor, a gigantic, nine-foot, nine-year-old boy, plays with language at every possible level, only finally to be consumed by it and die on his birthday. Victor is "l'enfant précoce, doté d'une cruelle lucidité, personnage qui va très vite incarner un mythe" (Hubert 14) [the precocious child, endowed with an exceptional lucidity, a character who very soon will incarnate a myth]. Indeed, Victor, with his extraordinary size and precocious linguistic abilities and comprehension of things adult, embodies a new myth and represents a unique case in the history of theatre. Children's roles were rare even after the eighteenth century, when, thanks to Jean-Jacques Rousseau, more attention was paid to children.[10] Gifted with an exceptional lucidity, this "terribly intelligent" boy "mène rondement le jeu, presse de faire jaillir l'amère vérité, tout au long du premier acte où il n'épargne personne" (Hubert 20) [takes the lead and pushes in order to force out the bitter truth, throughout the first act, sparing no-one]. The first victim of Victor's audacious use of language, loaded with profane allusions against the pillar of Christianity, the Holy Mother, is the maid of the house, Lili, who occasionally sleeps with Victor's father. The play opens with the following word play by Victor that makes Lili feel uneasy:

> VICTOR. ... et le fruit de votre *entaille* est béni.
> LILI. D'abord, c'est le fruit de vos *entrailles*, qu'il faut dire.
> VICTOR. Peut-être, mais *c'est moins imagé* (9; my emphasis).

> [VICTOR. ... And blessed is the fruit of your *cut*.
> LILI. First, it is the fruit of *your womb* that you must say.
> VICTOR. Maybe, but *it's less colorful*.]

The playful substitution of the signifier *entaille* (=cut) for *entrailles* (=womb) in French, sounds more colorful to Victor's ears. Reversing the technique of his predecessor Ubu Roi, who added the letter "r" in the infamous word "merde" that opens the play *Ubu-roi*, Victor deletes here the letter "r" in the word "entrailles" (the letter "s" is silent) in the opening of Vitrac's play, to create the same scandalous effect in both Lili's and the audience's ears.[11] Indeed, "*Victor* is the closest of Vitrac's plays to the mode of Jarry, and it is its childishness of tone, rather than more sophisticated devices, which creates both formal and thematic disruption" (Levitt 517). Already from these opening lines, Victor shows his determination to trick everyone through his language, a language that not only proves his extreme intelligence, but also his loss of childlike innocence, and which is placed in the service of a creative project-game. This kind of game turns in an astonishing manner "from puerility to a form of perversity" (Piret 344), endowed with the value of experience. Victor continues tricking Lili with his skillful puns, daring even to accuse her of cracking an expensive piece of Sevres china, worth 10,000 francs, an act that he himself committed on purpose. Lili responds with the only defense at her disposal: she slaps him in the face. This "small monster" decided "à être quelque chose" [to be something] this day of his ninth birthday, September 12, 1909. As he completes his "neuf ans" [nine years], he wants to be "neuf" [brand-new],[12] that is, he wants to quit his old child-model that he has been up to this moment, and the game-*agon* enables him to fulfill his goal. When the servant Lili indignantly asks him "what he has," he replies again in a spirit of mockery, juxtaposing concrete objects with abstract ideas:

> VICTOR. J'ai neuf ans. J'ai un père, une mère, une bonne. J'ai un navire à essence qui part et revient à son point de départ, après avoir tiré deux coups de canon. J'ai une brosse à dents individuelle … J'ai la vue bonne et le jugement sûr, et je dois à ces dispositions de t'avoir vu commettre, sans motifs, un acte regrettable (12–13).

> [VICTOR. I am nine years old. I have a father, a mother, a maid. I have a motor boat which departs and returns to its point of departure, after having shot two canon shots. I have my very own toothbrush … My vision is good and my judgment is sound, and thanks to these attributes I saw you commit, without reason, a regrettable act.]

The allusion to this "regrettable act" of adultery becomes more obvious when Victor starts a game of mimicry, imitating his father's voice and the words his father would use, as he addresses a crying Lili: "Ne pleurez pas, Lili, ne pleurez pas, chère petite fille" (14) [Don't cry. Lili, don't cry, dear little girl]. Meanwhile, still imitating his father's voice, Victor embraces Lili and continues in these words:

> VICTOR. … Je vous sauverai. Comptez sur moi, et au petit jour, je vous apporterai moi-même la bonne nouvelle dans votre chambre. … (*Il se lève d'un bond et se met à crier de toutes ses forces, les bras levés.*) Priez pour nous, priez pour nous, priez pour nous! (*Puis il part d'un grand éclat de rire*) (14–15).

> [VICTOR. … I will save you. Count on me, and tomorrow morning, I myself will bring you good news to your room. … (*He stands up and starts wailing, with arms raised.*) Pray for us, pray for us, pray for us! (*Then he bursts into great laughter*).]

Victor's spontaneous pretend play ends with his laughter as he ridicules his father and Lili, particularly in the act of praying.

A similar mimetic language in another child's mouth reveals in the following scene that Victor's father, Mr. Charles Paumelle, has committed adultery again. His mistress is Mrs. Thérèse Magneau, the mother of Esther, Victor's best friend:

> ESTER. Alors, voilà. Je reste, on me jette un livre: "Bonjour Charles, bonjour, Thérèse. Où est le cher Antoine?" Papa dormait. Ils se sont assis sur le canapé, et voilà ce que j'ai entendu. Mamam disait: "Friselis, friselis, friselis." Ton papa: "Réso, réso, réso …" (19).

> [ESTHER. Well, here it goes. I stay, they throw me a book: "Good morning Charles, good morning, Thérèse. Where is your dear Antoine?" Dad was asleep. They sat on the sofa, and here is what I heard. Mom was saying: "Friselis, friselis, friselis." Your dad: "Réso, réso, réso …."]

Esther recounts the lovers' scene for Victor in which the adults use children's language. The repeated, apparently meaningless words ("friselis" and "réso") are spoken by the children in a mocking fashion. This parody becomes a harsh criticism of the adults' hypocritical behavior, when Victor and Esther decide to perform it for all the adult characters as entertainment. One of the characters,

General Etienne Lonsegur, had suggested that the two children are a perfect match and should "jouer papa et maman" [play daddy and mommy], which is when Victor and Esther decide to play the scene:

> LE GENERAL. C'est cela, jouez-nous papa et maman. Ah, quelle bonne idée. Là, Victor, tu es le papa. Esther, tu es la maman. Et c'est la femme qui commence, bien entendu.
> *Un longue silence, pendant lequel Victor parle bas à Esther. Esther et Victor vont jouer la scène que la petite fille surprit entre Charles et Thérèse.*
> ESTER. Friselis, friselis, friselis.
> VICTOR. Réso, réso, réso.
> ESTER. Carlo, je m'idole en tout.
> VICTOR. Treize, ô baigneur muet.
> ESTER. Mais si Antoine, là d'un coup.
> VICTOR. Ton cou me sauverait (34–5).

> [THE GENERAL. It's this, let's play daddy and mommy. Ah, what a good idea. There, Victor, you are the daddy. Esther, you are the mom. And of course it's the mom who gets started.
> *A long silence during which Victor whispers into Esther's ears. Esther and Victor will act out the scene that Esther witnessed between Charles and Thérèse.*
> ESTHER. Friselis, friselis, friselis.
> VICTOR. Réso, réso, réso.
> ESTHER. Carlo, I am passionate about everything.
> VICTOR. Thirteen, oh silent swimmer.
> ESTHER. But if Antoine there suddenly …
> VICTOR. Your neck would save me.]

The General has defined the rules of the game: he states which game the two children should play in the first place, what role each should play, and who should begin. In the meantime, the players, like monkeys, obey these rules strictly while at the same time enjoying the freedom to act at will. Thus, they imitate their parents' words and assume their images. They do a successful job, judging from the effect of this scene. In their pretend play, while Esther plays her mother and Victor plays his father, they guide us toward a better understanding of "how children come to construct, experience, and implement their models of the world" (Goldman xvi). Despite the fact that everyone pretends to have understood nothing from the childish dialogue, a dialogue that uses a lovers' code, everyone is profoundly disturbed and they remain silent. The most disturbed of all is Antoine Magneau, Esther's father, who, in addition to being the cuckold, is treated by all as a fool due to his recurrent, vivid, and disturbing memories from the Franco-Prussian War of 1877. More precisely, Antoine is considered crazy "because he constantly retells the story of Bazaine, the French marshal known as a traitor for surrendering the town of Metz to the enemy during the Franco-Prussian war" (Beachler Severs 124). Victor's laughter alone disturbs the silence and exacerbates the newly introduced crisis in this small bourgeois friendly circle, which has gathered for a festive evening to celebrate the boy's ninth birthday. Interestingly, the two children, without yet knowing they are half-sister-and-brother (both being Charles' children), commit the most intelligent act of disobedience in their obedience. Victor triumphs, as his name suggests, thanks to his games. He began with his games of signifiers, and proceeded to mimicry games that now culminate in a "dada" game (an allusion to Dada), an *alea* type of game. Victor plays the latter with the General and here are the rules of this game, in which imagination plays a seminal role:

> VICTOR. Eh bien, je voudrais jouer à dada avec vous.
> LE GENERAL. Quoi?
> VICTOR. Oui, comme Henri IV. Vous vous mettez à quatre pattes, j'enfourche ma monture et on fait le tour de la table. Et qu'importe qui frappe, les ambassadeurs du roi d'Espagne peuvent attendre (37).

> [VICTOR. Eh, well, I would like to play horse with you.
> THE GENERAL. What?
> VICTOR. Yes, like Henri IV. You crawl, I sit on your back on my horse and we go around the table. And whoever knocks at the door, the ambassadors of Spain can wait.]

The General, having promised to play with Victor, takes the role of a child and plays the horse, despite Victor's father's objections that the General should not feel obliged to engage in this belittling behavior. The first act ends with the triumph in which both Victor and Esther (who observes the scene) have a great time. Equally, the General, who incarnates Duty, loses his inhibitions momentarily and offers the most satisfying idea to the children: a reversal of roles. In this reversal, Victor commands the General-horse, called "cocotte," and the latter obeys his orders:

> *Le général se prend au jeu, et imite le cheval. Il hennit, rue, se cabre, etc. On assiste à une sorte de dressage.*
> VICTOR. Arrière, arrière, là, là.
> *Il lui donne un morceau de sucre dans les creux de la main. Le cheval se calme, Victor monte en selle.*
> Hue! Hue!
> *Gêne pour tout le monde, sauf pour Esther qui se tord* (38).

> [*The General gets wrapped up in the game and mimics the horse. He neighs, rears up and charges, etc. We witness a form of horse breaking.*
> VICTOR. Back, back, there, there!
> *He gives him a piece of sugar in his hands. The horse is calm. Victor gets into the saddle.*
> Hue! Hue!
> *Everybody is annoyed, except for Esther, who bursts into laughter.*]

Victor continues breaking in his horse by giving it sugar, and at times, the spur. This game manifests Victor's ultimate goal for his party: to free, for better or worse, the adults from their hypocrisies and the constraints that their logic imposes on them, as the General's following words demonstrate: "Je dis toujours le contraire de ce que je pense" (42) [I always say the opposite of what I am thinking]. Through his mastery of games, Victor himself now becomes the director of a theatrical scene, in which all adults are forced to act out their true selves. At this point, he is the one who sets the rules of the game, as he proceeds to distribute the adults' roles in the third scene of the first act:

> VICTOR (*annonçant*). Les voilà: L'Enfant Terrible, le Père Indigne, la Bonne Mère, la Femme Adultère, le Cocu, le vieux Bazaine (20).

[VICTOR (*announcing*). Here they are: The Terrible Child, The Indignant Father, the Good Mother, the Adulterous Woman, the Cuckold, the old Bazaine.]

In this mimetic game, Victor finds correspondences between the members of his surroundings and these roles. Such correspondences constitute the logical background of Victor's new game that discloses the adults' absurd behavior. In the next scene of the second act, Victor spies on his father and his lover, Thérèse, interrupting their romantic interlude. Interestingly, during this scene, Victor learns that Esther is his half-sister. Victor uses his imaginative vocabulary to the full and addresses Thérèse as his "maman" in a form of supplication. In Victor's speech, we discern his orgiastic imagination but also his mixed feelings toward the new noun: a sense of betrayal and frustration, a desire to get revenge and to ridicule Thérèse and his father, who, like Lili, responds by slapping him in the face. When his father asks Victor to finish all his games and comedies and go to bed, Victor expresses his wish to sleep with Lili, a most scandalous request to everyone present. The adults' reaction provokes Victor's identity crisis:

VICTOR. … Ah, mais à la fin, qui suis-je? Suis-je transfiguré? Ne m'appelle-je plus Victor? Suis-je condamné à mener l'existence honteuse du fils prodigue? Enfin, dites-le moi. Suis-je l'incarnation du vice et du remords? Ah! S'il en est ainsi, plutôt la mort que le déshonneur! Plutôt le sort tragique de l'enfant prodigue! (*Il se prend la tête dans les mains*) (44).

[VICTOR. Ah, but in the end, who am I? Am I transfigured? Am I no longer called Victor? Am I condemned to live the shameful existence of the prodigal son? At last, tell me. Am I the embodiment of vice and remorse? Ah! If this is the case, better death than dishonor! Better the tragic fate of the prodigal child! (*He takes his head in his hands*).]

After a series of identifications through his games, these words come naturally to Victor. For, in a pretend play, "we overlay one identity onto another such that both are immediately and simultaneously recognizable" (Goldman 5). The question "Who am I?"—reminiscent of *Nadja*'s opening lines and of the game played between the couple, Martha and Yves, in *The Nightfall Hotel*—brings the problem of human expression to the center of Victor's concerns. His games finally invest him with an illusory power. There is a sense of something lacking in each one of the ludic avatars that Victor performs. The frantic game ends in a revelation for him: that there is something missing in his identity. Was his game playing a desperate attempt on his part to acquire a sense of wholeness? In other words, was it an identity game? Yet Victor's identity crisis is not the only one that occurs in the play. Everyone seems confused and embarrassed to the point that only a miracle could reverse the situation. According to Charles, "Il faudrait un miracle" (46) [It would take a miracle].

The miracle does indeed happen shortly, when a woman of extraordinary beauty, dressed in an evening gown, appears in the middle of this chaos. Her name is Ida Mortemart and, despite her beauty, she has a defect; she is a "pétomane" (a farter), something that makes everyone present laugh heartily:

IDA. Riez! Riez! Je sais bien, allez, on ne peut pas s'empêcher d'en rire. Je ne vous en veux pas. Riez donc! Il n'y aura après ni gêne de votre côté, ni gêne du mien. Cela nous calmera tous. J'ai l'habitude. Il n'y a qu'un remède, c'est le rire.

Ils rient de toutes leurs forces pendant qu'elle pète toujours, la tête dans ses mains. Graduellement les rires s'arrêtent. On attendra que ceux de la salle s'arrêtent aussi pour continuer la scène (50).

[IDA. Laugh! Laugh! Laugh! I do know, come on, we cannot prevent anybody from laughing. I don't mind. So laugh then! Soon there will be no embarrassment on your behalf or on mine. This will appease us all. I am used to it. There is but one remedy, and that is laughter. *They laugh with gusto while she keeps breaking wind, her head in her hands. Gradually laughter stops. We will also wait for complete silence to continue the scene.*]

Ida's words sound much like those in the brochure "Le Théâtre Alfred Jarry and Public hostility" (1930), where Vitrac and Artaud set absolute laughter as their final goal: "we propose … as our goal: the absolute laughter, the laughter that goes from the conspicuous immobility to bursting into tears" (Béhar, *Théâtre ouvert* 191). This is exactly what Ida Mortemart brings about in this play with her affliction. Through her unavoidable breaking of a social code of decorum, she leads everyone to absolute laughter and thus creates the perfect situation for the playing of "jeux d'esprit" in which Victor, the prodigy, excels. When Ida suggests that she tell her own story from A to Z, she says they already know A and Z. Victor, however, counter-argues that they only know her P (that is, her being a "pétomane") thus far:

VICTOR. Nous connaissons P. (*Gêne*.) Votre pâleur, votre peine, vos perles, vos paupières, vos pleurs, votre privilège. Nous connaîtrons votre passage … (51).

[VICTOR. We know P. (*Embarrassment*.) Your pale color, your pain, your pearls, your cheeks, your cries, your privilege. We will recognize your footsteps ….]

Here the limitations of translation do not convey the full range of word play; the final element in Victor's list of "p" words, "passage," is loaded with the sense of passing from one world to another, as well as with the play on Ida's "passing," both in the sense of walking by, and passing wind. These words create another wave of shame among the adults, who think Victor a bizarre child, a child whose fervent imagination talks to "angels," or a child who deserves punishment. This conversation leads to Victor's premonition that he is going to die. Addressing his mother, Émilie Paumelle, he says: "Maman, tu es enceinte d'un enfant mort" (52) [Mommy, you are pregnant with a dead child]. No one understands these words, yet somehow they are related to Ida Mortemart's coming, as her name also suggests.[13] This is why she also scares little Esther, who disappears in the garden, leading everyone on an anguished search for her. This search reminds us of the search for the little girl that disappeared in the play *Les Détraquées*. While the adults are searching for Esther, Victor has a conversation with Ida, in which he asks her to instruct him on how to fall in love. Ida whispers something in his ear and then departs while addressing these words to him:

IDA. Monstre! Monstre! Tu te présenteras de ma part demain aux Magasins du Louvre, rayon des jouets. Il y aura pour toi une petite carabine, une petite carabine à balles (55).

[IDA. Monster! Monster! You will go on my behalf to the toy section of the stores in the Louvre. There is a small gun, a small loaded gun for you.]

Ida's words—an invitation to Victor to commit suicide—are followed by a truly incomprehensible scene. Antoine, Esther's father, returns on stage and behaves with unprecedented violence under the pretext of being insane:

> ANTOINE. Oui, je suis fou, et après? (*à Thérèse*). Allez, toi et la gosse, en route, et adieu. Adieu à tout le monde. Encore heureux que je ne vous massacre pas tous!
> *Il entraîne sa femme et sa fille vers la porte. Tout le monde est atterré; mais Antoine reparaît tout à coup, suivi de Thérèse et d'Ester.*
> ANTOINE (*à Charles*). Espèce d'idiot. Il ne comprend rien à la plaisanterie. Hein? Était-ce réussi? Était-ce bien joué? (58).

> [ANTOINE. Yes, I am a fool, so what? (*to Thérèse*). Come on, you and the kid, go, and goodbye. Goodbye to everyone. You should be happy that I do not massacre all of you!
> *He drags his wife and his daughter to the door. Everybody is caught by surprise; but Antoine suddenly reappears, followed by Thérèse and Esther.*
> ANTOINE (*to Charles*). Idiot, he doesn't understand the joke at all. Huh? Was it successful? Was it played well?]

Victor's role as leader of the game is now played by an adult, Antoine, who plays the fool in order to get back at his rival, Charles. The game's function has accomplished its goal at this point. From now on, a bourgeois drama is really enacted with Emilie and Charles torturing each other with words, while reading excerpts from the newspaper *Le Monde*. They argue and they are ready to kill each other, while Victor repeatedly enters their room to tell them, to no avail, that his stomach aches. In the end, a doctor is called to verify Victor's feverish delirium that leads to the boy's death:

> LE DOCTEUR. Et voilà le sort des enfants obstinés.
> *Le docteur sort, tandis qu un rideau noir tombe. On entend deux coups de feu. Le rideau se relève. Emilie et Charles sont étendus aux pieds du lit de l'enfant, séparés par un revolver fumant. Une porte s'ouvre, et la bonne paraît.*
> LILI. Mais c'est un drame! (89–90).

> [THE DOCTOR. And this is the destiny of recalcitrant children.
> *The doctor exits while a black curtain falls. We hear two gunshots. The curtain rises again. Emilie and Charles are lying at the foot of the child's bed, with a smoking revolver between them. A door opens, and the maid enters.*
> LILI. How tragic!]

Lili's closing words confirm that a drama has been enacted as part of Vitrac's play, "to create that self-conscious awareness of the mocking of a theatre, the awareness of a game being played," a very modernist attitude (Melzer Henkin, *Latest Rage* 192). The multifarious game that Victor started, ended as a drama and proved to be more than a serious act. It affected various functions in this play, the most important of which is the emphasis on the revelatory/liberating power of words and their subsequent capacity to generate laughter. As such, games are a weapon that enables the children to come to power in *Victor or Children in Power*. The game is ultimately an instrument of role reversal between children and adults. Vitrac has taught his audience that, through play, it is possible for automatism to be staged and effective; to borrow Beachler Sever's words,

[t]he concept of automatic writing for the theater, however, as it is interpreted by Vitrac, *becomes a game* in the belief that words, when dissociated from their literal meanings and from rational thought, can renew contact with the unconscious and with the world of dreams. Dialogues based upon these new and fresh verbal associations produce the non-sequiturs and the unexpected verbal puns are typical of most of Vitrac's plays (91; my emphasis).

Such dissociation of words from rational thought obviously subverted normal power relations. Since surrealist dialogue gave free rein to the players' imagination, it enabled them to see something as something else (like the "one into another"), and in this way, to change their view of seeing and thus of perceiving. Victor, through the childish games of his dialogues, passed from one ludic pole to the other, from *paidia* to *ludus*. In each case, this terrible child mastered the rules of the games until the moment he gave in to them. In *Victor*, "game" has been employed in the way surrealist games functioned, but also as pure improvisational children's games, in the form of pretend play in which "we witness behavior that moves between *mimesis* and *mythos*" (Goldman xvii). "Play as pretense emerges very much as an imaginatively constructed and linguistically realized pathway between simulation and mythologization" (ibid.). This combination functioned as a vortex that engulfed everyone involved in this play. Like Hamlet, who states during the dumb show, "the play is the thing," Victor and Esther prove that "their play is the thing" when they play their lovers' scene, a scene purely grounded in reality. Basically, Vitrac shows how complex "game" is and how manipulative a tool it can be, even when it appears as pure *alea* at the hands of children. "Game" has the potential to effect change and, therefore, can prove to be the best means of carrying social change; *Victor* was, in the end, one of the most subversive creations of the late 1920s.

The history of the reception of this play's various productions is the best guide to appreciate its final effect, from its first performance in 1928 to its latest one in 1998, which placed Victor next to Hamlet.[14] The first performances of *Victor or Children in Power* as part of the program of the Théâtre Alfred Jarry took place in La Comédie des Champs-Elysées on December 24 and 29, 1928 and on January 5, 1929, under Artaud's direction. Most of the spectators were scandalized by the irreverent character of this first production—precisely Artaud's goal (Hubert 182–3). It was Artaud's surrealist direction, in particular, that shocked the audience, as Jarry's *Ubu-roi* had in 1896. For instance, in the first act, an enormous birthday cake covered almost the entire table, decorated with huge candles that created a macabre rather than a festive ambiance, anticipating, of course, Victor's death. "Faithful to Dali, this surrealist image," Hubert informs us, "announces to the spectator that he/she is perhaps attending a funeral" ["elle annonce au spectateur qu'il est peut-être convié à un enterrement" (182)]. However, a few critics saw this production favorably for its sense of originality, an originality that "is its surreality itself" (Metzidakis, *André Breton Today* 35).[15] For instance, a German journalist named Paul Block, wrote in the *Berliner Tageblatt*:

Roger Vitrac a écrit un drame incroyable, un drame incroyablement insolent, et dans les détails incroyablement comique. ... Ce fut la représentation théâtrale la plus curieuse qu'il m'ait été donné de voir pendant mes huit années d'après-guerre à Paris (quoted in Hubert 182).

[Roger Vitrac wrote an unbelievable drama, an incredibly insolent drama with incredible details. ... It has been the most curious theatrical representation that I happened to see during my eight post-war years in Paris.]

Through the surrealist symbols of the gigantic prodigy at play and the unforgettable Ida Mortemart, Vitrac ridiculed all ill-founded ideals of a bourgeois society, such as religion, family, and patriotism—the very ideals that Breton loathed. In *Victor*, according to Artaud, "[l]e titre seul indique un irrespect de base pour toutes les valeurs établies" (quoted in Hubert 183). This drama, Artaud continues, "tantôt lyrique, tantôt ironique, tantôt direct, était dirigé contre la famille bourgeoise, avec comme discriminants: l'adultère, l'inceste, la scatologie, la colère, la poésie surréaliste, le patriotisme, la folie, la honte at la mort" (quoted in Hubert 182) [This drama, at times lyrical, at times ironic, at times direct, was directed against the bourgeois family with these characteristic features: adultery, incest, scatology, rage, surrealist poetry, patriotism, folly, shame, and death.]

Henriette after *Victor*

Valaoritis emulated the subversive effects of *Victor or Children in Power* in his *Henriette où est-elle passée?* (*Henriette Where Did She Go?*), a loose adaptation of the former, and a parody of gothic dramas in general. Valaoritis himself calls it "a machinery of free associations."[16] Like *Victor*, *Henriette* is a drama in three acts that also unfolds in a bourgeois environment and is equally full of miraculous events. The main character is Mervyn Debout,[17] who is not a child but who behaves like Victor. Like him, he entraps everyone around him through his mimicry games. Also, like Victor, Mervyn prefers to disappear rather than live a miserable life. This is why he endlessly disguises himself. However, in the end, it is not he but a little girl, his own daughter, Henriette, named after her mother, who emerges as the victor of the play.

The problem starts when Mervyn's wife, Henriette, abandons him. Various people visit Mervyn's apartment looking for her. The first person is a woman called Zinaide Lisbonne, who is on a mission for the sake of Mervyn's father, who is looking for his son. The second person is Henriette's ex-husband, Molitor de Semblable, who at some point shocks Mervyn when he shows him a picture of Henriette. Convinced that he cannot escape his destiny, Mervyn tries once more to liberate himself but another man appears, Adrien Lecoureur, who is also looking for Henriette, but for another reason. She was the bet he placed in a game he played in a casino the previous night:

LE COUREUR. Je ne suis pas venu pour l'argent, mon cher comte. Je suis venu, comme vous l'avez sûrement deviné, un homme du monde que vous êtes, pour la femme. C'est elle que j'ai perdue. C'était elle l'enjeu de ma mise (11).

[LE COUREUR. I have not come for the money my dear Count. I came, as you might have already guessed, since you are a man of the world, for the woman. It is she whom I have lost. She was what was at stake in my bet.]

The next person to enter the stage is a young woman called Max, or Maximiliane, a fashion designer. She brings a costume for Mervyn and while she is waiting to be paid in the hall, Henriette's father, Mr. Buisson, enters the scene, full of rage and ready to punish his son-in-law:

> BUISSON. Je viens voir ma fille que mon beau-fils—dit-on—a dissimulé depuis deux ans dans la cave de cet immeuble. On dit que c'est un criminel, un vicieux, un sadique, un anormal, un être lunaire épileptique et détraqué (15).

> [BUISSON. I have come to see my daughter whom my son-in-law—they say—has been hiding for two years now in the basement of this apartment building. They say that he is a criminal, a vicious man, a sadist, an abnormal, epileptic, and deranged lunatic.]

Mervyn, disguised as a "suffragette," escapes his father-in-law's wrath. Moreover, he presents himself as Henriette and tells her story, that she married Mervyn only to be abandoned by him so that he could explore the world. At this moment, Mervyn, disguised as his wife Henriette, goes to the other room with Max, while Buisson reads a note that has dropped from Max's bag. It reads:

> Ma chère Maximiliane,
> Je vous ai convoquée ici pour vous dire que je vous aime à la folie. Si vous ne vous abandonnez pas à moi instantanément, je partirai pour les Indes avec le prochain vaisseau. J'ai tué une femme pour vous. Henriette est morte ce matin à huit heures dans la cave. Apportez la robe. Il faudra l'habiller pour l'enterrer. N'en parlez à personne. Car vous savez il y a des curieux. Faites-moi confiance. A tout à l'heure mon amour, mon adorée.
> Signé.
> Romanoff (18–19).

> [Dear Maximiliane,
> I have summoned you to tell you that I am crazy for you. If you do not give yourself immediately to me, I will take the next ship to India. I killed a woman for you. Henriette died this morning at 8 o'clock in the basement. Bring the funeral dress. Don't talk about this with anyone. For you know there are nosy people. Trust me. See you soon, my love, my beloved.
> Signed
> Romanoff.]

This note leads one to believe that Mervyn could also be disguised as Romanoff.

The second act takes place in a Vatican cave (an allusion to André Gide's *Les caves du Vatican*),[18] where all the men who are looking for Henriette are enacting a scene of Sainte Henriette's canonization and resurrection. Mervyn plays the role of a cardinal while directing this scene for television:

> MERVYN. Adrien, vous avez été admirable. Votre discours impromptu est un bijou. Et vous Molitor, vous êtes un acteur superbe. Jamais on n'a vu une telle possession sur la scène. Mes félicitations! (23).

> [MERVYN. Adrien you have been admirable. Your improvisational discourse was a gem. And you, Molitor, you are a fabulous actor. I have never seen such possession on stage. Congratulations!]

However, while the scene continues, Mervyn, the cardinal, begins insulting everyone. Instead of reacting, they accept Mervyn's vicious behavior simply as a well-acted role. At this point, Max appears to display her baby (that she will soon deliver) as Henriette's infant. In the end, she plays the macabre role of Henriette in the coffin while everybody calls for Henriette. The scene ends with a Grand-Guignol type of episode: Mervyn is beaten to death by Zinaide and Buisson.

The third act is the closest to *Victor*. Part of the décor is even similar to *Victor*'s. An enormous birthday cake appears, with 20 gigantic candles, for Henriette's twentieth birthday. Her parents, Zinaide Lisbonne (step-mother) and Mr. Buisson, are present while the incestuous relationship in the family is revealed. Max, Henriette, and Mervyn are half-brothers and sisters. At this moment, the lights change and show the house of a giant, while a pair of scissors hangs on the wall, echoing the knife-like image in the painting of the opening scene of Vitrac's *The Mysteries of Love*. In this setting we hear Mervyn and Henriette's voices through a megaphone:

> MERVYN (*Avec une voix de géant*). Hola, qui me chatouille le petit doigt du pied. Il y a des puces par ici.
> LA VOIX D'HENRIETTE (*Une voix de petite fille*). Anisette et coca cola. Je veux de l'anisette et du coca cola.
> MERVYN. Tu l'auras, mon chéri, quand ces imbéciles auront cessé de nous importuner. On m'a volé ma montre. (*On voit sur le coin de la scène une montre énorme*).
> LA VOIX D'HENRIETTE. Tue-les tous. On en a assez de cette racaille.
> MERVYN. Pas encore. Le moment viendra de les punir. Pour l'instant, je les laisse bien dormir. Hé hé hé (60).

> [MERVYN (*With a voice of a giant*). Hola, who is tickling my toe? There are fleas here.
> HENRIETTE'S VOICE (*A voice of a little girl*). Anis and coca-cola. I want anis and coca-cola.
> MERVYN. You'll have them, my dear, when all these stupid people stop bothering us. They stole my watch. (*We see on the corner of the stage an enormous watch*).
> HENRIETTE'S VOICE. Kill them all. We have had enough of this mess.
> MERVYN. Not yet. The moment will come to punish them. For the moment, I let them sleep well. Ha ha ha.]

Suddenly, a gigantic knife appears and Mervyn touches the cake, from which emerges a fairy doll which says:

> LA FEE. Je sais, moi, où se trouve Henriette. Sur le toit, transformée en chatte par le patron. Le toit brûle: il neige. Dépêchez-vous (63).

> [THE FAIRY. I know where Henriette is. On the roof, the boss changed her into a cat. The roof is burning: it's snowing. Hurry up!]

Then Mervyn takes a revolver out of his pocket and forces everyone to sign a contract of collective suicide. Only at this point do we understand that we face yet another scene, since Mervyn addresses all of them in these words: "Vous m'entendez? Vous mourrez tous. Dans la scène précédente vous m'avez assassiné! À présent c'est votre tour. Alignez-vous au mur, hauts les mains. Allez-y" (65). [Do you hear me? You will all die. In the previous scene you assassinated me. Now, it's your turn. Backs to the wall! Hands up. Come-on!]. In fact, these words confirm that Valaoritis modeled this play after another surrealist game called "Murder" that Breton used to play during his exile in Marseilles, from June 1939 to July 1941. As Mary Jayne Gold states, this game "acted as a great catharsis to our [their] troubled souls" (quoted in Polizzotti 489). In this game, with lights out, a secretly designated assassin would "kill" a chosen victim; it was then up to the other players to determine who did it (ibid). The play's game within the game continues until the revolver is out of order and Mervyn suggests that in the meantime they play other games:

> ADRIEN. Qu'est-ce qu'on peut faire pour passer le temps?
> MERVYN. On joue aux billes.
> ADRIEN. Ou aux quilles.
> MERVYN. Alors jouons aux billes.
> ADRIEN. On joue l'héritage?
> MERVYN. Mais je suis déshérité.
> ADRIEN. Aucune importance. Moi aussi.
> MERVYN. Alors jouons à l'héritage.
> *Ils se mettent à genoux et commencent à jouer* (70).

> [ADRIEN. What can we do to pass our time?
> MERVYN. Let's play billiards.
> ADRIEN. Or lawn bowling.
> MERVYN. Well let's play billiards.
> ADRIEN. Shall we play the inheritance game?
> MERVYN. But I am disinherited.
> ADRIEN. It doesn't matter. Me too.
> MERVYN. Well, let's play the inheritance game.
> (*They bend on their knees and they start playing*).]

Soon a knock is heard on the door and the light fades. Henriette finally appears, while all the others stop playing games. The surprising thing is that instead of a woman, Henriette is a little girl of only five years. Addressing Mervyn as her father, she kills him with the newly repaired revolver. If the surrealist element reached its peak in Victor's gigantic size at just nine years of age and in Ida's Sibylic appearance and disappearance, here it reaches its peak in the disclosure of Henriette's complicated identity. She is Henriette/Max's and Mervyn's baby, born only the previous day. Henriette's mysterious messianic appearance is symbolic. Like Victor, Henriette attains a mythological quality. In fact, she may be another incarnation of Mervyn himself. After all, as Valaoritis admits, he was intrigued by "a theatrical alchemy,"[19] mainly shown in the successive transformations of his main characters. As Nicole Ollier claims,

> the psychic metamorphosis is fundamental for the surrealist alchemist. Marked by Rimbaud's "Je est un autre" and Breton's "existence est ailleurs," the interlocutor [in Valaoritis's work] never ceases to change person, number, gender, substance and identity ... The self is multiplied *ad infinitum*, 'I' is the addition of its successive selves ... The subject lives numerous lives in just one life ("Métamorphose" 153–4).

This theatrical alchemy occurs too when Valaoritis reverses Greek myths by making a young girl a patricide. This cruel child, like Victor, shows no mercy at all:

> HENRIETTE. Finies les plaisanteries d'autrefois. Je suis ici moi et je représente l'Âge Nouveau, l'âge impitoyable et cruel, l'âge du diamant où les actes et les paroles ne seront plus interchangeables. Je suis Henriette. Je suis votre héritage (73).

[HENRIETTE. Gone are the jokes of the past. I am here in person and I represent the New Age. The merciless and cruel age, the diamond era when all acts and words won't be interchangeable. I am Henriette. I am your legacy.]

This is indeed Henriette, the symbol of a new heritage. The mystery of her absence has been solved. She, like Victor, embodies the myth of the precocious child, and like him, she does not stand for hypocrisy and incestuous relationships in her family. However, she is luckier than Victor as she remains in command of the game, in contrast to Victor, who is eventually consumed by it.

In *Henriette*, indeed, it is the *mimicry* game form, in Caillois' sense, that is employed most of all, visualized in the endless play with Mervyn's successive transformations. The excessive use of mimicry deliberately creates confusion in the play and aims at ridiculing long-established bourgeois values, such as religion and family. Disguise, doubles, and innumerable "theatre within the theatre" scenes constitute Valaoritis's endless experimentation with the concept of play itself. In the end, mimicry gives way to a traditional children's game, the game of heritage, that prepares for the arrival of the new Henriette.

Her miraculous appearance puts an end to the question of her disappearance, yet introduces a new question about Mervyn's identity: Who is he really? Thanks to the use of ludic techniques, Mervyn's identity has once again become unraveled. Henriette's character was but a pretext for the formation of a new version of a surrealist game invented by Valaoritis. Named "Henriette où est-elle passée?" it was based on the *leitmotif* formed by the same question, which was spoken by each player throughout the play. This "searching" game appealed to each player's imagination, as Henriette "represents everyone's ideal and proves to be the master of the game" (Bosnakis 97). Henriette is invented by each character, only to appear finally like another Victor—a mature and terribly intelligent girl who kills the past to announce a pitiless new future.

Playing Ping-Pong with Language: Valaoritis's *Round Tables*

Valaoritis undertakes a similar experiment with ludic strategies in another of his surrealist plays; *The Round Tables*, a three-act play, has never been performed and was written shortly before *Henriette Where Did She Go?* In fact, although it draws on the absurdist Arthur Adamov's play *Le Ping-Pong* (1955), which fascinated Valaoritis, *The Round Tables* is presented by the Greek playwright himself as a purely surrealist experiment with games. The two epigrams placed at the beginning of the play serve to inscribe it in the surrealist context. The first epigram concerns Breton's definition of surrealist dialogue as two simultaneous monologues that free the speakers from the obligations of politeness; and the second is Breton's phrase "these unprejudiced interlocutors," which emphasizes the interlocutors' free imagination (Seaver and Lane 35). Both epigrams introduce the reader to the ludics of the play and set the frame within which *The Round Tables* will unfold. With the epigrams, the title of the play also offers advance information to the audience. *Les Tables rondes* is an allusion to yet another game cherished by the Surrealists, the so-called "Who is a medium?" borrowed from the Romantic tradition. Victor Hugo's account of spiritualism in "Les Tables tournantes de Jersey (1853–55)" is an account of Hugo's experiments with medium sessions after the death of his daughter Léopoldine. It offers a detailed description of the mission of these sessions, during which people sat around a table and invoked spirits of the dead, in order to cross into another world and achieve a sense of unification with the cosmos.[20]

A frantic game conceived by some child-like interlocutor-players serves as the frame in *The Round Tables*. The game starts as an innocent joke (in response to a chance happening) and ends as a tragic farce. This protean game that takes and changes shape through dialogue as opposed to action, is the organizing principal of the "tragic comedy" *The Round Tables*. The play is about three young men, Anastase, André, and Pierre Ponce, who spend their time in a cafeteria. There they play tricks on two strangers whom pure chance procures for their entertainment. Their first victim is a country girl, Anabelle. Her name alludes to "la Belle Helene" (Helen of Troy), and it immediately marks her as a target to be conquered. Their second victim is a robust and strange man called Nero. He is endowed with the prophetic power of a medium at best, but also with insanity like his namesake, the Roman emperor, a connection that is strengthened by the play's Nero calling himself "august" (17). The young men weave a romance between the two victims and entangle themselves in an antagonistic way in this romance of their making. They initiate an endless game, the rules of which are constantly shifting and, in the end, turn against those who started the game.

The Round Tables is essentially about trivial events. Action is simulated because nothing really happens except for the constant talk about action. This simulated action unfolds in a café, which is referred to as "Two Pearls," or "Three Peals," or "Two Laurels," or "Little Babylon." The name constantly changes and the incongruent time references confuse the reader and function as a reminder of the surrealist setting where all contradictions are absorbed and where there are no boundaries between reality and dream, or life and death.

The first surrealist game that Valaoritis explicitly employs in *The Round Tables* is modeled after the now well-known metaphor game of "one into another." It is played according to the following rules, as Mel Gooding explains:

> one player withdraws from the room and chooses an object (or a person, an idea, etc.) for himself. While he is absent, the rest of the players also choose an object. When the first player returns, he is told what object they have chosen. He must now describe his own object in terms of the properties of the object chosen by the others, making the comparison more and more obvious as he proceeds, until they are able to guess its identity. The first player begins with a sentence, such as, "I am an (object)" … (31).

This game, that draws on the notion of the surrealist object, is at work when Anabelle's limbs erotically excite the imagination of Anastase and André as follows:

> ANASTASE. Elle a la jambe en éventail!
> ANDRÉ. Et l'oreille trop courte!
> ANASTASE. Des mains champignons!
> ANDRÉ. Des cheveux en carrosse! (6)

[ANASTASE. Her leg looks like a fan!
ANDRÉ. And her ear is too tiny!
ANASTASE. Her hands look like mushrooms![21]
ANDRÉ. Her hair is the hair of a coach!]

Anabelle is treated as a "being-object," whose qualities of the marvelous become obvious after their "baptism" by these young men. Anabelle becomes a toy or, at best, a stimulus for men's imaginations, reminiscent of Breton's poem "L'Union libre" (1931), as well as Valaoritis's own later poem "Golem" (1987), in which "a female doll is evoked through its components" (Ollier, "Cultural Cross-Breeding" 45). Each part of Anabelle's body, scrutinized by the male gaze, activates these men's creative potential. Their linguistic ability is so intensely inspired by Anabelle's physicality that it gives expression to the competitive character of these men. We find here another surrealist game—introduced in 1922 and in which Vitrac himself also participated—where each participant responds to the question: "Why do you prefer this?" The question is applied to a list of 37 objects/subjects, including the categories of "woman," "body part," and "love" (Garrigues 53). The compiled answers constituted an anti-poem, similar to the anti-blazon form. The male friends sitting at the café's round tables undertake a similar contest, full of erotic allusions referring to Anabelle's body parts. These images surprise both the dramatis personae and the audience with their extreme arbitrariness and their poetics of fragmentation. In this "masculine discourse par excellence," to use Jeffrey Charles Persels' words, "[w]oman suffers further displacement from fetishized body part to abstracted stimulus for self-gratification and glorification. The blazon is not a poem about women at all, it is about men" (133). On the level of player versus player (or character versus character), this contest among males provokes an inflammatory discourse that irritates Anabelle. Uneasy under their gaze, she engages in the game in order to avenge herself.

Soon this surrealist game shifts to a childish mimicry that simulates sounds from all kinds of vehicles, from boat sirens and train whistles to car horns. Anastase and André imitate these sounds to irritate Anabelle. Jazz music plays on a juke-box in the background, stressing the improvisational nature of their game. Valaoritis alludes here to the raw material available for poetic composition in terms of rhythm and sound patterns. At this point, the two young men regress to puerility as though convinced that if one game does not work, another might. They continue to talk over each other, as they try to guess who it is that Anabelle is expecting:

ANASTASE. C'est l'Empereur de Chine, qu'elle attend!
ANDRÉ. Non, c'est le roi des Esquimaux!
ANASTASE. L'Aurora Borealis en personne!
ANDRÉ. Le Dalai lama en personne!
ANASTASE. Non, elle attend l'autobus!
ANDRÉ. Tu as tort! Le tramway!
ANASTASE. Il n'y a plus de tramways, Mademoiselle! Et les autocars sont parties!
ANDRÉ. Mais voyons, elle attend l'avion!
ANASTASE. Le train!
ANDRÉ. Le bateau! (9–10).

[ANASTASE. It's the Emperor of China she is waiting for!
ANDRÉ. No. It's the King of the Eskimos!
ANASTASE. The Aurora Borealis in person!
ANDRÉ. Dalai-Lama in person!
ANASTASE. No, she is waiting for the bus!
ANDRÉ. You're mistaken! For the tramway!
ANASTASE. There are no tramways, Miss! No buses either!
ANDRÉ. Let's see, she's waiting for the plane!
ANASTASE. The train!
ANDRÉ. The boat!]

The ironic juxtaposition of well-known, real and fictionalized persons with means of transportation suggests Valaoritis's effort to apply another of Breton's premises, based on Pierre Reverdy's statement that the more arbitrary the juxtaposition of images, the more effective it is. In fact, the above dialogue is barely a dialogue at all, in the sense that no communication is achieved between the two interlocutors. Instead, each character's words are repeated by the other character, slightly modified, only to function as springboards to the most audacious images of Anabelle. The appearance of Nero, who has a muscular body and a suspect self-absorption, calls for a change of game plan. Despite his overt strength, Nero will nevertheless become entrapped in their malicious plan, which attempts a more sophisticated make-believe as they invent a story about Anabelle. They pretend they are ready to save her from suicide. Here we have a reference to the scene "Is Suicide a solution?" from "Dialogue in 1928." Nero falls into their trap when he makes the decision to save the girl.

Protracted convulsive laughter seals the triumph of the three young men who end this part of their game by writing a love letter, supposedly from Anabelle to Nero, delivered by a waiter. The message, a parody of romantic literature, marks a turning point in that writing and reading have now become part of the hitherto purely spoken game. The three young men momentarily feel guilty, but their game has acquired a kind of autonomy that makes it impossible for them to end it. They are all under Anabelle's spell. When she "confesses" that she desires them only as a composite of each of their traits that satisfy her standard of masculinity, they suddenly feel their masculinity threatened and want to withdraw from the game. Anabelle dismembers each young man in her imagination and creates, from their limbs, a "perfect man" who is suitable to her tastes. Whether Anabelle makes fun of the three young men or tells them the truth is left vague. She may indeed be a liberated woman, like Breton's Nadja,[22] an "errant soul" (Breton, OC1 688). Anabelle later explains to one of them that she is a creature of chance:

ANABELLE. J'ai toujours été la créature d'une seconde. Je suis semée aux quatre vents. Je porte en moi des secousses auxquelles je n'ai aucune résistance. Je frappe à toutes les portes. Finalement je me porte bien. Je suis à l'aise. N'importe quoi me convient pourvu que ça ne dure pas. Je ne suis pas dure. Mais me durcis contre tout ce qui est permanent. J'aime changer. Même de train. Ça m'est égal. Ça me convient (95).

[ANABELLE. I've always existed for only one second. I am scattered to the four winds ... I knock at all doors. I actually feel good. I am comfortable with everything provided it does not last. I am not tough, but I am resilient against everything that tends to be permanent. I like change. Even taking a different train. I don't care. It suits me.]

Anabelle is no ordinary woman, but the personification of freedom itself. Her freedom propels her desire to play with these men. Her involvement with their game does not come merely from a desire to get revenge for having been the target of their mockery, but also from a gratifying feeling of being the object of a contest that justifies her existence. Her desire to be desired and, at the same time, remain unattainable, appears in the wordplay that constitutes her name: An/Ana/Belle/Elle. In Greek and French in succession, her name means "If/Again/Beautiful/She," calling to mind another surrealist game called "The Game of Syllogisms," in which actual syllogisms were used for all sorts of subject matters, including the most trivial. In this game, sentences beginning with either "If" or "When" were circulated among the surrealist players around a table.

After Anabelle's self-description, a game of "Hide-and-Seek" follows which is accompanied by a strange incident. A woman appears and disappears three times on top of a music box when a waiter rings a bell. The waiter says: "C'est un jeu de cache-cache! On se cache, on se retrouve. Nous nous cachons, on nous retrouve. Vous vous cachez, on vous retrouve!" (39) [It's a game of hide-and-seek! One hides, the other finds them. We hide, they find us. You hide, we find you!].

This is perhaps the most surrealistic and important scene in the play. It evokes the permanent concern of the Surrealists to bridge the gap between reality and imagination by inventing a different reality. It applies the surrealist game "Ouvrez-vous?" (Would you open the door?), which appeared in 1953 in the French review *Medium*. In it, the participants recorded their reactions each time they imagined a famous person suddenly appearing and asking them to open the door. The originality of this game, in Garrigues' view, lies in "the effect of surprise and the free interplay between the real and the imaginary, as well as in the degree to which each one of the participants is willing to reveal himself" (35).

The play ends with a switch to a vertiginous game (*ilinx*) planned by Nero in order to entrap all the other characters. He pretends he knows where a secret treasure is hidden, marks the whole parquet of the café with various signs, and then gives a message to the waiter, who first reads it and then tears it into small pieces. The five men all frantically pick up the pieces to try to reassemble the note and find the hidden treasure, but to no avail. In this frantic activity, the vertigo game reaches its peak, when the curtain falls leaving all of them out of breath.

This last episode combines all of the four types of games classified by Roger Caillois: *agon*, *alea*, *mimicry*, and *ilinx*. Throughout *The Round Tables* a number of game combinations are used that stretch along a continuum between *paidia* (the pole of spontaneity) and *ludus* (the pole of disciplined structure) (Cohn, "Godot's Games" 184). For Valaoritis, the power of game is a protean process of transformation that stretches in a non-linear way from the pole of free improvisation to the more sophisticated pole of games structured by rules that generate new forms of dialogue, acquiring their meaning only in their use.

The ludic model examined in *The Round Tables* permeates Valaoritis's entire dramatic output, written mostly in Paris in the late 1950s. It represents an aspect of the surrealist revolution, which was an expression of vital and spiritual needs.

In *The Round Tables*, Valaoritis creates a play that is not really a play, but a genre located somewhere between the theatre and the novel, in the same way that Breton's *Nadja* is located among several genres. In the latter, Breton embraces the concept of game as a dynamic interplay between novelistic norms and conventions and the anti-novel. Likewise, Valaoritis consciously experiments with anti-theatre, a form that despises action within the realist tradition, to replace it with another kind of action—one of playing all types of games as an end in itself. This way, he challenges the Aristotelian notion of drama, especially tragedy, as an imitation of a complete and serious act. In its place, he favors a constant play with the most trivial events, in which both actors and spectators participate. Thus, play ceases to be an imitation and becomes instead an unlimited semiosis in the here-and-now, exemplified in the coincidence of "play" as a theatrical piece with "play" as an activity. In other words, Valaoritis pulls the play element back to its origins as a theatrical performance-ritual. The Greek playwright exploits the disruptive power of game by putting all the characters in *The Round Tables* on trial with no apparent winners or losers.

Valaoritis attempted to write *The Round Tables* as a purposeful exercise of style based on Breton's definition of surrealist dialogue and its magic. This magic forms a maze, in terms of both structure and theme, through which the audience may experience the marvelous. By so doing, Valaoritis pays homage to Breton, while at the same time challenging Breton's idea that poetry and even the novel were better adapted than drama to express "surreality" as generated by juxtapositions. For Valaoritis, playing with language is solely what matters. The creative process in both *Henriette Where Did She Go?* and *The Round Tables* was governed by the rules that guided surrealist ludic activities, endowing it with something that is not entirely nonsense, yet passionately seeks the irrational and the revelation of the subconscious. These games, in short, confirmed Breton's idea that language may anticipate thought.

In the end, Valaoritis's plays and ideas about playwriting show how well the largely dialogic surrealist games can be rendered on the stage. For Breton, the purpose of surrealist juxtapositions was to create a sense of the marvelous for readers and audiences. Valaoritis, in contrast, wants his readers and audiences to recognize that the seeming irrationality of his characters' dialogues is generated through rational means (rule-bound games), and that an awareness of the combinatory and transformational nature of these behind-the-scenes rules can only reinforce their experience of the marvelous. Valaoritis is convinced that if audiences can understand the overlapping and criss-crossing rules of the games, they will be able to grasp the inner logic of the texts by reassembling them step by step, scene by scene, in the manner of the characters that try to reassemble the pieces of Nero's torn note in the last scene of *The Round Tables*. By understanding how the plays *Henriette Where Did She Go?* and, particularly, *The Round Tables* echo the rules that guided surrealist ludic activity, actors and audiences may also find a key to approach any surrealist theatrical text. More importantly, the members of the audience are invited to participate actively in the rebus-game of discovering which rules of the surrealist games form the underpinnings of his theatrical dialogues. In this way, Valaoritis transforms trivialities into a sophisticated *ludus*, despite its appearance as *paidia* in the sense of a frivolous activity.

In other words, Valaoritis takes the ludic strategies employed in his model—Vitrac's *Victor or Children in Power*—a step further, especially in *The Round Tables*. While Vitrac uses games as a means of revealing the problem of human expression, Valaoritis uses them as an end in itself. While Vitrac uses language to deconstruct language, in order to "undermine all rational presuppositions of society and culture" (Beachler Severs 136), Valaoritis plays with its patent nonsense and creates something new from it. While Vitrac's Victor performs a variety of mimicry and *alea* games to dismantle the ill-conceived bourgeois values, Valaoritis's characters focus on the performance of these games as a language-game. We use the term here in Ludwig Wittgenstein's sense, as examined in his *Philosophical Investigations* (1954), in which he developed his theory of "language-games." For Wittgenstein, although he never fully gave a precise definition of the term, a "language-game" is a real or imagined situation in which words play a role, as they are integrated in a certain way, in a pattern of activity, or in a context that comprises both linguistic and non-linguistic elements. Or, to use Steven Winspur's definition, "[l]anguage-games are the overlapping codes that make up the semiosic field of a particular language and as such they are the temporary limits imposed by social conventions on the indefinite play of semiosis" (49). For Wittgenstein the meaning of a word is its use in the language. To illustrate this seminal idea, Wittgenstein finds recourse in the game-concept. Thus, in his seventh aphorism, he claims: "I shall call the whole, consisting of language and the actions into which it is woven, the 'language-game,'" while in his twenty-third aphorism he adds: "Here the term 'language-*game*' is meant to bring into prominence the fact that the *speaking* of language is part of an activity, or of a form of life." Language, then, is conceived of in its specific uses and, like game, is rule-governed. However, according to Winspur, who treats Wittgenstein as a semiotician, what this philosopher brings to light is the fact that,

> words in a language do not derive their meaning from a fixed logical structure ... or from an "essence" of language which would contain the semantic building-blocks for all possible words in the lexicon of language. On the contrary, there can be no "stable structure underlying the complex of links and branches of every semiosic process" ... since each word in a language forms part of a "complicated network of similarities overlapping and criss-crossing" ... or a "maze-like network of intertwined sign-functions ... (49).

Due to this lack of a fixed logical structure, Winspur continues, it is only social convention that freezes the movement of unlimited semiosis and gives the appearance of fixity to our semantic universe (48). Wittgenstein thoroughly examines countless examples of language-games, all of which stress the inherent performance of words, and the creative and combinatory aspect of language, common in the play-concept. Wittgenstein then enlists the following "language-games": play-acting; riddles; making a joke and telling it; inventing a story and telling it. All these language-games are present in the surrealist games and in their avatars employed by Valaoritis. Like Wittgenstein, Valaoritis shows that language is living, rule-governed, and full of "family resemblances," and he attempts to bring some of its underlying rules to the fore in their performative and combinatory aspects. By doing so, he dares to make the trivial interesting and endows it with an aura of the marvelous. Through these games, poetry, even incantation, is emphasized, as the following piece, "Ode to Pythagoras"—written by Valaoritis during the same period when he wrote both *Henriette Where Did She Go?* and *The Round Tables*—shows:

> BUDDHA GURE Buddha gura Buddha gurun budha gorra Bud agora Pytha guru Puthagura Buda Buda Buda Pest Buddha Abouda Ouda-Boura-Gora Pytha Pest Buddha-Guru Boudagoras Buddhagora Puthabuddha Buddhapytha Buca Rest Bucu rest Beddha Grad Belhi Grad Delhi Grad Stylo Grad Retrograde Perachora peragora Paragoura Guru Pest Pestigrad Gradipest Gradiva Vadi Gra Mardi Gras Gramardi Gramerci Madrigrade Omnedi Conpani Panico Oncle Niko On Cleni Cleniko Nikokles Konicles Le Lapin Lelape Ain Etc (1).[23]

In this text-incantation, reminiscent of Hugo Ball's Dadaist "sound poem," the play with language reaches paroxysm to the point that it cannot be translated; it is almost like an undecipherable code created out of the deconstruction (in three languages; Greek, French, and English) of the name of Pythagoras, the famous ancient Greek philosopher, mathematician, and mystic, who seems to have taken the form of Buddha. Out of this playful deconstruction of Pythagoras' name, a series of famous cities emerge. All these allude to a possible influence of this old and new Guru, such as Buddhapest, Bucurest, Perachora ("A Place in the Other Edge"), as well as other proper names, or meaningful terms such as Gradiva or Mardi Gras. Basically, this Ode functions as a carnival dance in which the words are its main players, as they endlessly mask and unmask themselves, obeying the Rimbaldian rule of "the alchemy of the word." Through such a process, a musical harmony is created, suggesting that the concept of play unearths the inner quality of language that is called primordial rhythm, whether it pushes the words "to make love with each other," or "to treat each other as an enemy," as Breton suggested in both cases. Valaoritis pushed the limits of language in this "Ode to Pythagoras," anticipating his American creative phase in the early 1970s, when he was deeply influenced by Allen Ginsberg and the Beat Generation. Later, during the 1980s and '90s, he experimented with language-centered poetry, always remaining faithful to his surrealist background, particularly the surrealist concept of metamorphosis that allowed him to constantly mix genres and writing styles: "The surrealist metamorphosis, like the postmodern metamorphosis later on, grants him [Valaoritis] the freedom to do this kind of mixing of genres; or language-centered poetry and lettrism, the freedom to pass to an autoreferential poetry" (Ollier, "Métamorphose" 160).

Today, living in Greece, Valaoritis reshuffles his old French surrealist sketches, and plays with them through their spatial and temporal distance: at times he is himself caught by surprise, recognizing the deep impact the surrealist games had on him in terms of creativity; at other times, he re-appropriates these old ludic strategies to create new plays that test once again the concept of surrealist dialogue. His most recent play *To Φιλί* (*The Kiss*, 2005), is a rendition of the surrealist dialogue-game in a new version of *The Nightfall Hotel* that this time unfolds in the open-air and is more overtly playful. At other times still, he is tempted to theorize his passionate engagement with the surrealist ludic activity of his youth.

Ultimately, Valaoritis's experiment with surrealist games had a two-fold purpose: on the one hand, he set forth a poetics of surrealist theatre, based on a game-theory that led to a reevaluation of surrealist theatre on the basis of its poeticized language. On the other hand, he opened the path to the post-surrealist on-stage games of transformation, which the following chapters will further explore in the work of well-known American playwrights and performance artists, Robert Wilson and Megan Terry. By making use of the most characteristic features of the surrealist games, such as "their privileging of chance over necessity"; "their commitment to the dynamic production of an extremely contingent reality by the subject in *errance*"; and "the construction of a reality formed by intertextual and intersubjective representation" (Laxton, *Paris as a Gameboard* 528); Valaoritis opens the way to post-structuralist and language-centered theatrical techniques. Ultimately, like Wittgenstein, Valaoritis had one aim: to show his audience how "to pass from a piece of disguised nonsense to something that is patent nonsense" (Wittgenstein's aphorism #464). Yet, paradoxically, such patent nonsense is, in fact, full of systematic rules and thus of meaning.

Notes

1 Part of this chapter appeared in earlier versions in: Vassiliki Rapti, "Surrealist Ludics in Nanos Valaoritis' Play 'Les Tables Rondes'," *The Charioteer: An Annual Review of Modern Greek Culture* 43 (2005): 99–113, published by PELLA Publishing Co., New York, NY; and *Text and Presentation* (2004) © 2005 edited by Stratos E. Constantinidis by permission of McFarland & Company, Inc., Box 611, Jefferson NC 28640. www.mcfarlandpub.com.

2 Susan Laxton, in her book *Paris as a Gameboard*, states that "the regulated action of surrealist games reactivates the parameters of ritual" (534).

3 I refer to my first interview with Nanos Valaoritis in Oakland, California on May 22, 2001.

4 See Sewell, *The Field of Nonsense*.

5 Roger Caillois joined Breton's group during the years 1932–34. For more details on his relationship to the surrealist movement, see Caillois, *The Edge of Surrealism*, ed. Claudine Frank.

6 Hereafter referred to as *Henriette*.

7 All quotes from this play have been translated by the author and have been approved by the playwright to whom I address my warmest thanks for his advice and for kindly offering me access to his archive.

8 Nanos Valaoritis stayed in Paris during the years 1954–60. In 1954 he joined André Breton's surrealist circle along with the surrealist painter Marie Wilson, later his wife. During these years he wrote more than 40 plays and skits in French and Greek, both of them being his mother tongues, since he was born in Lausanne, Switzerland and both languages were spoken in his home. Later, when the author moved to the United States, he also wrote plays in English. In the archives of Surrealism his name appears in the "Who is it about?" game that belongs to the series of the "cards of analogy" game, which appeared in *Le Surréalisme même* (No. 5, Spring 1959). These cards were modeled after identity cards in which the participants were asked to identify some celebrities, including Freud, Chateaubriand, Huysmans, Watteau, Rousseau and Nietzsche, among others, with the ultimate goal of showing the participants a "state of sensory and affective resource" (Garrigues 38).

9   This term is borrowed from Warren F. Motte's book *Playtexts: Ludics in Contemporary Literature*. This book is a collection of essays that explore the concept of play as "necessarily and fundamentally creative," and therefore, as inseparable from writing itself, a statement made since Plato's time (Motte 15).

10   See "Le cas est unique dans l'histoire du théâtre où les rôles d'enfants sont rares, pour des raisons techniques évidentes, même à partir du XVIII siècle où l'on commence à s'intéresser à l'enfance, grâce à Rousseau" (Hubert 14) [The case is unique in the history of theatre, where the roles of children are, for obvious technical reasons, rare, even in the eighteenth century when, thanks to Rousseau, interest in childhood began.]

11   This blasphemous pun, invented by Victor, anticipates the tone of the text *L'Immaculée conception* (*The Immaculate Conception*) that Breton would write with Louis Aragon two years later, in 1930.

12   A new pun is suggested by the use of the word "neuf," which in French has a double meaning: a) nine and b) brand-new.

13   One wonders if Vitrac borrowed from the ancient Greek verb "οἶδα" (ida), which means "to know," to create the character of Ida Mortemart. In this light, Ida would be the one who knows about love and death, a role which is relevant to the attitude in the play. Vitrac's following words support such a view: "ici le destin s'appelle Ida Mortemart. Un sphinx ... Ida Mortemart est le sphinx de la gloire et de la honte à l'échelle des petits gens" (quoted in Beachler Severs 131). Of course, other interpretations could apply to Ida's name, such as perhaps one related to Montmartre, a place of rebels and revels, cherished by the Surrealists, or even one that could be related to a combination of the words "le marteau de la Mort," in the sense of a vivified coup of Death.

14   *Victor* was staged again on November 10, 1946 in the Théâtre Agnes Capri by the company Thyase under Michel de Ré's direction. Interestingly, both Artaud and Breton attended the performance but overall it did not receive a better reception than its first performance in 1928. However, Jean Anouilh, who undertook the endeavor to stage *Victor* again with Roland Piétri on October 3, 1962 in the Théâtre de l'Ambigu, applauded the 1946 performance. Critics were almost unanimous in judging its success which placed Vitrac next to Shakespeare by aligning Victor with a modern Hamlet, as Bertrand Poirot-Delpech wrote in the *Monde* of October 5, 1962 (quoted in Hubert 184). From this moment on, *Victor* became a classic of the French theatrical repertoire staged again in 1982 in the *Comédie Française* under the direction of Jean Bouchaud and Marcel Bozonnet, while in September 1998 it was staged in the Cartoucherie de Vincennes by the Théâtre de la Tempête under Philippe Adrien's direction. In this production Victor was portrayed again like a modern Hamlet.

15   André Gide and Giorgio de Chirico also claimed that they found originality in this production, which they attended during all three of its performances, only regretting that there were no more performances of this unique spectacle (Hubert 182).

16   This information was given in a phone conversation on January 5, 2006. During the same conversation, the playwright stated that all his characters, despite the fact that they were based on real persons—mostly his friends—were always changing.

17   With regard to the choice of the name Mervyn or rather, the multi-faceted character of Mervyn, Valaoritis stated that he was inspired by a poem from Lautréamont's *Chants de Maldoror*. Mervyn also suggests the marvelous.

18   The author confirmed this allusion to *Les Caves du Vatican* during a phone conversation I had with him on January 5, 2006. He added that, like Vitrac, he himself at that time was very interested in the late medieval *mystères* (mystery plays). Beachler Severs lists a series of common features in the work of Vitrac and the mystery plays: "the grotesque

humor and violence, the lack of concern for sequential time and action, the invitation to audience participation, the stock characters from everyday life, and the farcical nature of the action" (113).

19 Information given during a phone conversation on January 5, 2006.

20 For further details, see Francis Lacassin's edition *Les Fantômes de Jersey* (1991). Another inter-textual reference is the medieval fellowship of the Round Table in the King Arthur legend, where all the knights have equal status around the egalitarian round table. See Barber, *King Arthur*, 39–40. The well-educated Valaoritis (particularly in the field of French literature) was familiar with both Victor Hugo's work and the Arthurian tradition. His overwhelming erudition is present in all of his works, including his plays and has been considered a shortcoming for staging his plays. Marcelle Capron (*Le Combat*, April 29, 1959), for instance, as Valaoritis admits, saw his erudition as an obstacle in regard to the staging of his play *L'Hôtel de la nuit qui tombe* (*The Nightfall Hotel*) in Paris in 1959 (Personal Interview).

21 Valaoritis borrows here Breton's image of a woman's hair-mushrooms from *Poisson soluble* and applies it to Anabelle's hands. The relevant passage from Breton's work reads: "Her hair was nothing but a patch of pink mushrooms, among pine needles and very fine glassware of dry leaves" (Seaver and Lane 88).

22 The approximation of Anabelle and Nadja is also suggested by their association with Helen (of Troy). Anabelle is etymologically speaking of "la belle Ana" (the beautiful Anna), which alludes to the beautiful Helen of Troy. As for Nadja, there is stronger evidence of her association with a certain Helen. In a note in *Nadja* Breton states that the medium Mme Sacco told him that at some point his mind was preoccupied with a certain Helen. Puzzled, Breton noted: "La conclusion à en tirer serait de l'ordre de celle que m'a imposée précédemment la fusion dans un rêve de deux images très éloignées l'une de l'autre. 'Hélène, c'est moi', disait Nadja" (*OC1* 693).

23 This short text remains unpublished along with another similar short text entitled "Un drame léttriste." Both come from a unnumbered original.

4

PLAYING WITH LANGUAGE: ANTONIN ARTAUD'S *PAIDIA* AND ROBERT WILSON'S *LUDUS*

A Jarry Theatre production will be as thrilling *as a game, like a card game* with the whole audience taking part (Artaud, quoted in Schumacher 35; my emphasis).

In the second chapter we explored the way the Théâtre Alfred Jarry implemented André Breton's tacit ludic dramatic theory. By relying on the mechanisms and the effects of games, Roger Vitrac and Antonin Artaud paved the way for a different concept of theatre, in search of a new language for the stage. This type of a new theatre would ensure the thrill of a game. More precisely, like a card game, it would embrace both the whims of chance and the card-players' (actors') well-calculated moves, while at the same time being constantly fueled by the audience's active involvement. Moreover, Artaud's theatre would abandon the notion of dialogue with its reasoning value as the primary constitutive element of a well-made play. In its lieu, Artaud would place the images issued forth by the actor's body language that functions as a multisensory stimulus bridging the stage with the auditorium. In a lecture Artaud gave at the Sorbonne on December 10, 1931,[1] he explicitly scorned the dialogue-bound Western theatre and advocated a new tangible stage language, independent of speech:

Dialogue—something written and spoken—does not specifically belong to the stage but to books ... I maintain the stage is a tangible, physical place that needs to be filled and it ought to be allowed to speak its own concrete language. I maintain that this physical language, aimed at the senses and independent of speech, must first satisfy the senses (quoted in Schumacher 92–3).

Thus, dialogue would be replaced by the actors' physical language which would become a tool for exploration of the player's inner mind, since, according to Artaud, it always plays the most important role on stage. This new concept of theatre, briefly, would have the qualities of "a thrilling game" that attempts to extend life "to be a sort of *magical operation*, open to any development, and in this it answers a mental need which audiences feel are hidden deep down within themselves" (Artaud, quoted in Schumacher 35).[2] Artaud attempted to put this conceptualization of theatre into practice in his playlet *Le Jet de sang* (*The Jet of Blood* or *The Spurt of Blood*), first published in his collection *L'Ombilic des limbes* (*Umbilical Limbo*) in 1925 and included in the first bill of the Théâtre Alfred Jarry in 1927, under his own direction. Despite the fact that *The Jet of Blood* remained subsequently unstaged until Peter Brook rediscovered and included it in his 1964 London Theatre of Cruelty production (to a much debated reception),[3] it is necessary to examine it here, since it "plants many of the seeds" of Artaud's seminal study *The Theatre and its Double* (Bermel 14). For both fundamental concepts of Artaud's dramatic theory—the concept of "the double" and that of "cruelty"—blend here with the surrealist principle of the unification of contraries (ibid). The Artaudian principle of "the double" represents the foundations of Artaud's theory, and "refers to a specific aesthetic principle—the relationship between art and the world of reality" (Benisson 128). The term "cruelty," on the other hand, is defined by Artaud himself in a letter to his friend Jean Paulhan on November 14, 1932: "I use the word cruelty in the sense of hungering after life, cosmic strictness, relentless necessity, in the Gnostic sense of a living vortex engulfing darkness, in the sense of the inescapably necessary pain without which life could not continue" (quoted in Schumacher 107). "Cruelty" thus "indicates danger, in the sense that the rational processes are short-circuited, and the shock aimed directly at the spectator's viscera" (Bennison 128–9). Artaud's supposedly "failed drama" *The Jet of Blood* takes Artaud's "call to revolution farther than he could have ever imagined," "in fact, past the realm of modernism and into the postmodern—into, as Jameson would say, 'some new, as yet unimaginable, perhaps ultimately impossible, dimensions'" (Kornhaber 57). These "yet unimaginable dimensions" that Artaud imparted in *The Jet of Blood* can be better understood through the lens of one of its multiple contemporary stagings that remained faithful to Artaud's surrealist stage principles. I refer to the performance of February 14–17, 1996 at Wickham Studio Theatre in Bristol, UK, under the direction of Günter Berghaus. After examining Berghaus's experiment with the *Jet de sang* in the next section of this chapter, we can then better trace Artaud's supposedly "unperformable" conceptualization of the stage in the work of contemporary, American man of the theatre, Robert Wilson.

Gunter Berghaus's experiment with *Le Jet de sang*

Günter Berghaus's stage experiment with Artaud's five-page play *Le Jet de sang* occupies a particular place here because it concerns the key theoretical issue addressed in this study, namely, the presumed incompatibility of surrealist theatre and the stage. Taking as a point of departure the conviction that Artaud's supposedly unperformable play *Le Jet de sang* can indeed be staged, Berghaus's experiment takes the form of a collaborative reflection upon Artaud's theatrical concepts during his surrealist phase, and tests their validity and the limitations of their applicability. In his illuminating article "Artaud's *Jet de Sang*: A Critical Post-Production Analysis" (2001), Berghaus begins his critical analysis of his 1996 student production of Artaud's *Jet de sang* by distinguishing Artaud as the only Surrealist with actual stage experience:

> he had worked with Lugné-Poë, Dullin and Pitoëff; he was an experienced actor in a variety of modern and classic rôles; he knew the conventions of contemporary theatre practice and was familiar with the aims of the stage reformers of his time. He was therefore well-qualified to map out an alternative theatre system and set signals for a different kind of product to be presented in it. Even if in the end the existing conditions of theatrical production did not allow him to realize his intentions, at least Artaud knew what he was aiming for. Therefore he could act as stimulator and catalyst for following generations of theatre artists, influencing their thinking in a number of ways:
>
> * abolishing the rhetorical and ornamental style of acting
> * discovering the prime importance of the actor's physical means of expression
> * translating raw emotional states into the symbolic language of the stage
> * making the theatrical event real by centering it on the actors' mental and physical experiences and joining these with the spectators' emotional world (5–6).

All these principles of the Artaudian stage vision that Berghaus discerns here can indeed already be traced in the *Jet de sang* and are explicitly explored by Berghaus in his own version of the play. Another important point that Berghaus makes about Artaud's approach to theatre is his precision. He quotes a letter that Artaud had sent to his friend Jean-Richard Bloch, in which he asks not to be judged by the hurried and unpolished performances, due to financial and time restrictions, of the Théâtre Alfred Jarry: "[t]hese performances did not indicate exactly my true intentions, nor did they reveal my technical and professional abilities as director" (quoted in Berghaus 9). For Artaud, Berghaus continues, "[c]hance and improvisation have an important role to play in the rehearsal phase, but not during the run" (9).

Berghaus set out to explore with his students all of the above issues raised by Artaud's surrealist play during an entire academic year, first in the format of seminars and workshops and then during the rehearsal process. In all these phases, the scenic design—an early designed miniature proscenium-arch theatre erected in a studio—was a crucial component, meant "to offer the audience a peep-show, a view into a weird and wonderful world, where all perspectives were strangely distorted" (5) (see Figure 4.1). At the same time, this monstrosity of the physical stage was meant to throw the actors "off their centre of balance," while at the same time producing the Artaudian "equivalent of vertigo in the mind of the senses of the spectators" (ibid.). Their rehearsal process started with numerous exercises involving the surrealist notions of "automatism," "chance," and the "marvelous," all of which led to dream transcripts that, in turn, triggered the actors' personal responses to Artaud's play, shaping their feelings and emotions. The latter, it must be emphasized, were further affected by the technical aspects of the show, including the sound that served as a rhythmic skeleton for the performance. Among the emotion-inducing technical elements, the powerful olfactory dimension was used to great effect; every scene was accompanied by a very specific smell, such as cheese or perfume, generating "subliminal responses that create an intimate bond with the spectators' other emotional reactions to the events presented on stage" (8).

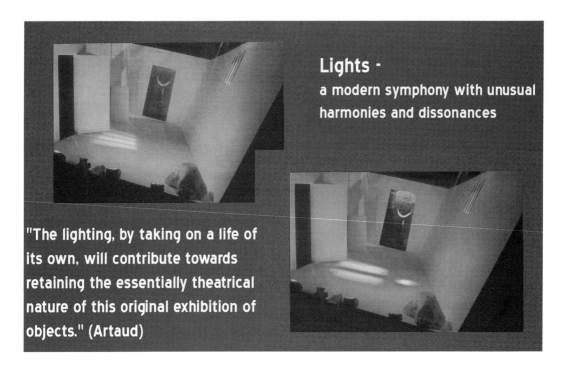

Lights -
a modern symphony with unusual
harmonies and dissonances

"The lighting, by taking on a life of
its own, will contribute towards
retaining the essentially theatrical
nature of this original exhibition of
objects." (Artaud)

4.1   Günter Berghaus's lighting setting in his stage experiment with Artaud's *Le Jet de sang (The Spurt of Blood)*, performed February 14–17, 1996 at Wickham Studio Theatre, Bristol, director: Günter Berghaus. Photographs copyright of Günter Berghaus. Berghaus Archive, Overath / Germany

Also, lighting played a major role, in the sense that it functioned as a poetic and physical core element of the production. To quote Berghaus, the lights "gave the *physical* space of the stage a strong emotional resonance and opened up a *mental* space for the audience, into which they could project their own feelings and inner visions" (11). What mostly counted in that production was not a unified interpretation of Artaud's script, but a multi-layered approach to it which encompassed each actor's own personal response. These responses, initially prompted by improvisation (*paidia*), took shape in the form of startling images and mesmerizing stage actions, which "possessed a suggestive power without being too fixed in their meaning" (ibid.), and were personal elaborations of some rudimentary, psychoanalytical directorial guidelines. As Berghaus states,

> I felt inclined towards psychoanalytical readings of Artaud's state of mind, of the symbols and archetypal actions in the play. In my view, the development of the plot related to Artaud's own rites of passage: his discovery of sexuality; his rebellion against his father and mother; his attempts at assuaging his anxieties by romantically wooing a virginal girl; his successive acceptance of his sexual urges in contact with a mature, erotic woman and the subsequent conflict with the remnants of his own oedipal attachment to his mother (ibid.).

All these states of mind were presented to the audience in seven scenes, a prelude and two interludes. Without a clearly discernible start, the performance would get the starting cue from the audience: "when they had sufficiently settled and immersed themselves into the atmosphere, we were ready to lead them into a dream world that was real and surreal at the same time" (Berghaus 12). In this real and surreal world, a vast gamut of emotions was triggered in the audience in a polysensory event: confusion, irritation, frustration, bewilderment, all created by their encounter with a materialization of a dream. That stage dream began with the first scene's "hurricane of feelings and desires," set free during the encounter of the two protagonists, a Young Man and a Young Girl. Their encounter was followed by an explosion of the whole stage that gave way to the first interlude—a shadow play, in which the inner world of the young couple was projected onto a screen (ibid.). It is interesting to notice here how Berghaus managed to accommodate the "impossible" actions of Artaud's script in this disturbing scene that required pieces of human body to fall down, including hands, feet, scalps, and masks, by using a wide array of puppets to represent the body parts. Some of the puppets used were related to Oriental theatre which also influenced Artaud in his later career. Equally disturbing was the appearance of the Whore on stage in the fourth scene, which was the turning point of the production. Accentuated by lighting effects and an entirely different profusion of smells, it introduced the fifth scene that aimed at "showing how the overwhelming force of sexuality leads society into disarray" (14). Berghaus particularly stressed here each character's different response to "the provocative sensuality of the Whore, ranging from fear to fascination and enchantment" (ibid.). Particularly telling was the following scene, in which sex and religion were directly confronted:

> Like Zeus firing his thunderbolt, "God" threw a red beam of light towards the Whore and set her hair on fire. Other lighting effects from underneath the stage turned her clothes transparent and revealed her naked body to the assembled society figures. They stumbled back, blinded by the light and the demeanour of the Whore. She responded to the threat of church and religion by biting God's wrist. Immediately, the whole scene was bathed in a dark-red light, brightened up by flashes of lightning occasionally zig-zagging across the stage (14).

Figure 4.2 illustrates how Berghaus overcame the challenges of Artaud's script. Even more challenging was Artaud's requirement in the subsequent scene: "An army of scorpions comes out from under The Nurse's dress and swarm over her sex, which swells, cracks open, becomes glassy and shimmers like a sun" (quoted at 15). To realize Artaud's stage directions, Berghaus used an 8mm film, projected onto a balloon, which was inflated between the woman's legs. This is only one example of the many innovative devices that Berghaus used in this performance, a performance that attempted to implement Artaud's physical language of the stage. As Figures 4.2 and 4.3 show, language here is channeled through the body and not through verbal communication. What is important to notice here is that Berghaus made clear that what Artaud had in mind back in his time was not, in fact, impossible or unperformable. On the contrary, he showed that Artaud was well ahead of his time, envisioning a theatre of the future, which unfortunately Breton—another player of the future—failed to recognize. Playing with light, the five senses, the actors' transcribed dreams and visions, and the audience's disorientation vis-à-vis a fixed meaning, Berghaus translated Artaud's surrealist conceptualization of the theatre into a concrete language of the stage. Here, once again, the concept of play is an underlying guiding principle in the sense of a constant interaction between life and dream, between the actors and the spectators, and between the actors and themselves.

4.2   The Whore and the Knight, from Günter Berghaus's stage experiment with Artaud's *Le Jet de sang* (*The Spurt of Blood*), performed February 14–17, 1996 at Wickham Studio Theatre, Bristol, director: Günter Berghaus. Photographs copyright of Günter Berghaus. Berghaus Archive, Overath / Germany

Characteristic is the following testimony by one of the actors in that production, who discovered an unknown freedom on stage that allowed for a transcendence of his physical actions, which however were fully controlled, and far from delirium or abandonment: "This transcendence of self during the moments of performance creates an emptiness. I am devoid of subject, I am object; I am not a character, I am a notion, an archetype. I approach hollowness like a marionette, a pure symbol of abstraction" (10). Another actor, who also attempted never-tried-before improvisations that gave free rein to the projection of intense emotions, confirmed this experience—one during which the objective form merged with subjective impulse. This new stage language is fully-fledged on the contemporary stage and finds a major ally in Robert Wilson, whose work bears clear marks of the Artaudian surrealist theatrical poetics. The following section traces the game techniques that Wilson employs on stage in Artaud's manner, as Berghaus has shown us in his self-aware experiment with Artaud's *Jet de sang*. Berghaus's experiment—well documented on film in its every permutation— took the form of a "true reality" (17) and "unrepeatable as any act of life" (ibid.); it was "as thrilling *as a game, like a card game* with the whole audience taking part," to recall this chapter's opening quotation from Artaud's manifesto on the Théâtre Alfred Jarry.

Although Robert Wilson claims various influences and not a specific one,[4] the affinities between his work and Artaud's concept of new theatre that draws on Surrealism are salient and have already been noted by various scholars. Louis Aragon, in a 1971 letter to his dead friend André Breton, heralded the performance of Wilson's theatrical work *Le Regard du sourd* (*Deafman Glance*),

which he attended during its opening tour in France, as something that far
exceeded what they had hoped for thus far:

> The miracle we were waiting for has happened, long after I had stopped believing in it:
> *Deafman Glance*. I have never seen anything so beautiful. No other spectacle can hold a
> candle to it because it is, at the same time, waking life and life seen with the eyes closed,
> the world of every day and the world of every night, reality mixed with dream. Bob Wilson
> is not a surrealist. *He is what we, from whom Surrealism was born, dreamed would come
> after us and go beyond us* (quoted in Holmberg 154; my emphasis).

Continuing to praise *Deafman Glance*, Aragon added: "This strange spectacle,
neither ballet, nor mime, nor opera (but perhaps a deaf opera) calls forth new
ways with light and shadow. It seems to criticize everything we do out of habit. It
is an extraordinary freedom machine" (quoted in Blank 2). In this work that runs
for seven hours on stage, Wilson collaborated with Raymond Andrews, a young
deaf-mute boy with whom he explored a world of visual, rather than verbal logic.
An architectural arrangement in pictures, with no reliance on any script, it is a
play of images that evokes fluidity and freedom and aims at the disorientation
of the spectators' senses, similar to the effect of the surrealist image. As Arthur
Holmberg states, "[w]atching *Deafman Glance* was like smoking a hookah: one
slipped easily, peacefully over the edge into the beatitude of dreams. In the blink,
the exterior world fades into mist. One floats on the dark sea of the mind among
shadows and reflections of reflections (156). Indeed, "both the surrealistic and
the oneiric make their presence felt in Wilson" (ibid.).

4.3   Mother and Knight, from Günter Berghaus's stage experiment with Artaud's *Le Jet de sang* (*The Spurt of Blood*), performed February 14–17, 1996 at Wickham Studio Theatre, Bristol, director: Günter Berghaus. Photographs copyright of Günter Berghaus. Berghaus Archive, Overath / Germany

Alain Jouffroi, an ex-member of Surrealism, seconded Aragon's view with regard to the proximity of *Deafman Glance* and Surrealism:

When I was very young I met Antonin Artaud and André Breton and I participated in the surrealist movement until I was twenty. I found the memory of these things again in the dream of this play. The spectacle of Bob Wilson was very new but with special roots in French art. We find this connection. Maybe it's not true but we find it. And we think, how is this possible? Astonishment (Shyer 258).

This same connection was also detected by Michel Guy who saw in it the ideal surrealist theatre: "I happen to know that Bob didn't know anything about European art or surrealism yet strangely *Deafman Glance* was like the ideal surrealist theatre" (Shyer 258). Nor was the resemblance detected in Wilson's work to surrealist theatre limited to *Deafman Glance*; as theatre critic Theodore Shank remarks, some of Wilson's productions on a grand operatic scale "resemble large surreal paintings with moving figures and objects" (125), as, for example, Figures 4.4–4.8 from the *Alcestis* production at the American Repertory Theatre show. Regardless of scale, Shank continues, Wilson's "collage-like works incorporate invented material as well as material from the real world" (ibid.). Talking about the full retrospective of Wilson's working vision mounted by the Boston Museum of Fine Arts in 1991 after several years of collaboration between Wilson and curator Trevor Fairbrother, Johannes Birringer also notices the dreamlike Surrealism of Wilson's poetry: "In this exhibition the dreamlike surrealism of Wilson's poetry clearly suspends the linear 'vision' of conventional museum displays of an artist's collected works" (80).

This chapter seeks to identify better the affinity between Wilson's work and Surrealism, as illustrated in Artaud's early experiment *The Jet of Blood* as regards the similar process that both Artaud and Wilson adopt when dealing with the language of the stage, that is, as an ongoing, thrilling game in which both actors and audience are wholeheartedly engaged as players. Wilson, in particular, "has been playing games with language, like a kid with a new bag of marbles, but, as Wittgenstein assures us, meaning is use and the games we play with language and language plays with us are infinite" (Holmberg 47). These games, in his case, range from aphasia and experimentation with deaf-mute and brain-damaged children, to an on-stage screen, infused by letters in all their physicality to the point that language becomes an autonomous actor that interacts with the audience in a new and infinite play. In this new play, language is transformed into images, thus placing at the fore a visual rather than a verbal logic. This chapter will show several characteristic examples of experiments/games with language that the American director, dancer, performer, architect, and painter Robert Wilson has introduced to the stage in order to interrogate language and in which he far exceeded the Surrealists' ludic expectations. Through a comparative approach, these games will find a predecessor in Artaud's own games with language and images in *The Jet of Blood*.[5]

Like the Surrealists, Wilson constantly plays on stage with language, with light and shadow and the images related to the states of dream and waking. However, where the Surrealists favor the random juxtaposition of their images, Wilson arranges his images on stage in a precise and calculated manner.

4.4   Scene from American Repertory Theatre's 1986 production of *Alcestis*, directed
by Robert Wilson. Photographs by Richard Feldman, courtesy of A.R.T.

4.5   Scene from American Repertory Theatre's 1986 production of *Alcestis*, directed
by Robert Wilson. Photographs by Richard Feldman, courtesy of A.R.T.

4.6   Scene from American Repertory Theatre's 1986 production of *Alcestis*, directed by Robert Wilson. Photographs by Richard Feldman, courtesy of A.R.T.

As František Deák claims, "instead of a dramatic concept, he uses a visual one: the juxtaposition and assemblage of images. … The juxtaposition of images on different horizontal planes, their focusing and defocusing, is the main principle of Wilson's theatrical assemblages" (67–8). So, if the main surrealist mode of playing with images aspires to improvisational *paidia*, Wilson's play with language resembles rule-bound *ludus*. The following description of *Deafman Glance* by Wilson himself, one year after its performance in France in 1972, bears proof of his affinity with Surrealism, all the while stressing his sense of *ludus*, located in the chess-like preciseness of the well-defined zones of the stage. Referring to his work "in somewhat surrealist terms" in the *Cahiers Renaud-Barrault* (Romero 492), Wilson describes his work as "un collage visuel d'images et d'activités [qui] se produisent par couches dans des zones scéniques stratifiés et clairement définies qui sont, de temps à autre, juxtaposées par rapport au centre et par là même, mises en relief" (ibid. 492) [A visual collage of images and activities (which) are produced by layers in the stratified and well-defined stage zones, which are, from time to time, juxtaposed in regard to the center and from there even they are put into relief]. On another occasion, he describes his work as the work of a painter and explains how pictures matter more than any story in his work, just like in any surrealist work:

> Go like you would go to a museum, like you would look at a painting. Appreciate the color of the apple, the line of the dress, the glow of the light … My opera is easier than *Butterfly*. You don't have to think about the story, because there isn't any. You don't have to listen to words, because the words don't mean anything. You just enjoy the scenery, the architectural arrangements in time and space, the music, the feelings they all evoke. Listen to the pictures (Shyer xv).

4.7   Scene from American Repertory Theatre's 1986 production of *Alcestis*, directed by Robert Wilson. Photographs by Richard Feldman, courtesy of A.R.T.

4.8   Scene from American Repertory Theatre's 1986 production of *Alcestis*, directed by Robert Wilson. Photographs by Richard Feldman, courtesy of A.R.T.

In effect, Wilson, surpassing Surrealism and Artaud, achieved a transmutation of Surrealism on stage. His stay in Paris during a crucial period for his formation[6] played an important role in this transmutation and offered new perspectives on the art of theatre in general, opening up to him the painter's realm even on the stage.[7] It is in particular the first phase of Wilson's work that bears closer affinities with Surrealism. I refer to "the private fantasy performances of the 1970s, followed by a more varied combination of historical/literary stagings beginning with CIVIL warS in 1981" (Romero 488). During this phase, Wilson stressed the visual as a viable language, as he was convinced that "conventional linear speech was a very limited conveyor of sense and meaning beyond everyday exchanges" (490). Disregarding a theatre of words, Wilson was instead interested in developing a visual theatre with its own language that renews itself as if in a game: "I think what you do in theater is that you can invent a theatrical language, a vocabulary. And once it becomes discernible, then you can destroy it and with the deconstructed parts you can reconstruct another language" (Wilson, quoted in Bell 23). From *Deafman Glance* to *Edison*, as Lawrence Romero states, Wilson's first phase remained consistent, that is, "an unorthodox, idiosyncratic, self-referential work, *essentially imagistic and surrealist*" (490; my emphasis). This "essentially imagistic and surrealist" work will become clearer in the next section of this chapter, which highlights the common surrealist thought in both Wilson and Artaud in their early work.

Antonin Artaud's and Robert Wilson's common ground: In search of a new language for the stage

In any comparison of Artaud and Wilson one cannot neglect their common adventure with language from their early stages. On the one hand, we have Artaud's suffering of meningitis at the age of five, and his subsequent life-long struggle with nervous disorders significantly affecting his relationship with language itself. On the other hand, as Lawrence Shyer informs us, at the age of 17, Wilson was cured of a stammer with the help of Miss Bird ("Baby") Hoffman, a local dance instructor (at Waco, Texas), who taught him to speak slowly and free the tension from his body through dance (289).[8] Language, then, arose as a challenge for both Artaud and Wilson and, little by little, they realized the need to experiment with it in an alternative manner in order to minimize the precedence of reason-driven language and articulated speech, using the body's liberating energy. Searching for a new language for the stage, both Artaud and Wilson, each one by different means, realized the necessity for placing at the foreground two interrelated aspects of language, both of which were originally pointed out by André Breton: first, the emancipation of traditional dialogue from its communicative value together with its transformation into a highly esteemed generator of audacious images, and second, the significance of dreams.

As early as 1925, when he was still an active member of Surrealism, in an attack against "style" and all kinds of literature, Artaud writes: "Then you will understand why my mind is not here, then *you will see all language exhausted*, all minds dry up, *all tongues shrivel up*, all human figures collapse, deflate, as if drawn up by shriveling leeches" (quoted in Schumacher 23; my emphasis).[9] According to Artaud, such a concrete language that appeals to the senses is related to the actual space of the stage and the actors' gestures rather than to their speeches, and is capable of unleashing poetry: "There must be poetry for the senses just as there is for speech, but this physical, tangible language I am referring to is really only theatrical insofar as the thoughts it expresses are beyond spoken language" (quoted in Schumacher 93). Such spatial poetry, as opposed to language poetry, Artaud adds, assumes many guises: "first of all it assumes those expressive means usable on stage such as music, dance, plastic art, mimicry, mime, gesture, voice inflection, architecture, lighting and décor" (ibid). It becomes evident, then, that the concrete language Artaud envisioned for the stage would be conceived as an interplay among each one of the aforementioned guises that would give place to a total theatre, in which words give way to signs. This is what Artaud stresses again in a letter he wrote to the theatre critic Benjamin Crémieux on September 15, 1931, a text that was later included in *The Theatre and Its Double*:

> word language must give way to sign language, whose objective aspect has the most immediate impact on us. Viewed from this angle, the aim of stage reassumes a kind of intellectual dignity, words effacing themselves behind gesture, and from the fact that the aesthetic, plastic part of theatre abandons its role as a decorative interlude, to become a *language* of direct communication in the proper sense of the word (ibid. 112).

These views of Artaud's, elaborated in a span of several decades, come in agreement with Wilson's own view of stage language. An enemy of realistic language, Wilson claims: "Realistic dialog doesn't work for me. What time is it? Five o'clock. How boring" (Holmberg 67). The following anecdote, provided by Arthur Holmberg, is also telling in this regard: during the rehearsals of *When We Dead Awaken*, Wilson told two actors running through an Ibsen conversation not "to bounce dialog back and forth like a ping-pong ball. Let the words fly past each other. Don't pick up each other's rhythms. Follow your own line. Each of you is lost in a separate world" (67). These words, similar to Breton's definition of surrealist dialogue as two simultaneous monologues, decenter conventional dialogue, often suspending "a sentence midair before it arrives at a conclusion" (ibid. 67). Like Artaud, "[b]y disturbing the flow of ordinary conversation, Wilson unravels the social fabric, disrupts interpersonal relations, and intensifies the mood of alienation" (ibid. 67).

Moreover, Wilson experimented with language by collaborating with children and in particular, with brain-damaged children who offered him a different perception of language. Also, Daniel Stern, author of *The Interpersonal World of the Infant* (New York, 1985) who showed Wilson approximately a hundred films on the relationship between mothers and their babies, was a seminal influence. Through this experience Wilson learned that infants (literally meaning "unable to speak") are an inexhaustible source of creativity. Within their toy theatre, children discover their realm: "theatre and dreams" (Morey and Pardo 21). Equally revealing was Wilson's collaboration with the deaf-mute Raymond Andrews and the autistic actor Chris Knowles with both of whom Wilson was amazed, because they spoke by way of visual form, always seeing images as they spoke, as if they organized language through an inner screen. Thus, Wilson was willing to accommodate Raymond Andrews' view of the world, "the idea that, to the extent that he thinks in images rather than in words, he can penetrate a whole range of aspects that tend to go unnoticed by those of us who live in a predominantly verbal world" (ibid. 24). Similarly, Wilson admits that from Chris Knowles he learned to use language differently, from another point of view: "I began to explore the sound and division of words themselves again" (ibid. 20). For,

> [h]is speech reflected a linguistic organization that was not ordered by syntax. His systematizing was based, quite spontaneously, on categories that Wilson intuits as mathematical, numeric and geometrical. ... From the ephemeral geometries of the body, language becomes, with Chris, formalization, spontaneous abstraction on his inner screen (ibid. 145).

Indeed, the way this 11-year-old boy organized language was remarkable and helped Wilson, as he admits, to "rediscover the hidden. That for me (him) is avant-garde" (ibid. 26). The desire for making the stage the realm of a revelation of the hidden (as in the "one into another" game) was something that Artaud had already expressed in 1928 in these psychological terms:

> The Jarry Theatre will endeavour to express what life has forgotten, has *hidden*, or is incapable of stating. Everything which stems from the mind's *fertile* delusions, its sensory illusions, encounters between things and sensations which strike us primarily by their physical density, will be shown from an extraordinary angle, with the stench and the excreta of unadulterated brutality, just as they appear to the mind, *just as the mind remembered them* (quoted in Schumacher 35).

Uncovering the hidden goes hand in hand with brutality, a brutality that is typical of dream, all the while these elements form the quintessence of the "thrilling game" that is the stage, according to Artaud. In the above statement, Artaud articulates for the first time his later notion of "the theatre of cruelty." By this term, it is by no means meant a theatre in which "blood and sadism predominate, but one which draws upon the passionate in life, the violent rigor—this life that exceeds all bounds and is exercised in the torture and trampling down of everything, this pure implacable feeling is what cruelty is" (Zeps 130). This notion of cruelty is inherent in the dreams, as Artaud states in his first manifesto of the Theatre of Cruelty (1932):

> *If theatre is as bloody and as inhuman as dreams*, the reason for this is that it perpetuates the metaphysical notions in some fables in a present-day, tangible manner, whose atrocity and energy are enough to prove their origins and intentions in fundamental first principles rather than to reveal and unforgettably tie down the idea of continual conflict within us, where life is continually lacerated, where everything in creation rises up and attacks our condition as created beings (quoted in Schumacher 101; my emphasis).

In other words, Artaud wanted "to bring to light all that is obscure, buried deep and baffling within man. The theatre must be a solid material projection of our internal drama" (Knapp 93). The same kind of brutality or cruelty is typical of Wilson's work, as well. Exemplary is the murder scene in *Deafman Glance*, which has been performed many times, all over the world since its initial conception in 1967, not only as part of *Deafman Glance* but also as part of the various productions of *Medea* that Wilson attempted.[10] Wilson looks at this murder scene as one of those fascinating moments "as germs or points of heightened attention around which orbit—as their dynamic centers of attraction—the component parts of his mises-en-scène" (Morey and Prado 25). Wilson is aware of his *mises-en scènes* as his art, distinct from life, no matter how often he uses non-professionals for his productions. For Artaud, however, the idea of separating life from art was intolerable. Hence his seminal idea of "the double," "defined as a shadow in the sense of the famous Platonic analogy, indicated the absolute unity of art and life. Expression of this unity was the aim of Artaud's theatre" (Bennison 128). Yet there is another similar notion that Wilson seems to share with Artaud: he believes that there are two kinds of screens through which one perceives the world: an "exterior," through which we experience sensations of the world around us, and an "interior" screen through which we become aware of dreams and daydreams (Shank 126). In his long performances, Wilson argues, "the spectator's interior audial-visual screens become one. Interior and exterior images mingle so that they are indistinguishable" (Shank 126). Reminiscent of the surrealist game "one into another," if there is "life into art" and "art into life," equally there is "an interior screen into the exterior screen" and an "exterior screen into the interior screen." In other words, as the Surrealists did not separate one's life in a state of wakefulness and another of dream, similarly Artaud and Wilson embraced one's whole existence on stage. Drawing on cinematic techniques they both were able to present such wholeness in one's life on stage. Interestingly, they were both attracted to the seventh art as both actors and film directors.[11]

Embracing a new language for the stage "somewhere between gesture and thought" (quoted in Schumacher 101) that has as common denominators the collapse of dialogue and the preeminence of images and dreams, both Artaud and Wilson materialized and extended some of the most crucial surrealist tenets. They materialized them because they accepted the stage as the ideal playground where all experiments were allowed and thus served as a constant source of thrill for every player involved. Such experience became possible due to the fact that both Artaud and Wilson accepted that both play and theatre have something in common: *the mise-en-scène*, and that they also are both intimately related to the metaphor. As Jacques Henriot states in his study *Sous couleur de jouer: la métaphore ludique* (*Under the Color of Playing: The Ludic Metaphor*), "tou jeu possède à des degrés divers ce caractère de mise en scène" (259) [every game possesses at various degrees this character of representation]. Both play and theatre have an intimate relation with metaphor in the sense of transposition or transfer from one plane to another one. For, "la métaphore est un mouvement, une démarche brève et presque soudaine par laquelle la pensée passe d'un plan à l'autre" (268) [the metaphor is a movement, a brief and almost sudden procedure through which the thought passes from one plane to another]. During both theatre and play, Henriot adds, "la transposition affecte l'objet transposé, le rend différent, tout en lui conservant mystérieusement son identité" (264) [this transposition affects the transposed object, it renders it different, all the while mysteriously keeping its identity]. At the same time, this transposition also affects the subject, both player and actor: "c'est le joueur qui, par la pensée, se déplace, change de position par rapport au monde qui l'entoure et à lui-même, adopte un point de vue différent du point de vue habituel, met les choses et se met lui aussi en perspective—se 'métaphorise' en quelque sorte" (ibid.) [it is the player who, through his thought, is displaced, changes position in relation to the surrounding world, adopts a different point of view from the usual one, puts things in perspective and along with them himself/herself—he/she is "metaphorizing" himself/herself somehow]. This process of "metaphorizing themselves" during their games with language enabled both Artaud and Wilson to constantly reinvent themselves, and thus, to reinvent the language of the stage. In the next section of this chapter, I will explore characteristic examples of such experiments with the language of the stage from both Artaud's *Jet of Blood* and Wilson's various performances mainly from his "surrealist" period.

Robert Wilson's play with language

According to Arthur Holmberg, Wilson uses the following 10 strategies to interrogate language: "discarding it; disjunction; discontinuity; the play of meaning; the collapse of dialogue; decontextualization; *reductio ad absurdum*; jamming; dissolving into sound; ritualization" (48). Interestingly, traces of almost all of these techniques can be found in Artaud's *The Jet of Blood*. In the pages that follow, I will illustrate each one of these techniques in Wilson's work juxtaposing them with similar examples from *The Jet of Blood*.

DISCARDING LANGUAGE

Wilson discards language by privileging silence. He called his early works "structured silence" (Holmberg 48). The most characteristic of all is *Deafman Glance*, a silent opera or a "deaf opera," as Aragon named it, or to use Laurence Shyer's words, "a haunting construction of silence and time" (ibid. 6). The following description of the silent murder scene from its prologue that Lawrence Shyer offers, constitutes the signature piece of Wilson's theatre:

> A young black woman in a dark, high-collared Victorian dress stands motionless before a cracked gray wall, her back to the assembling audience. On a white rectangular platform beside her are two small children dressed in white night-clothes—a boy seated on a low stool reading a comic book and a girl asleep on the floor under a white sheet. To her left is a small table, also covered with a white sheet, on which are arranged a pitcher of milk, two glasses, a napkin, a black glove and a large knife whose blade gleams in the light. She moves silently to the table, puts on the black glove and pours milk into a glass. Every action is measured and deliberate, at times unbearably slow. She takes the milk over to the little boy, who drinks. When he has finished she moves back to the table, takes the knife and carefully wipes it with the cloth, and then returns to the boy. With the same care and impassive concern, she slowly pushes the blade into his chest. He falls from the stool without any show of fear or pain and she gently cradles him to the floor, calmly sliding the knife into him one more time. She now returns to the table, pours a second glass of milk and wakes the girl. The sequence is repeated: the child drinks, the glass of milk is exchanged for the knife, the knife pushed gently into the child's side, each task performed with concentrated energy but also a curious inattention (5).

In the original version of the *Deafman Glance* prologue, an older boy named Raymond appears at the edge of the stage during the first murder and begins to scream repeatedly, "the high-pitched, impotent utterance of a deaf-mute. The figure crosses to the boy, puts her black-gloved hand on his forehead and then moves it down over his mouth, stifling his cries" (Shyer 6).

The exemplary in the movements of the female murderer slow-motion technique is also used by Artaud in *The Jet of Blood*, a six-page script that was intended to make a full staging. Also, the screams of the deaf-mute boy when witnessing the ineffable could find a parallel in the words of the young boy who also faces another kind of ineffable: "*An army of scorpions comes out from under The Nurse's dress and swarms over his sex, which swells up and bursts, becoming glassy and shining like the sun*" (Benedikt and Wellwarth 226). As "*if suspended in mid-air and with the voice of a ventriloquist's dummy,*" he cries out: "Don't hurt Mummy" (ibid.). The screams of both young boys, as expressions of speech impediments, interrupt silence when confronting traumatic experiences, making it clear how both Artaud and Wilson discard language. As Nina Sundell states, words are used mainly for their sonic and associative content. Here is a telling description of Sundell's account of Wilson's vision:

> For Wilson, even dramatic structure is based on vision. Neither narrative nor episodic, it consists rather, of the unfolding of a slow sequence of the stage effects: apparently un-related images that seem almost hallucinatory in their vivid strangeness. These images are endlessly astonishing. Rich, lucid, and sensual, they possess a dream-like density and proceed with orderly elaboration. They are connected by a mysteriously convincing inner logic: not the logic of causality, but that of aesthetic coherence. Action and speech or song are subordinated to this visual scenario. Fragmented, dislocated, woven into a recurrent pattern of sound, dialogue seldom conveys literal meaning. Drained of the power to describe, analyze, or communicate directly, words are used mainly for their sonic and associative content. In the absence of normal discourse, the action seems at once incomprehensible and intensely, almost painfully significant. What is memorable is not what happens but what is seen (7).

DISJUNCTION

Wilson's second strategy to interrogate language is disjunction, that is, the disassociation of theatrical codes. His theatrical codes—"lights, costumes, make-up, movement, proxemics, set, sound, language, props—all speak different languages. Each tells a different tale" (Holmberg 53). By deliberately juxtaposing all of them on stage simultaneously according to Lautréamont's example of an "accidental meeting of an umbrella and a sewing machine on a dissection table," he creates unexpected surrealist images (ibid. 175). These surrealist images go beyond a shocking effect—they amplify the spectator's perception. In other words, "Wilson's theatre dramatizes the 'simultaneous perception of multiplicity'—language as both sense and nonsense" (ibid. 57). Layering the theatrical codes against each other, Wilson states: "Usually in theatre the visual repeats the verbal. The visual takes second place to language. I don't think that way. For me the visual is not an afterthought, not an illustration of the text. It has equal importance. If it tells the same story as the words, why look?" (ibid. 53).

Or, on another occasion, Wilson states: "Theatre can be a gesture, it can be a light, it can be a sound, can be a word, can be a color. It can be anything, and there are all of these stratified zones that you are layering together and structuring, *in my case often through counterpoint*" (Schechner, "A Dialogue" 125; my emphasis). A typical example of such disjunction comes from the very successful *Einstein on the Beach*, first performed in 1976, in which the visual and the verbal coexist in disjunction yet strangely interpenetrate and inform each other. In act II, scene 1B, a trial scene is enacted. Lucinda Childs plays a witness who walks to a huge white bed incongruously nestled in the middle of the courtroom, while Einstein plays the violin. Then the witness starts a nonsense monologue (repeated hypnotically 35 times), while "the jury sings a chorus of numbers over Philip Glass's obsessively repeated rhythms" (ibid. 54).

A similar disjunction of the verbal and the visual takes place in *The Jet of Blood* when the young man claims: "Ah, how well ordered this world is!" (Benedikt and Wellwarth 223). Yet, ironically, the facts contradict the young man's statement as the world immediately falls into pieces as the following stage directions illustrate. Disjunction between the verbal and the visual makes its full appearance here, giving room to a larger than life spectacle:

> A pause. Something that sounds like an immense wheel turning and blowing out air is heard. A hurricane separates the two. At this moment two stars crash into each other, and we see a number of live pieces of human bodies falling down: hands, feet, scalps, masks, colonnades, porches, temples, and alembics, which, however, fall more and more slowly, as if they were falling in a vacuum. Three scorpions fall down, one after the other, and finally, a frog, and a beetle, which sets itself down with a maddening, vomit-inducing slowness (Benedikt and Wellwarth 223).

This overwhelming spectacle may have been unimaginable in terms of its *mise-en-scène* in Artaud's time, but not in our time, which boasts an incredibly advanced stage technology.

DISCONTINUITY AND THE COLLAPSE OF DIALOGUE

This term refers to the fragmentation on the level of words, sentences, and narrative. Wilson "violates grammar, semantics, syntax, pragmatics, and the rules of rhetoric that enable a coherent argument to unfold" (Holmberg 58). A characteristic example of such discontinuity is *A Letter for Queen Victoria* (1974), stimulated by Wilson's work with Christopher Knowles. The opening lines of this text have become something of a refrain, having been used by Wilson at a number of his press conferences:

> DIAN DIENA KAASOWRD
> THE DINA DYE KNEE THE DINA
> DYE EYE THE DINA DIE DIE
> DIEING DINA SORE SORE SORE
> THE DINA DYE KNEE THE DINA
> DYE EYE THE DINA DIE THE
> DIEING DINA SORE SORE SOWRDKS!
> THE DINA DINA SORE SORE SOWRDS (Morey and Pardo 143).

The words in this piece do not recount a story; they "do not construct the images of a development that would spell out their meaning. The word is not split between the saying and the said. Language is sound expression that follows the graph of the inner screen" (ibid. 145). The words are like a mantra that hypnotize the audience through both their visual display and their sound patterns.

The collapse of dialogue is the result of such discontinuity. Wilson frequently uses on-stage word games to illustrate the collapse of dialogue, as in his musical *Alice* (1992), in which the title character explores the shifting boundaries between sense and non-sense by playing word games. In this play, Wilson also uses word games to illustrate Alice's traumatic experience as an abused child. Likewise, in the *CIVIL warS* (1981), instead of continuous dialogue, there are tatters of sentences. Here is an example, in which numbers refer to the actors who speak the phrases and E is a recorded voice-over:

> 5E: don't be nervous I'm just scared to death one two three four five six seven eight a thousand dollars / 21: mama / 20: he looks pale / 19: yeah / 18: sister / 17: pages sewn in signature / 19: signatures / 17: daddy / 19: a spot in known / 18: boys / 17: a stopping place / E (*sound of coyote in distance*) / 16: nearest place / 17 please / 18: family makes two no / 19: many others / 10: still pictures are forever records results of family incredible ears in a field of many shows signatures made others still (quoted in Holmberg 58).

This discontinuous dialogue among many voices may not be a coherent logical dialogue but it best captures the tragic outcome of a civil war. The collapse of dialogue that Breton fervently advocated as early as 1924, also makes its appearance in *The Jet of Blood*, as the following example shows:

> THE PRIEST (*in a confessional tone*). To what part of her body would you say you refer most often?
> YOUNG MAN. To God (Benedikt and Wellwarth 225).

This is by no means a coherent dialogue and it resembles two simultaneous monologues that produce misunderstanding, humor, and even blasphemy; yet such misunderstanding allows for a play of meaning, the next common strategy in Wilson's work of questioning language.

THE PLAY OF MEANING

Dramatizing the play of meaning is a key ludic strategy for Wilson through which he shows that meaning is a process and that there might be plural readings of the same words, phrases or sentences. Such is the case of *I Was Sitting on My Patio this Guy Appeared I Thought I Was Hallucinating* (1977), a play that "dramatizes the way consciousness works, constantly slipping back and forth between different levels of reality—perhaps one should say levels of unreality" (Holmberg 61). According to Stefan Brecht, in this performance, Wilson "built up a powerful image of a lone individual, of the autism in all of us, of someone beset by encroaching shadows, or simply by too many concerns, harassed to the edge of disintegration, or rather, not of any individual, but of that state" (380–81). In the first act of this play, Wilson delivered the following discontinuous, stream-of-consciousness monologue: "I was sitting on my patio this guy appeared I thought

I was hallucinating / I was walking in an alley / you are beginning to look a little strange to me / I'm going to meet them outside / have you been living here long ..." (ibid). In the second act the same monologue was delivered by Lucinda Childs, who directed it herself. The result was that she generated completely different meanings and emotions to the point that the audience hardly believed they heard the same monologue twice. "Movements, gestures, tone of voice, music, lights, costumes—all these paralinguistic systems of communication shifted the semantic weight and destabilized the texts' meaning" (ibid. 61). The same play of meaning also exists in the following scene from *The Jet of Blood*:

> THE YOUNG MAN. I love you, and everything is beautiful.
> THE YOUNG GIRL (*with a strong tremolo in her voice*). You love me, and everything is beautiful.
> THE YOUNG MAN (*in a very deep voice*). I love you, and everything is beautiful.
> THE YOUNG GIRL (*in an even deeper voice than his*). You love me, and everything is beautiful (Benedikt and Wellwarth 223).

This dialogue is by no means a progressive dialogue. Instead, the voices of the two protagonists progressively shift from a lower tone to a higher one. From the opening of the play, Artaud shows his concern with the physicality of the stage and sets an early example of his attempt to rediscover a "unique language halfway between gesture and thought" (quoted in Brandt 191). Such a concrete language of the stage exists here in the specialized use of intonations applied to the same set of words four times with a slight shift in the grammatical subject of the young man's utterance "I love you," which becomes "You love me" in the young girl's mouth. Without the intonations, a purely theatrical device that stresses the dissolving into sound, and in turn, the young couple's strength and passion for life, the audience would have probably burst into laughter, as the words seem to parody the genre of romances on stage, especially Armand Salacrou's play *La Boule de verre*, as Eva Baranska has convincingly shown. Whether a parody aiming to abolish the ornamental style of acting or not, the audience can detect the play of meaning in this dramatization, residing primarily in the actor's physical means of expression. Such play of meaning is also extended through the other two strategies that Wilson uses to interrogate language: decontextualization and *reductio ad absurdum*.

DECONTEXTUALIZATION AND REDUCTIO AD ABSURDUM

Decontextualization refers to the use of a preexistent text in a new context that renders it strange. For instance, the use of an archaic language in *A Letter for Queen Victoria* served to defamiliarize language. Or the use of a quasi-apocalyptic scene, reminiscent of relevant Biblical passages in the following tableau from *The Jet of Blood*, generates a strange effect on the audience:

> A pause. Something that sounds like an immense wheel turning and blowing out air is heard. A hurricane separates the two. At this moment two stars crash into each other, and we see a number of live pieces of human bodies falling down: hands, feet, scalps, masks, colonnades, porches, temples, and alembics, which, however, fall more and more slowly, as if they were falling in a vacuum. Three scorpions fall down, one after the other, and finally,

a frog, and a beetle, which sets itself down with a maddening, vomit-inducing slowness (Benedikt and Wellwarth 223).

As far as the *reductio ad absurdum* is concerned, Holmberg refers to the questioning of any original use of language by placing at the foreground the cacophony and the banality of everyday conversation, as the famous scene "Chitter, Chatter" from *A Letter for Queen Victoria* exemplifies, in which the cocktail party syndrome is dramatized. More precisely, "[a]gainst a chorus who repeats the words 'chitter chatter,' we pick up rags and patches of conversation: 'it's such a charming place; how very touching; it's slipped my mind entirely; yes isn't it a shame; how dreadful'" (Holmberg 69). As these patches of conversation are put together in the foreground they seem nonsensical but they alert the viewer-auditor to the futility of such an emotionally charged assemblage of words. Perhaps there is no better example of a parallel of *reductio ad absurdum* than the image of the knight calling for his cheese in a threatening voice in *The Jet of Blood*: "Where have you put it? Give me my Gruyère!" (Benedikt and Wellwarth 226). The response of the young man to the priest's cynicism is another example of everyday banalities: "Ah, yes, there we are, that's life! Oh, well, it all goes down the drain sooner or later" (Benedikt and Wellwarth 225). The next strategy of Wilson's undermining of language is jamming.

JAMMING

This term refers to triumph of the interference of many other disturbances over language, thus rendering language unintelligible. Such was the case in *Alcestis* (1999) for which Wilson collaborated with composer Hans-Peter Kuhn who made a collage of voices for this production. Here is how he describes this endeavor:

> I used eighteen speakers. Everyone recorded one word, so every nineteenth word was said by the same person. The sound structure was based, not on the text, but on an acoustic curve: a symphony of vocal sounds. When the ritual started you could follow the words, but it got more and more dense, and in the end it was pure noise (quoted in Holmberg 72).

Perhaps there is no better expression of the experience of death that *Alcestis* represents than this jamming of vocal sounds that end up as pure noise. A similar jamming of natural sounds dissolving any human voice is the following scene in *The Jet of Blood*, described by the stage directions:

> Night suddenly falls. Earthquake. Thunder shakes the air, and lightning zigzags in all directions. In the intermittent flashes of lightning one sees people running around in panic, embracing each other, falling down, getting up again, and running around like madmen (Benedikt and Wellwarth 225).

While sound overwhelms the stage in both Artaud and Wilson, there is another ludic technique that both of them favor: playing with the sounds of words. Perhaps this is why Artaud directs the young boy and the young girl to repeat in different voice inflections the words "I love you and the world is beautiful!"

However, Wilson goes far beyond Artaud in this regard. As Holmberg states, "Wilson toys with words to pulverize meaning into sound" (72). For him "the pleasure of language involves the sensuous experience of sound" (ibid. 73). The words reverberate in the body and in themselves, as they do in this exercise in reverberation, from a text written in 1971:

THE OVER REVERBERATIONS THE BODY
GESTICULATE A LAYERING A RING, A LING
A DING THE OVERREVERBATIONS
THE BODY OVERREVERBERATION A ZATION
REVERBALIZATION A NATION REVERBARAR
ING A RATIONING OF ALL NATIONS
THE BODEE REVERBATES
THE GESTICULATE A LAYERING VIBRATES
A RING A LAYER ANOTHER GESTICULATING
ANOTHER LAYER LAYERING I SING
THE BODY OVER OVER OVER
OVER REA REA REA VIB
THE BODEE GESTICULATE A
LAYERING ARING A LING
THE BODY GESTUKLE YOU LATES
A LAYER THEN RINGS THE
OVER RE BA RATION THE BODEE
REVERBATION A NATION RATIONING
CATIONING THE BODY GESTICULATE
A LAYERING RING SINGING

As Morey and Pardo state, "[i]n the reverberation of the sound through the body, language transformed into waves, into sound strata that seem to weave lines, sound lines" (143). And they add: "The body that vibrates with the sound does not lend its ears to the meaning, it seeks the positions of the word as if speaking in another tongue and listens, listens to its sound" (145). In the above examples, the text, written to be heard, works the sound. The impossibility of picking out a meaning becomes an invitation to linger over the sound:

> a lingering that derives from a concentration on the positions of the body that will make hearing possible, perhaps an also stupefied hearing of an unrecognized term. The movement of the body that is made audible in the voice dislocates the meaning in order to make the word physical, to feel it with the body (ibid.).

In all of these examples language is organized not only by sound but also by visual patterns, functioning thus as "concrete poetry" (Holmberg 45). "By molding language into a pictorial composition, Wilson emphasizes the visual beauty of written script and fuses word into image. … The director focuses on language in its brute physicality" (ibid. 45–6). Both visual and sound patterns lead to the last strategy that Wilson uses to challenge language: the release of its magic. This strategy bridges the gap between Artaud and Wilson. If Artaud expressed the need for the magic of language on stage as early as in his manifesto for the Théâtre Alfred Jarry, Wilson managed to restore "to language its primitive power to make visible the invisible, to reach beyond ordinary experience into extraordinary realms of consciousness where the spirit, instinct with godhead, establishes contact with the divine" (Holmberg 73). Ritual language, stylized and formal, becomes ecstatic, incantatory, magic, for instance, in the use of language in the *CIVIL warS*, in which Wilson incorporates fragments of well-known canonical texts including the Bible, Shakespeare, and the Brothers Grimm to stress one thing: the slaughter of the innocents. In *The Jet of Blood*, Artaud aimed to restore language to its magical power by evoking the apocalyptic, beyond the human scope of events.

Conclusion

All of the above examples of techniques with which Artaud and Wilson in particular played with language, prove that the stage for both of them became a toyland, open to experimentation. In this new realm serious and thrilling games take place that render the experience of the stage for both actors and audience a methectic experience, albeit, a living initiating experience. To use Wilson's own words,

> I think there will always be a place for live theatre … It's a forum where people can come together and share something. … It's a place where madness can happen, and where political ideas can be viewed, or social ideas can be viewed. Aesthetics, Poetry, dance, music, architecture, all the arts can be seen in the theatre, in this forum, in this palace of exchange (quoted in Morey and Pardo 40–41).

In other words, both Artaud and Wilson dared literally to "metaphorize themselves" as actors and directors and ultimately as players on stage. In so doing, they transformed themselves into mediums that revealed to the audience the hidden, encapsulated in a series of images or dream-like visions. Like Nadja and Alice in Wonderland, they both dared to pass "through the looking glass" by experiencing innumerable metamorphoses, having always as their point of departure a game that targeted language. Each one of these games brought them closer to a pre-linguistic stage out of which they felt a language more suitable for the stage would emerge. To use Julia Kristeva's words, it is in such revolutionized theatre "that the mobile *chora* of language is most completely liberated: the word becomes a drive which is thrown out in enunciation, and the text has no other justification than to give rise to this music of pulsions" (quoted in "Subject in Process" 122). By *chora*, a term borrowed from Plato's *Timaeus* to refer to the matrix that existed prior to the formation of cosmos, Kristeva means the pre-linguistic mobile-receptacle of the process prior to the formation of the subject, defined by the body's pulsions and the mechanism of expulsion. Thus, quoting Artaud, Kristeva continues:

> [l]anguage, always and already a detour of expulsion, under the pressure of a renewed expulsion, becomes divided, fragmented, discredited; it is no longer language as such, and can only be understood by "aphasiacs, and in general all the rejects of words and speech, the pariah of Thought." But it is only in this way that it can take on the possibility of presenting matter in discourse: "All matter begins with a spiritual disturbance" ("Subject in Process" 124).

Thus, both Artaud and Wilson redefined the language of the stage, linking it to the actor's body, dream, silence, and images. Therefore, both Wilson and Artaud, like the Surrealists, challenged the dominant culture of the West, founded on rational thought. As Arthur Holmberg claims, one cannot understand Wilson, latter-day incarnation of this tradition (of the Romantics through the Symbolists to the Surrealists), without understanding how he questions the dominant culture of the West—the positivist, rational culture that expresses itself in newspapers, locomotives, and realistic drama (120). In the final chapter, we will examine a different type of stage games that take the actor's physical language to the extremes. I refer to Megan Terry's so-called *theatre games*.

Notes

1 This lecture was entitled "La mise en scène et le théâtre" and was published in the *Nouvelle revue française* 221, February 1, 1932. For more information, see Schumacher 97.

2 This excerpt is from the eight-page pamphlet published in 1928 under the title "The Alfred Jarry Theatre (1928 Season)," included in Artaud, *OC2* 29. The translation here is by Victor Corti from Artaud's *Collected Works*, vol. 2, 26–9, reprinted in *Artaud on Theatre*, ed. Claude Schumacher, 35–6.

3 Brook's production of *Le Jet de sang*, as Günter Berghaus confirms, "has been judged a total flop (Hunt & Reeve 77)." Christopher Innes also offers some details about this production. See *Avant-garde Theatre* 128–9.

4 When John Bell asked Robert Wilson what effect his predecessors had on his work including Louis Aragon who in his famous letter to André Breton talks about his work as the fulfillment of the surrealist project, Wilson answered: "Well, I think the world's a library and that we draw from all sources" (21).

5 The struggle with language in the early stages in the lives of both Artaud and Wilson makes their approximation more relevant.

6 Wilson studied painting under George McNeill at the American Center, Paris in 1964. McNeil was an American abstract expressionist on faculty at Pratt (Fairbrother 110).

7 Gilles Anquetil, the literary editor of *Nouvel observateur* describes Wilson's work as "a meeting of the new world and the old world, of American culture and European art" (Shyer 258). Pierre Gardin describes the first days of Wilson when a guest at his house in Paris: "Bob came and lived in my house for three months and he was always looking through my books on painting. He was very inspired by pictures. He would look at the work of Paul Delvaux and make a scene with a Delvaux look. He discovered, he was surprised. Bob was not really very cultivated but he was intelligent and sensitive. He came to Europe and saw so *many* different things. And he would take from everywhere and put into his shows" (Shyer 259).

8 Wilson talked about Miss Byrd in these words: "[She] talked to me about the energy in my body, about relaxing, letting energy flow through ... she would play piano and I would move my body. She didn't watch ... she never taught a technique, she never gave me a way to approach it, it was more that I discovered it on my own" (Fairbrother 109).

9 I refer to Artaud's text "Toute l'écriture est de la cochonnerie" (All Writing is Filth), published in *Le Pèse-Nerfs* (*The Nervometer*), Leibowitz, August 1, 1925 in the collection *Pour vos beaux yeux*, edited by Louis Aragon. The relevant citation is in Schumacher 23.

10   In 1984, Wilson first staged *Medée* (a baroque opera with music by Marc-Antoine Charpentier and text by Thomas Corneille) and *Medea* (with a libretto by Robert Wilson based on the Euripides play and music by Gavin Bryars, preceded by a prologue constructed from the Heiner Muller texts *Despoiled Shore*, *Medeamaterial* and *Landscape with Argonauts*). For more information, see Morey and Pardo 35.

11   In 1924 Artaud also began a career as a film actor. As Susan Sontag states, "Artaud was never given the means to direct a film of his own, and he saw his intentions betrayed in a film of 1928 that was made with another director from one of his screenplays, *The Seashell and the Clergyman*. ... He continued acting in films until 1935 ..." (84). Wilson, on the other hand, from the early steps in his career, experimented with cinema. His first film, *Slant*, was an abstract film, produced in 1963, approximately 10 minutes long. Since then he has made numerous filmic versions of his theatrical performances including *Deafman Glance* and *Einstein on the Beach*, among others.

5

LUDICS IN MEGAN TERRY'S "THEATRE OF TRANSFORMATIONS"

At the core of the constant search for new forms in postmodern drama is *the notion of play*. Postmodern drama *plays with forms and genres*, and thus, brings about new constellations and opens up new theatrical spaces (Schmidt 69; my emphasis).

I found it fun to play with audience expectations. Change one or two elements of what they were expecting and they may find it fun to reorder their expectations and thus *"get in" on the game* or they may walk out on what they see before them (Megan Terry).[1]

In the previous chapter, Robert Wilson's "theatre of images" or "theatre of vision," which is informed by the surrealist ludic spirit, illustrated how postmodern theatre plays with language, forms, and genres and opens up new theatrical spaces, as Kerstin Schmidt states in the above quotation. Likewise, this chapter will focus on another seminal American postmodern playwright—this time female—in whose work not only affinities with Surrealism have been detected but also in which play is a core element that allows "for playing with audience expectations." I refer to Megan Terry, playwright, director, and actress, whose multifarious theatrical work, both in theme and style, is driven by the ludic principle. In an e-mail communication dated February 17, 2011, Terry admits that "playing games" either athletic or jokes is something that she has inherited from her family[2] and that she has tried to bring all that festive family tradition of fun and laughter generated by playing games onto the stage, since she has "always considered theatre a conservative act, in the best sense of 'conserving' what had gone and what might be going on after the other arts have reached some sort of zenith." Terry's deep involvement in team games has shaped her overall approach to theatre as both a playwright and a director. She sees herself in both those roles as a coach who regulates her actors' energy and plays with the audience's expectations in order to engage it in the game that is the play each time she directs. Indeed, the concept of play is inherent in each one of the three major techniques that constantly reappear in her dramas, that is, transformational characterizations, a montage-like structure, and politically surrealistic satire (Larson 9). It is in the first of these—transformational characterizations—in particular that both the concepts of play and game find all their amplitude and this is why it will be the focus of our attention in this chapter. The choice to include Terry in this chapter, from a pleiad of other American playwrights who also experiment with the concept of play and who have, to a greater or lesser extent, affinities with Surrealism (such as Edward Albee or Sam Sheppard), was dictated mainly by the fact that, in the span of a long and successful career as a playwright, stage director, and actress, Terry never stopped experimenting with the concepts of play and games, on both the level of stage language and that of the actors' body movements, in an ultimate attempt to investigate the function of the ever-elusive "self" in the frame of a feminist agenda. Her "theatre of transformations" (or sometimes "theatre of metamorphoses"), which cannot be imagined without the play concept, best expresses her ties to surrealist theatre.

"Transformations" is of course a term that has always existed in the world of art, known since Ovid's time when he completed his *Metamorphoses* (in 7 A.D.). This work uses the term "metamorphoses" or "transformations" in the sense of "a whole range of wonders" or "miraculous changes," applied to all the stories of classical mythology, and linked together in an artistically harmonious whole (Miller x). This term, however, although it kept much of its Ovidian sense, was enhanced with a new dimension in the Open Theatre of New York, co-founded by Joseph Chaikin and Megan Terry. It refers to an improvisational acting technique developed within the frame of this theatre that meant "the abrupt taking on and dropping of different roles without any accompanying changes in setting, costume, or lighting" (Schmidt 12). The technique itself is said, however, "to go back to the famous Chicago workshop of Viola Spolin, renowned theatre teacher, whose handbook of teaching and directing was soon to assume quasi-biblical status for theatre groups of the time" (Schmidt 12), such as the well-known Chicago-based Steppenwolf Theatre Group.[3] For in her theatre game directing techniques, the word "game" displaced "problem solving," while "the logical, rational brain seeking such information had been transcended by the theatre game focus" (Spolin, *Theater Games* 2). Thus, playing freed both the director and the actors-players "from the fear-producing trap of memorizing, characterizing, and interpreting" (ibid.). Instead, improvisation, intuition, passion, and discovery play major roles in this new directing technique, in which everyone in the same playing space stands *in waiting*. "To stand in waiting is allowing the unknown, the new, the unexpected, perhaps the art (life) moment to approach" (ibid. 4).

Such openness to the unexpected brings Spolin's theatre games close to Surrealism's constant quest for the marvelous, prompted by the play element. One among the great variety of theatre games used by Spolin is the so-called "transformation of relation game." The purpose of this game is "to allow players the exciting experience of the new relationships they are capable of playing," while the focus of this game is "on movement, constant interaction, relation between players within a series of changing relationships" (ibid. 93). In this game, players are not to initiate change but are to let it happen, while dialogue should be minimized since transformation of relation requires a great deal of body movement for the transformation to emerge.[4] Often in playing, sounds such as grunts, shouts, etc. will emerge. Sound in this case is part of the play's rising energy and a continuation of body movement. "In the course of changing relationships, players may become animals, plants, objects, machines and enter any space and time" (ibid.).

Terry was greatly influenced by Spolin's theatre games techniques and applied them to her own theatre of transformations. Richard Schechner offers a telling description of what exactly her theatre contains:

> The basic construction block for *both* playwright and actor is the beat, those discrete units of actions which make up a scene. In transformations each scene (sometimes beat) is considered separately; there is no necessary attempt to relate one scene to the next through organic development: one scene *follows* another but does not logically grow out of it. The relationship between beats, or scenes, is para-logical or pre-logical—a relationship of free association or arbitrary cue ("The Playwright" 14).

This para-logical or pre-logical relationship between the scenes of a play is, I believe, one of the main elements that tie the "theatre of transformations" to the surrealist theatre. In both cases, like dream work, the scenes succeed one another without logical connection, yet they reveal another kind of logic, one that is elicited by the unconscious. Also, like the surrealist theatre, the "theatre of transformations" relies heavily on the visual—as does the "theatre of images"— and, in particular, on games appealing to both the actors' improvisation and the audience's imagination, whether this results from the interrogation of language or from an emphasis on the actors' bodies. In each case, the ludic transformational principle is at stake, finding a precursor in Nadja's transformational game that she performed for Breton's sake.

This chapter will focus on the specific games Terry implements on stage in several of her transformational plays and, in particular, in one that has been acknowledged at several reprises as bearing a surrealist mark due to its fluid structure and its open form—one that "is no longer a consistent set of interrelated units" (Schechner, "The Playwright" 14). I refer to her work *Keep Tightly Closed in a Cool Dry Place* (1967), in which both character and situation constantly change.[5] "In *Keep Tightly Closed* the characters are continually being transformed into other characters, all based on the play's themes of entrapment, escape, torture, and expiation. The play develops through a set of concrete free associations" (Schechner, "The Playwright" 15). This technique I interpret to be very close to the surrealist principle of the "one into another" game that we have explored in earlier chapters. To borrow Schechner's words, "[t]he form of a play thus conceived and acted is one of contained and containing boxes in which the 'lives' of the characters are axes" (ibid. 14). Also, like the surrealist pieces we have examined in the previous chapters, the transformational principle in *Keep Tightly Closed*, "besides questioning our notion of 'reality' in a very graphic way, also raises certain questions about the nature of identity and the finitude of character" (Feldman, quoted in Terry 201). Thus, this final chapter will offer a demonstration of some ludic stage techniques that find their precursor in Surrealism. Mainly operating on the level of the actors' bodies, these techniques challenge our notion of reality, the nature of identity of the character, and the nature of the relationship between stage and auditorium.[6]

The technique of transformations was already introduced, although moderately, in Terry's most famous play, *Viet-rock: (A Folk War Movie)* (1965), a political play overtly against the Vietnam War, conceived out of the rules of the game basketball in terms of playing with the audience's expectations.

Developed in a playwright's workshop at the Open Theatre and premiered at Ellen Stewart's Café La Mama Experimental Theatre Club, this play grew out of improvisation in which stage games play a major role. Opening with a blissful scene where childlike laughter is heard and sounds like when children play vigorous games, and where the actors free their imaginations by immersing themselves in free associations of playtime, this play gradually unravels to reveal the unprecedented cruelty of war. For example, in the opening stage directions one reads: "Playtime material, especially of war games, cowboys and Indians, cops and robbers, should be allowed to come to the surface and explode into sound, sounds of weapons, horses, tanks, planes, guns, troops, orders, marching, bugles, songs, etc." (29). These children's mimicry games are employed in all their amplitude, soon to be equated with the brutal *reality* of war, brought up on stage in a variety of bitter tableaus. The latter, such as fighting on the battlefield, the death of a young soldier, a mother's mourning, a callous sergeant's training of novices, a massive massacre of youth, young students' protests, among others, resemble the cuts of daily newspapers and TV news. In the meantime, still in this opening scene, the actors continue drawing on the repository of children's games. In an instant transformation they play "mamas" and "boys" and experience a "feeling of play, discovery and contentment" (30).

Such theatre games were largely due to Terry's experimentation with children. As she herself confesses, "I ran a playschool in Canada for two years, and I learned a lot about transformations from them" (Hardison Londré 141). In another interview, led by Dinah L. Leavitt, Terry offers more details about the way she incorporated children's games in her theatre of transformations:

> I worked with children for many years, three-and-a half to six-year-olds, and there's no mystery to it. It's just the basic way children play. You just apply the principles of creative dramatics to adult drama and you get a whole new technique, cuttings, a juxtaposition, and it's all jammed together with film techniques, cutting, jump cuts. I said, "What if you do this on stage?" Well, in *Comings and Goings* and *Keep Tightly Closed* you get a new kind of comedy just because of the jump cuts (292).

These theatre games rely on the constant slippage of meaning that is the outcome of the interplay between the imagination of the playwright, the actors, their roles, and the members of the audience. Such a technique "as opposed to a motivationally connected narrative, allows for greater compression, rapid pacing, freedom to digress and comment through counterpoint, and unlimited perspective on the topic" (Hardison Londré 139). As Richard Schechner states, "Miss Terry's plays are made with her actors. They begin as 'notions,' *move through a chrysalis stage of improvisation*, become 'solidified' in a text, and are produced. But this solidification is not final; the plays themselves, like the performances, *evolve*" ("The Playwright" 9–10; my emphasis).[7] I would add that Terry's plays evolve in the same manner as a basketball game evolves, which no matter how well the actors/team players are prepared, they always embrace the moment and inevitably shift focus and thus the audience's horizon of expectations. Talking about the acting technique in *Comings and Goings*, for which every actors needed to know the entire script, Terry explains in her aforementioned e-mail communication: "Just as team players have to know their game, the actors had to be ready to go into the play when the Coach or

Director sent them, picking up their dialogue perhaps in the middle of a sentence that had been started by the actor they were replacing. This is not only fun for the audience; it shows the power of the actors, the power of their belief to be there in an instant, but also their mind power." The essence of this fun creative process that opens itself to the unexpected is reminiscent of the surrealist "small papers" game, which we had encountered in the previous chapters. The final outcome is the product of a gradual change achieved through endless replacements. Such gradual change and development into different forms is well illustrated in one of the most representative of Terry's transformational theatrical works, the one-act play *Keep Tightly Closed*. Like *Viet-rock*, this play was developed in collaboration with the Open Theatre of New York, under the direction of Peter Feldman, and it is devoted to Joseph Chaikin, the leader of the Open Theatre. It premiered at the Sheridan Square Playhouse on March 29, 1965, on a double bill with *Calm Down Mother* and was later produced by the Firehouse Theatre of Minneapolis. This play is animated through the ludic transformational principle and is literally open to the coach's/director's free choice. In its production notes, Terry claims that "[t]he play should be directed literally or as a fantasy or dream" (5). The fluidity of the form of the play therefore opens up many possibilities for the director to play with each one of the aforementioned options and finally choose one of them. The director, in essence, Terry continues, "should decide if a murder has been committed, or, if it is the desire to commit the murder, or if it is a dramatization of relief" (ibid). To understand better how each of these options could work a brief look at the plot is needed.

Keep Tightly Closed: A chain of transformations

The play revolves around three inmates, linked by murder. "Jaspers hired Michaels to hire Gregory to kill Jaspers' wife. ... Gregory botched the job and all three are serving out life sentences. Jaspers wants to force Gregory into signing a confession that would exonerate Michaels and Jaspers" (Schechner, "The Playwright" 12). A series of tortures at the hands of the two other prisoners then begins for Gregory, represented by a series of transformations. These transformations are complemented by mechanical transformations. In the latter, "the actors become part of a machine, interacting with each other and incorporating the dialogue into the workings of the machine" (Walter, quoted in Terry, *Viet-Rock and Other Plays* 207). There are three mechanical transformations in total in *Keep Tightly Closed* as if each one corresponded to each one of the three characters.[8] The first mechanical transformation is "characterized by extreme tenseness, by jabbing and slapping motions. The second is patterned after the animated machines of TV. ... In the last mechanical transformation we tried to inform the machine with human joy" (ibid.). Thus, "the play begins with an archetypal transformation in which the three male actors combine to become a machine" (Keyssar, *Feminist Theatre* 61):

> MICHAELS. Press here ...
> GREGORY. Tear back ...
> JASPERS. To replace ...

TOGETHER (*locking arms*). Insert lip. But we may be opened. But we may be opened. But we may be opened for ...
JASPERS. For inspection (7–8).

The language used in this sequence, as Schmidt suggests, "imitates the sound and working rhythm of a machine; it follows the short, cut-up sequences that Cecelia Tichi has associated with the literature of the so-called machine age," while "the characters' short utterances resemble torn-off parts from an instruction manual" (141). This mechanical transformation that occurs three times is ironically the only one that connects the three prisoners so tightly, to the point that they can be seen as aspects of one personality, and prepares the three initial characters for their final reconciliation scene. As Terry states, "[t]he actors must come to understand that they are connected with one another by muscle, blood vessels, and nervous structure—impulses felt by one member may be enacted by another" (156). These mechanical transformations frame the other "situationist"[9] transformations in the sense of "created, organized moment(s)" that include "perishable instants, ephemeral and unique" (Hammond 1). Or, to borrow the definition of the *Situationist Manifesto* of the Situationist International, these "situations are the realization of a better game, which more exactly is provoked by the human presence" (Thompsett 1). In Terry's case, the situationist transformations are constructed indeed by the human presence and seem to be avatars of the same theme, that is, of a torture scene, with the exception of the last scene, which is an expiation scene that makes up for all the previous scenes. In these situationist transformations the interesting thing is that the three characters seem to play self-consciously at their various roles all the while keeping their initial identities, as they continue calling each other by their real names, although the tone of their voices or their body gestures change. This theatrical device successfully displays the double plane on which play in general operates. For what reason the three characters engage in such a self-conscious ludic activity remains ambiguous. Do they enjoy playing the "other" (as do Breton's Nadja, or Martha and Yves in Valaoritis's *The Nightfall Hotel*), in order to escape the boredom of their prison cell by amplifying their space? Or, on the contrary, do they find the perfect tool to achieve their goals by exhausting the others' ability to play? A closer look at the various transformations, both mechanical and situationist, that Terry introduces in *Keep Tightly Closed* will better illustrate their inherent ludic character, their role in the play, and their impact on the audience; and ultimately, the way they call for a redefinition of theatrical "praxis" on the basis of ludic strategies.

MECHANICAL TRANSFORMATIONS VERSUS SITUATIONIST TRANSFORMATIONS

Keep Tightly Closed opens with the aforementioned first mechanical transformation (7–8) and after this scene Jaspers tries to persuade Michaels to torture Gregory into signing the paper exonerating them of their involvement in the crime plot. It is like an interval with a realistic scene in the jail (8–12). A situationist transformational scene (13–14) follows, in which Jaspers is transformed into General Custer, renowned for his unorthodox methods on the battlefield during the Civil War as well as for his wild fighting of Native Americans. Also, Michaels is transformed into a bluecoat and Gregory into a Native American chief, his hands and feet tied. With this first non-mechanical transformation the essence of each one of the inmates does not really change, since Jaspers is the initiator of the torture, Michaels is his medium of torture, and Gregory is the receiver of the torture. His stubborn claim, "I will never sign the treaty" (13), echoes his repeated claim, "I won't sign" (35). By this association Terry offers a harsh look at America's history, while illustrating more vividly what each one of the three characters represents in the play.

After a second realistic interval (14–18) during which Jaspers and Michael discuss the way in which they will make Gregory sign the paper, Gregory is shaken by Michaels and is asked to share his dream with them. The dream sequence that follows in this realistic scene, like "one into another," lies between reality and dream. It suggests the way Gregory committed the murder of Jaspers' wife— a murder that appears more like a sexual crime/rape that still excites Gregory, as in the end he climaxes and lies back moaning under his blanket.

The next scene (19–20) is not perceived immediately as a transformational scene but as another interlocking scene in which Gregory narrates a story about a girl (not necessarily the one he murdered in his dream) who accidentally drank water containing a snake egg that led to her death. Although it is difficult to decipher what lies beneath this story, the fact that the scene ends as a transformational scene in which Gregory hisses and moves in a snakelike fashion suggests that he is perhaps, metaphorically speaking, the snake that grows out of the girl's belly, forced, ready to "bite" those who force themselves upon him, as Jaspers and Michaels do.

Next is the second mechanical transformation (20), which has the same rhythm but, in addition, is composed of segments of commercials advertising mechanical products. Fragments, such as "Versatility of operation," "Easy to get at mechanism," "SAFE," "Self-closing," etc. are the commands of this mechanical transformation, which ends with the words "Self-closing"—a sharp contrast to the closing lines of the first mechanical transformation, which referred to "an opening for inspection." The next scene is a realistic one (20–23) in which, once again, Jaspers in an authoritative voice tries to force Gregory to sign the paper despite the latter's refusal.

There follows another transformational scene (23–6). Here Jaspers becomes a 15-year old English lad, dying in the swamps of Jamestown, Virginia. Michaels is one of Jaspers' dying colleagues and Gregory is Captain John Smith. The latter is seen bringing water to the two dying members of his expedition, while Jaspers has hallucinations. He sees a ship carrying Queen Elizabeth come to save them. In the end, all three are covered by the blanket. They become another semi-mechanical transformation as their movements are mechanical and well coordinated but the words they cry out are full of philosophical meaning, such as "Dust to dust, ashes to ashes" (26). These words soon are parodied in the following reversal: "Asses to asses, dust to dust" (27). Then they quickly lock arms under their blanket and sing. This transformation ends with Gregory trying to swallow the (unsigned) paper, thus preparing the audience for a new transformational scene.

Next comes what I refer to as the drag queen scene (27–30), in which Gregory tries to swallow the paper, which is now a love note addressed to him, written by another inmate in a neighboring cell. Jaspers and Michaels again conspire against Gregory and tease him to the point that he should feel "small." The interesting thing here is that the characters are aware of their true selves and they make explicit references to their prison cell. Therefore, one gets the impression that all three of them are playing at being drag queens as part of their torture game against Gregory, as depicted in the next scene as well.

This next scene is another transformational scene, in which the drag queen scene becomes one involving movie gangsters (30–36); Michaels talks as a movie gangster but the topic is again the description of the murder of Jaspers' wife. Michaels exchanges insults with Gregory until he annoys Gregory by repeating exactly the same words Gregory says, as in the following example that seems another form of torture, reminiscent of Breton's example of the Gang-syndrome use of language. The only difference here is that such use of language is deliberate and aims to exhaust the interlocutor's patience:

GREGORY. My voice is not high.
MICHAELS. My voice is not high.
GREGORY. It's not.
MICHAELS. It's not (33).

This repetitive talk continues until Gregory breaks into sobs and Jaspers joins their game as Bogart or Cagney playing the role of a referee between Michaels and Gregory. He tries another game with Gregory: to ally with him against Michaels in order to make him sign his confession. The scene ends with Jaspers wondering what his wife would have felt at the moment of her murder. His words lead logically to the next scene in which Jaspers is transformed into his wife, working in the kitchen rolling out pie dough, and Michaels becomes his eight-year-old son, Richard, and Gregory plays the criminal who holds the cord used in the murder (36–9). The scene ends with an exhausting fight between Jaspers and Gregory enacting the strangling of Jaspers' wife.

The next scene is a realistic one again in which Jaspers feels guilty for having hurt Gregory, while seeking Michaels' company in his bed. Michaels surrenders and Jaspers is sexually aroused under his blanket and at that moment he delivers a delirious speech confessing that he felt suffocated by his wife's presence: "I could no longer be a whole man" (41).[10] This talk ends with a verbal fight between Jaspers and Michaels, who accuses the former of being a failed lawyer who has lied to him. This makes Jaspers lean toward Gregory, whom he asks not to sign the paper because he has changed his mind; it is now Michaels who should be convicted alone and therefore he should be the one to sign the confession to exonerate the two of them. When Gregory asks him how he will change Michaels' mind, he answers: "The same way I convinced you. Come I'll teach you" (44). It is the end of this scene that leads to a new transformational scene in which Jaspers becomes a priest and the two others altar boys (44–8). He delivers his sermon in a confessional manner that leads him to a physical collapse that, in turn, leads to a new transformational scene.

In this new scene, Jaspers is the father while Michaels becomes his eight-year-old son, Richard, and Gregory his 10-year-old son, Mark. The two sons support their father by talking about their dead mother in terms of her finding peace in heaven. This scene functions on at least three levels: first, it plays on a symbolic level in which Jaspers is the Father/God; second, Jaspers is the father of the two children; and finally, Jaspers is the imprisoned lawyer who plays with the two other roles to find and console himself. This scene on the one hand ridicules Christian sermons, but also shows the despair of these three men who are in need of expiation and consolation. In such despair, the final scene comes as the only consolation by the mechanical transformation in which all three men roll like a machine wheel (48). The difference between this and the previous mechanical transformations is that now it turns to an entropic situation, as the following lines illustrate:

> TOGETHER. AND roller and roller and roller
> AND rocker and rocker and rocker
> AND roller and roller and roller
> AND feeder and feeder and feeder
> AND roller and roller and rocker! (48)

Compared to the two previous mechanical transformations, in which the machine opened for inspection and was then self-closed, this one focuses on one part of the machine: a machine wheel that rolls over to stop at a position directly facing the audience, with Jaspers impersonating this part of the machine wheel and addressing these words to the audience: "This side should face you!" As an attorney, Jaspers implicates the audience dynamically in their continuous transformative stage game.

All these transformations are in fact mimicry games that operate on the level of imagination, both the actors' and the audience's, since there are no props available except for a blanket that functions as a symbolic stage curtain that covers and uncovers the various transformations. Otherwise, the entire work is the work of the imagination, supported by the appropriate language and the actors' suggestive body movements. What the three characters in essence achieve is what Nadja does in her own game, except that her own transformations are not visible to the audience, but are assumed from the moment she states them. Instead, in the case of Terry's characters, not only do their mimicry games become vivid on stage with a minimal change of stage setting, but their games are collective and not individual. They are coordinated.

What is it that really happens in all these mimicry games that constantly transform characters into other characters? And why do they undertake such games? First, these efforts show the self's desire to escape from an unsatisfying static self. At the same time, they jump from one state to another, and then again to another, where reality shifts to another reality. Each self gains a new self and although one would think this protean transformation is an indication of *loss* of the self, it might actually be proof of the opposite: that the self finds its true identity only through experiencing multiple selves, just like Nadja does when acknowledging her endless successive "playing the other" through her game. This fluidity of self is the ultimate gain of these ludic transformations and is perhaps the main common element that both Terry's theatre of transformations and the "one into another" surrealist game embody. The concept of game not only liberates the actors and the characters from their physical constraints, but also allows them to explore new facets of their own selves, crossing borders of gender, time, and space, and ultimately changing them. As Joseph Chaikin explains, "[i]n former times acting simply meant putting on a disguise. When you took off the disguise, there was the old face under it. Now it's clear that the wearing of the disguise changes the person. As he takes the disguise off, his face is changed from having worn it" (quoted in Schlueter, 166).[11]

According to Schechner, Megan Terry in particular accomplishes three functions by using the liberating path of transformational games: "They explode a routine situation into a set of exciting theatrical images; they reinforce, expand, and explore the varieties of relationships among the three men; they make concrete the fantasies of the prisoners" (quoted in Schlueter, 164). I would add that they explore, in a very innovative manner, feminist issues by pinpointing key themes such as rape, crime, the relationship between men and women, and sexuality, among others. By eliminating the female element from the stage, Terry attempts an anatomy of male behavior in relation to the absent, yet omnipresent, female presence. As Schlueter argues, "Terry's understanding of transformational drama as more than an acting exercise, as an opportunity to explore with intelligence and with force the modes of self-definition in a contemporary arena, helped move American theatre beyond the cliché" (169). In *Comings and Goings* and *Calm Down Mother*, feminist issues are placed in the foreground. Here, the transformational technique is explicitly placed in the service of the feminist agenda, enhanced by the techniques used by a coach in a basketball or baseball game.

Calm Down Mother: A Transformation for Three Women

This is the first of Terry's transformational and dream dramas. It was produced by the Open Theatre and premiered in March 1965 at the Sheridan Square Playhouse in New York. The play consists of a series of seemingly non-linear, random, abstract juxtapositions, not prompted by cause-and-effect, very similar to the surrealist juxtapositions. It is organized in seven snapshots in which the three characters (woman #1, woman #2, and woman #3) initially unite as an organic whole in the form of a plant. They separate from one another, only to end up as another unified whole, yet this time dehumanized and mechanical, as that of a dishwasher. The latter is a mechanical transformation that appears in sharp contrast to the initial organic transformation of the three anonymous women/team-players, reinforcing the idea that that initial plant is "an emblem that parodies the notion of organic form" (Larson 226). In fact, the play could be interpreted as a parody of the entire issue of creation and procreation associated with women's bodies. For this reason, the seventh of the extant scenes is also significant, referring as it does to the seven days of Creation. In short, nurture versus nature debate, a hot topic of the 1960s, is represented here in an experimental way. In the meantime, the three women are transformed into numerous other characters in a variety of situations, in which each one of them lays bare some aspects of the ever-pressing feminist issues that surpass the obvious issue of maternity, and are at the heart of women's concerns. Issues such as their coping with sex, pain, aging, loss, or anger come to the forefront in each one of the seven tableaus that Terry captures in this one-act play. I have named the tableaus as follows, according to the main motif or subject matter with which each one of them deals: a) the "plant" scene, b) the "hair" scene, c) the "I want to hit" scene, d) the "cancer" scene, e) the "nursing home" scene, f) the "call-girls" scene, and g) the "contraception" scene.

In the first scene, the three women are clustered together to suggest a plant while a taped recording is heard covering the scientific topic of the genesis of the world out of three one-celled creatures that float under the sea, fighting ceaselessly with the waves, until the moment they take root on the shore. With this minimal device the three-woman-plant is put into context while their unison-separation, along with their fight against external forces, will remain basic thematic axes around which all the following scenes will revolve. An interesting movement happens in this first scene: as a tornado uproots and splits the plant, two parts fall away and the third one stretches toward the sun in joyous wonder. Woman #1 then emerges, introducing herself as Margaret Fuller:

> MARGARET FULLER. I am Margaret Fuller. I know I am because ... "From the time I could speak and go alone, my father addressed me not as a plaything, but as a living mind." I am Margaret Fuller. I am Margaret Fuller and I accept the universe! (279).

This is indeed an unexpected turnout. Where one would expect a primitive creature rising out of this primordial plant, one sees a fully self-aware female creature, the nineteenth-century literary critic and author, Margaret Fuller. Her name forms a pun on the full and intense personality of this historical feminist figure who proudly claims that because her father addressed her as a fully emancipated mind and not as a plaything, she is now able to accept the universe. To this boisterous claim of hers the other two women respond in a ritualistic, chorus-like voice: "... you had better. Better grab this universe, little daughter. Grab it while you can. You had better, you had better. You had better grab it before you melt" (280). These feminist lines obviously are addressed not only to Margaret Fuller but to the audience as well, who, as Terry describes it, is "in play," as it is seated in two opposite sides, as in a basketball game: "As they watch the action, they are seeing the reaction of the opposite audience" (e-mail communication).

After a brief freeze, the second tableau takes place in a delicatessen in Brooklyn. There, the first woman becomes Sophie; the third woman becomes her sister, Esther; and the second woman is transformed into a 19-year-old girl with thick hair, ordering ale. Her hair leads Sophie into a deep reverie of her mother's hair and of her own hair, which is missing due to anesthesia from open-heart surgery:

> SOPHIE (*smiling*). It's just like ... you see, your hair ... it's just like Mother's was. Just like it. Same color even. ...
> (*Reaching toward the GIRL'S hair*) My hair was like yours ... but now? (*She shrugs*). Surgery. (*She nods*). Major operations (280).

In the girl's hair Sophie finds the umbilical cord to her mother and a bond to her own previous self. The hair, symbolic of feminine beauty, leads to "her," the archetypal feminine figure of affection; all three women strike and comb each other's hair in this scene. This is how the second scene ends, and the third emerges out of it as an interlocking scene where the girl suffocates and addresses her anger directly to the audience. This is the "I want to hit" scene in which each one of the three women express her rage against anything that goes wrong in her life, sometimes not clearly defined as the following speech of the first woman illustrates:

> WOMAN ONE (*During this speech the other women run their hands together and hiss*). I want to hit. (*She doubles her fist*) I want to hit! (*She brings her fist up and shows it to audience*) I want to hit. I WANT TO HIT! (*She paces back and forth slamming her fist into the other open palm*) Hit, hit, hit, hit, hit, hit! Bang, screw! Screw this hitting (282).

It becomes clear that the audience is no longer safe when witnessing such aggressive confessions. This direct presentation of emotion is reminiscent of the goals of the Théâtre Alfred Jarry; this desire for aggression from the first woman is fulfilled when she beats down to the floor the third woman, who is being assisted by the second woman. This ends the third scene and leads to the following one, as Women #1 and #2 jump up and down, landing flat, making loud thumping noises, suddenly changed into New Yorkers in a charming flat. This is a rather realistic scene, like a soap-opera; Nancy from Oklahoma is visiting her sister Sally in New York. The latter started drinking heavily after her last divorce, following in her alcoholic father's footsteps. Now Nancy informs her of another disaster in their family: their mother has just been diagnosed with "terminal bone cancer"—a fact against which Nancy rails, frustrated at its unfairness. It is interesting to notice in the "cancer" scene how the value of woman in general is praised in direct contrast to man's value. For instance, Nancy speaks highly of her mother as courageous and a fighter, while she disdains her alcoholic father who gets all the attention because he feigns a heart attack:

> NANCY. Mother ... it's "terminal bone cancer." Sal, it's not fair. It is not fair. She's such a fighter. My God, she began a whole new career when dad retired to his bottle of booze. No training, only her guts ... good taste (284).

Nancy cannot cope with the idea that her mother has only 180 days of life left:

> NANCY. ... Oh God, Sal, how am I going to stand it? I'll be dying for her every day, every goddamned day from now till ... till ... (285).

At this point, the two sisters embrace and freeze while a new snapshot appears with the third woman speaking to the audience a kind of lament for lost youth, a snapshot that naturally leads to the next scene, "the nursing home" scene. Here, Woman #1 and Woman #2 become Mrs. Tweed and Mrs. Watermelon, residents of the nursing home. Mrs. Tweed starts their conversation in this way: "Ah, yes, Mrs. Watermelon, and the days go by and the days go by and the days go by and the days go by, and by and by the days go by. My God, how the days go by!" (285). These repetitive words convey a sense of boredom and frustration for Mrs. Tweed who soon gets angry at Mrs. Watermelon and threatens to have her relatives "commit" her to an institution, while she is already "committed."

Their entire conversation, at times indirect—"often expressing meaning through the sounds of their words rather than from any meaning intrinsic to the words themselves" (Larson 230)—and at times showing the marks of senility, evoke the audience's pity for the old women. These feelings become accentuated when their nurse, with her flat, mechanical voice and her cold, professional smile, enters with a tray to feed them their regular cream of wheat. "The scene turns surreal when the old women claim their food is worms. Also, they claim the nurse is worms. It links directly to the 'war is worms' scene in *Viet-rock*" (ibid.). This extended metaphor is a great application of the so-called surrealist metaphor, as Michael Riffaterre has defined it, in the sense of a cluster of images that all stem from an initial image. After this vivid metaphor it is not difficult for the audience to accept the two women's change to a mechanical transformation: a subway door that opens and closes while the two women chant the following motto 11 times in a chorus-like voice: "Please keep your hands off the doors" (287). These words become meaningful when read as a reaction against the previous extended metaphor of "worms." It is a protest claiming the old women's need for dignity and respect. The subway door alludes both to the underworld and the underground, the natural environment of the worms. The two old women's chant becomes, then, a claim for life despite their old age. Also, their chant, seen in light of the "war is worms" of *Viet-rock*, becomes another outcry of protest similar to the protest of the young student in this anti-war play.

From old age there is a return to young age when in the next scene the three women are transformed into three call-girls, Momo, Felicia, and Inez. They are in a lush apartment, dressing and applying make-up. Momo and Felicia are constantly bickering with each other, revealing the gloomy conditions of their life, while Inez tries to calm them down. It is here that the phrase "Calm Down Mother" occurs for the first time. It is spoken by Felicia to Inez when the latter threatens to tell everything to their pimp, Ricky. Of course, Inez is not their mother, but she is responsible for the other two call-girls assigned to work with her by their pimp. As Larson states, here "Terry insinuates that mothers are often responsible for training their daughters to be a 'legitimate' or socially sanctioned call-girl" (231). Larson's statement is strengthened by the following, sado-masochistic scene in which Momo and Felicia, as daughters who have regretted their behavior, ask Inez for a spanking:

> INEZ. I should blister you till you couldn't sit down.
> FELICIA (*Turns her bottom up for spanking*). Do it. We're bad. Bad, bad girls.
> MOMO (*Nearly on her knees, she does the same*). Bad, bad, bad, we should have a spanking (289).

In this controversial scene, two "surrogate daughters" behave in compliance with an old code of decorum, consisting of self-discipline and acceptance of punishment. Yet in their act of compliance a reaction on their behalf is natural. Such controversial behavior is blatantly seen in the clash of the two girls' locutionary and perlocutionary acts, reminiscent of Victor's similar behavior in *Victor or Children in Power*. For instance, there, Victor is aware that he is acting as a bad boy; nevertheless he deliberately breaks the Sevres china. Here, Terry poignantly criticizes the old-fashioned system of education passed on for centuries from mothers to daughters, according to which a daughter must always be attentive, disciplined, and obedient. Again, the substitution for a real mother by a "surrogate" mother in the world of call-girls magnifies Terry's intentions for parody. This "call-girls" scene builds to a snapshot in which the three women alternately repeat the words "You've been found" and "Have confidence:"

> WOMAN ONE. Have confidence.
> WOMAN TWO. Have confidence. You've been found.
> WOMAN THREE. You've been found. Have confidence.
> WOMAN ONE. Have confidence. You've been found.
> WOMAN TWO. You've been found. Have confidence.
> WOMAN THREE. Have confidence.
> TOGETHER. You've been found! (289).

Notice in these words how each woman takes up where the other woman stops, as if it were a team game. As these words echo again and again in the audience's ears, despite their truncated way of being uttered, they are linked with a cause-and-effect conjunction in the following manner: "Because you have been found have confidence." Such advice implies a mistake or a false step in each woman's behavior that has been brought to light, but because of "a merciful system" they should have confidence. It seems that such advice falls into the same pattern of behavior that we detected in the spanking snapshot of Felicia and Momo. The repetition of the same words reinforces the idea of these women being brain-washed into believing in the system of behavior bequeathed to them, according to which women should be quiet and disciplined and, if possible, confined in the household. At any rate the culminating moment of this scene is suggested by the snapshot during which the three women assume positions of cooperative dishwashing at a tenement sink.

Out of the "call-girls" scene the last scene of the play—the "contraception" scene—emerges. One of the three women puts the dishes away while trying to read a magazine. Her name is Sue and she is 23 years old. In an angry tone, she slaps down the magazine where perhaps she has read something about the use of birth control being wrong. In fact, she is trying to convince her sister, Sak, and their mother that there is nothing morally wrong with using birth control. To her conservative mother's words, "The Bible says you shouldn't cast thy seed upon the ground," Sue replies:

> SUE. See, I got enough eggs in me for thirty years, see. That's one a month for thirty years. Twelve times thirty is 360 eggs. Three hundred and sixty possibilities. Three hundred and sixty babies could be born out of my womb. So, if I don't produce each and every one of them, which is a mathematical impossibility, should I go to hell for that? ... And you two! You sit there in the church every Sunday, kneeling and mumbling and believing all that crap those men tell you, and they don't even know what the hell they are talking about. And I'll bet you don't know what I'm talking about. Because I'm the only one in this whole carton of eggs what's got any brains. And I'm taking my pills and I ain't kneeling on any beans or babies' brains to make up for it (292–3).

Despite her angry rant regarding a woman's right to use birth control, Sue is nevertheless still on the receiving end of her mother's disapproval. Her mother angrily tells her "to pack her things" and "pack herself" (292). Here Terry overtly places in Sue's voice the prominent feminist ideology of the 1960s, while showing at what cost each woman's revolt came; she had to pay dearly for her radical beliefs about her emancipation, including issues of sex and birth control. The play ends with an overt embracing of the feminist ideology as all three women resume their initial positions as Woman #1, Woman #2, and Woman #3; they address the audience with an incantatory speech that celebrates their bodies:

> WOMAN TWO (*On sides*). Our bodies
> TOGETHER (*Back on bellies*). Our bellies
> TOGETHER (*On bellies*). Our bellies
> WOMAN THREE (*On sides*). Our bodies
> TOGETHER (*On bellies*). Our bellies
> WOMAN ONE (*On breasts*). Our funnies
> TOGETHER (*Bellies*). Our bellies
> WOMAN TWO (*Sides*). Bodies
> WOMAN ONE (*Bellies*). Our eggies
> WOMAN THREE (*Bellies*). Our eggies
> WOMAN TWO (*Bellies*). The eggies in our beggies
> WOMAN ONE (*Sides*). Are enough
> WOMAN TWO (*Sides*). Are enough
> WOMAN THREE (*Sides*). Are enough
> TOGETHER (*Turn their backs on audience*). ARE THEY? (293).

In this final speech, the subject of creation and birth is treated by the three women in a funny, yet decisive manner. Emphasizing those of their body parts responsible for giving birth they conclude that their bodies and their eggs "are enough." As Larson states, "[t]he whole play comes together at that moment, as if the word 'enough' contained a magic which could fuse all the elements, both physical and verbal, both fictive and direct, both thematic and ideological, into one experience of wholeness. It is a hollow wholeness, a parody of organic form" (233). Indeed the word "enough" appears here in its double meaning, both positive and negative. As a positive value, the word "enough" reassures the audience of the three women's sufficiency, in their bodies and their ovaries, for guaranteeing the continuity of life, while giving them the breath of managing their own lives according to their will. As a negative value, the word "enough" implies the burden, which the women's anatomy has created for them, imposing on them ever-expanding duties of which they "have had enough" and which they finally realize it is time for them to control. Both these meanings are passed onto the audience in a very witty manner. I refer here to the concluding question addressed to the audience (which is in upper case letters in the script): "ARE THEY?" The significance of this question is best grasped if we think in terms of Roman Jakobson's six functions of language: emotive, referential, poetic, phatic, conative, and metalingual. The question stresses both the emotive and the conative functions of language, thus creating an open channel between the addresser(s) and the addressee(s). In other words, this question—stated so stubbornly by all three women—is not really seeking an answer, since they all have shown themselves quite determined in their decision to self-manage their bodies. Rather, it seeks the audience's active affirmation and active involvement in this major feminist concern. By addressing this open question to the members of the audience, Terry stresses the conative function of language by redefining the role of the audience, which, for her, should be politically engaged and responsible for decision-making. For Terry, the audience is not a passive congregation that seeks entertainment, but a body that must be brought to an inquisitive state and political engagement. Therefore, *Calm Down Mother* is not at all a "pure, de-politicized play," as Larson states (226); it may be less overtly politicized than *Viet-rock*, for instance, but it is indeed politicized. After all, the feminist issues that were brought to light in this analysis were an integral part of the broader political discourse that was at the heart of that very distinct decade, the 1960s.

The same feminist issues are also treated in *Comings and Goings: A Theater Game*, but in a subtler and funnier way. It is "Terry's transformational playwriting at its purest" (Larson 247). I would also add that it is the most representative of Terry's experiments with the ludic principle, as its subtitle makes explicit— a new theatrical genre which she calls "theatre games." This new genre is "a formalization of theatre games into viable play structures such as *Comings and Goings*" (Terry, *Viet-Rock and Other Plays*, 1).

Comings and Goings: A Theater Game

"Terry has said she wrote *Comings and Goings* as a gift to the actors of the Open Theatre because they had become such excellent virtuoso performers" (Larson 246). To borrow her own words, "[t]his play is meant for both actors and audience to be an enjoyment of technique—pure virtuosity on the part of the actors. The fun of the play is in how much and how involved the audience gets" (*Viet-rock and Other Plays*, 113). To ensure this effect, Terry equated the performance of this play with an actual game that ingeniously combined all of the four elements that we have encountered in Caillois' categorization of games: *alea*, *agon*, *mimicry*, and *ilinx*. The following rules, according to which Terry directed this play at the Café La Mama Experimental Theatre Club in 1966, leave no doubt about the unique way in which all the aforementioned elements of play were embedded in her performed play:

> We played it with *a small card* on which all the actors' names were printed. *A wheel was spun* by a disinterested party at intervals of thirty-five to ninety seconds. A name was called out and one actor *ran into the play and another actor ran out*. … We staged the play in the center of the café, with a small bench for the men on one side and another for the women on the opposite side. The person who spun and called sat in full view of the audience and *behaved with the attitude of an official at a tennis match or basketball game*. … I like to think of the play *as a trampoline for actors and director* (ibid. 113–14; my emphasis).

All the emphasized words in the above quotation clearly illustrate how the elements of chance, vertigo, mimicry, and contest are intertwined in this new theatrical genre of Terry's, surpassing Spolin's theatre games. This new technique, Terry admits, "[b]esides being great fun to watch and do," "can train the actor in concentration, focus, flexibility, and ensemble work" (ibid. 113). To better appreciate the effectiveness of this new acting technique and see what a long way it has come, one has to compare it to, and contrast it with, Denis Diderot's ideas about acting in his seminal work, *Paradoxe sur le comédien* (*Paradox on the*

Comedian), written between 1770 and 1778 and published much later in 1830. Diderot encouraged a totally different perspective on the great actor's task: he should be guided by an absolute coldness of feeling on stage and should not live on stage the various roles he has to perform; instead he should be a great imitator of all possible natural states of being, after observing and reasoning about each case: "Celui que la nature a signé comédien, n'excelle dans son art que quand la longue expérience est acquise, lorsque la fougue des passions est tombée, lorsque la tête est calme, et que l'âme se possède" (266) [He whom nature has assigned as a comedian does not excel in his art but when he has mastered a long experience, when the fugue of passions has fallen down, when the head is calm and the soul is master of itself]. Unlike in Diderot's theory, Terry allows her actors not only to live out on stage each role they perform, but also to take risks by getting involved in improvisational games. In essence, what *Comings and Goings* sacrifices in setting and developing conflict, it gains in:

> improvisation, pure spontaneity, and the honesty and intensity of its stage life. As in a game, the actors face each other, not knowing what the other's move will be. When they see the move, they must react to it with a total allegiance to the present moment, for their goal is to live on stage, to solve—without premeditation—the moment-to-moment problems that occur (Larson 247).

The element of surprise for both the actors and the audience is constantly at stake, much like in any surrealist work. Likewise, as in the surrealist plays, there is "no link between the various settings that suddenly erupt and then as quickly disappear" (ibid.). The following pages offer some details that will better illustrate in which scenes actors were involved in their trampoline-like theatrical game.

The first scene shows a man and a woman waking up—the man trying to arouse the woman. To his insistent words, she repeatedly replies, "In a minute." The scene repeats three times and each one of them "are to be transformed *one into the other* without pause" (Terry 115; my emphasis). As Larson states, "[a] major impact of scenes like this is their ability to strip away practically everything except the actor's subtext, which grows and changes as the scene repeats" (248).

The second scene shows He and She in a kitchen.[12] While She washes dishes, He cleans his gun. A dispute starts between them:

> SHE. You don't give me a moment's peace.
> HE. But that's all I want from you. (*He pats her fanny.*)
> SHE (*Slapping him with the dishcloth*). Stop that, you dirty old man.
> HE. I am your dirty old man. Your very own, very dirty old man. Come here. You want to clean me? Come on and clean me good.
> (*He hugs her and she responds, laughing*).

While this scene is realistic, focusing on a couple's daily routine, it suddenly breaks into one of the most unexpected of scenes—one that is "outside of traditional notions of reality" (Larson 248). He and She change into a faulty plug in a wall socket, yet they use realistic language, as in the following example:

> SHE. I can be constant, that's something. (118)

These words have a double reference "to behavior in a love relationship and to a law of electricity" (Larson 249). After all, the power socket alludes to the fact that it consists of a female and male pole.

The above scene transforms into another one in which a drunk female driver runs over the mother of the man who is sitting next to her. The man is furious, propelling the woman toward his car and forcing her head down, to look at the mangled body of his mother:

> HE. There! That's what you've done, you-you-you miserable! (119).

The woman, in a state of shock, is able only to notice that the woman is still holding on to her purse, while the man is about to take revenge on her by jumping on her head.

The next transformational scene is another unconventional one; He becomes a pencil, and She, the list He writes. She speaks it:

> SHE. Take car to be greased.
> Pick up shirts.
> Check on George.
> Go to Joe's workshop.
> Plan the next five years.
> Get new underpants.
> Mail letters on way home.
> Stop at Roger's to get the key.
> Check on Mozart Masses.
> Attend Mr. Jordan's funeral.
> Take car to be greased.
> (*He topples over to land beside her*).

This scene, as Larson states, "indicates that housewives think of themselves as the incarnation of errand lists, a record of petty deeds and not much more" (249).

The following scene is another morning during which She is trying to wake up the He so He is not late for work. This is a realistic scene that depicts in a funny way a couple's daily routine. It is He's use of language that fills the scene with humor as, half-awake, he cannot even articulate a coherent sentence:

> SHE. Honey?
> HE. Arhgghhhh.
> SHE. Alarm.
> He. Grrrrrrr.
> SHE. Get up.
> HE. Uhhhhhhhhhhhhh.
> SHE. Get up.
> HE. Ghhhhhhh (120).

This scene has a logical connection with the following one, in which He complains to She that She has too many expectations of him. He cannot understand what She wants from him, and She is crying:

> HE. Where do you want me? What do you want of me? Backward and forward, you want!
> (*SHE cries.*)

HE. That's what you wanted? That's what you wanted? That's all you wanted. Cry? That's too easy. You can't get out of it that way. It's another trick to get me off the track. I'm going to find out if it takes me the rest of my life. I'm going to find out what it is you want (121).

The misunderstanding between the couple is stunningly illustrated in these words, as well as in the pain He inflicts upon She.

Another confrontation begins between He and She in which the couple acts like kabuki performers. The first time, He asks She where she is going and She replies, "to wee-wee." Then He asks She to bring him a cigarette and She replies, "In a minute." In the second snapshot of this scene, She is asking He where he is going and He replies, "Bowling with the boys." Then She asks He to bring her a cigarette and He replies, "In a minute." These two snapshots should be repeated three times according to the stage directions. Life's ups and downs and the non-communication between men and women is well depicted here.

The next scene is a warm one. He and She transform into American Indians in a cave. She is named Morning Star. They speak in monosyllables. In this minimal scene, Terry captures one of the most tender moments in a couple's life, where He caresses the face of Morning Star, then strokes her hair, and finally He asks her if she prefers love instead of food. When She nods indicating the word love, He puts his blanket around them, "which is their civilization's dawning of erotic love" (Larson 250). Then follows a breakfast scene, which repeats five times in different tones, each time based on a different power relation. It starts casually and realistically, with He naming items he would like to have for breakfast while She, as the waitress, writes down his order and says "Yes" after each item that he orders. Suddenly, at the same café, the waitress and He trade lines, repeating the scene. The waitress, who is doing the ordering, has become the master, and He is the slave. When this rendition is complete, they again repeat the scene. Now the customer does the ordering. This time He is the master and the waitress is the slave.

A fourth repetition of the breakfast scene soon begins, during which He and She act like automata, to end up with a fifth repetition in which "customer and waitress have a symbiotic ecstatic relationship. Played with quiet warmth and secure joy" (Terry, *Viet-Rock and Other Plays*, 128). What can all these repetitive breakfast scenes possibly reveal? To borrow Larson's words, they "reveal several numerous complexities about human relationships, about the constant struggle in which people engage for the upper hand, and the transitoriness of one's personal power over others" (251). After the breakfast scene, He and She become desert wanderers desperately looking for an oasis. When She asks He, "How farther?" He responds, "Only a bit." They soon fall asleep and awaken in an amorous mood.

The next scene is a reprise of the earlier "Where are you going?" scene, in which He and She assume Kabuki postures, only this time their postures are more threatening toward each other. For instance, to each one's anxious question, "Where are you going? Where are you going?" the other replies, "Crazy, wanna come along? Crazy, wanna come along?" (133).

A love scene follows in a kitchen, where He appears after a long time and She welcomes him, during which they lie on the floor and embrace, showing excitement. The next scene takes place in a Hell where He is tormented and asks She—who is playing the God—to send Lazarus and give him some water. When the God denies his request, He begs him (She) again to send him to his home and let him persuade his siblings not to commit the same crimes as he did when he was alive so that they can avoid torture in Hell. Again the God appears merciless, since he (She) has already sent Moses and the prophets to preach faith in Him. This is an unusual setting that ends with a very significant series of hand movements between He and She that reveal all their anxiety about their future after the scary scene in Hell that preceded. He and She read their hands, interlock their palms and look deeply into each other's eyes, as if to suggest their desperate position in this uncertain world. The scene then breaks into a new scene that takes place in a police station.

She is accused of an armed robbery, using her grandson's fake gun. She has committed the robbery at an insurance company for her husband's sake— a husband she has served during all 40 years of their marriage to the point that she even cuts his meat into "small bites." When He, as the policeman, asks her to disclose where she has hidden the money, she refuses, and does so once more when she is asked to identify the items she used during the robbery. This comic scene becomes absurd when she claims that she gave away the money she robbed "in the hand of every bum on Third Avenue" (138). The most absurd part, however, is the scene's ending when She asks the policeman to wear the handcuffs so that she won't have to hug her husband back when he meets her; the scene finally reveals how complicated this woman's marital life is. The policeman now transforms into a comedian with a mike in a night-club talking about an event which occurred in a police station, or in a court room.

During this scene He, the comedian, is attacked by She, who is a drunk member of the audience who is bothered by the way the comedian speaks. Their confrontation ends up with insults on both sides:

HE. Back to your table, cow pie.
SHE. Greaseball.
HE. You're sloppy you have to home permanent your snatch.
SHE. Bastard, bastard.
HE. Beast, beast.
SHE. Bugger.
HE. Bug (140).

Exploding the conventional limitations of drama and pushing her experiment to its farthest reaches, "the rhythm and sound of He's and She's jibes throws them into an unearthly realm. They become galaxies sending radio signals to each other, using a kind of Morse code language that consists of 'bleeps' and 'blinks'" (Larson 254). This non-language, Larson adds, has the capability of communicating intentions, which depend on how the actors use their voices and bodies (ibid.). In the next scene, He and She become members of a cub-scout troop and, after a song, they transform into a new scene. Here She recites to He, who is now a small boy, a story like a lullaby about "the best clam we have ever had" (142).

The next scene shows He and She as American Indians, again in an intimate moment. He is called Red Feather and is about to leave and at this moment a greater understanding between them occurs. In the next scene, She is arriving home after a long time and He, as her father, gives her a tearful welcome. Their very simple, yet suggestive dialogue reveals an intensity of emotions. The scene ends with the daughter asking her father to take the boat out like old times and he nods positively to her. After this tender moment another conflict arises between He and She, as the latter packs her things to leave, while He is unpacking them and repeating that he forbids her to leave him.

The following scene shows He and She near the ocean. There, He asks She to comfort him that she will never abandon him, since they have been together for such a long time. She does so and the next scene follows logically out of this one. In a grassy field, they dance a polka in a joyous courtship. This is one of the most playful moments in this chain of comings and goings, ups and downs in a couple's life, and culminates in a more graceful dance in which all actors participate, singing these lines:

> TOGETHER. Then we'll dip,
> We'll slip
> We'll glide,
> We'll hide.
> We'll slide
> Into love time,
> Into love time,
> Into love time.
> Then we'll dip,
> We'll slip,
> We'll glide,
> We'll hide.
> We'll slide
> Into love time,
> Into love time,
> Into love time.
> Love time,
> Love time,
> Love time,
> Love time,
> INTO LOVE TIME! (150–51).

The play ends with these very optimistic lines. It continues to be one of Terry's most produced plays regardless of time or place. As Helene Keyssar states, "[t]he performance transcends the world portrayed and makes the mode of playing appealing to the spectator" (*Feminist Theatre* 66). Its success lies precisely in the fact that "its theme and its form are inseparable" (ibid. 65). Its theme and its form are, in fact, that of a theatre game and all the qualities of play are embedded in this new theatrical genre that Terry inaugurated with her play. *Comings and Goings* is a play about "role definitions and role change which relies on theatrical role transformations to move the play forward. Each of the mini-scenes presents a moment of encounter between two people, in which the tension of change, of coming and going, is central" (Keyssar, *Feminist Theatre* 65). In 22 scenes of varied length, several of which are repeated up to five times, Terry trained her actors to pay attention to minuscule details, and to convey in a new light even the most banal feelings in a couple's daily life, laying bare the complexities of gender relationships and their relationship to social roles. As Keyssar states, "actors stress the different meanings and infinite variety of interactions possible by varying modes of deliverance" (*Feminist Theatre*, 64). At the same time, she created some of the most original scenes that surpassed the notion of conventional reality, particularly when He and She transformed into objects located from the underground to the Milky Way, from power sockets to galaxies, corresponding perfectly to the title of the play, *Comings and Goings*—"a telling and very precise title for the transformational activities of the play" (Schmidt 150). In essence, the motif of displacement structures this play, as "stage directions urge repetition of some scenes, and require that the entire company be prepared to play any role at any time" (Keyssar, *Feminist Theatre* 65). The experimental and playful character of *Comings and Goings* is also stressed in these words in which Terry herself reminds readers that the number of actors may vary: "We played with three men and three women. But more or fewer would work. It could even be done as a straight transformation play with one man and one woman. The director should feel free to cut any scene he and the actors can't solve" (*Viet-Rock and other Plays*, 114).

In short, this play is the culmination of Terry's experimentation with the play concept. Here, form and content coincide and resume in the subtitle of the play "A Theatre Game" in terms of both content and theatrical genre. Terry realized the crucial role of the play concept in her theatrical work as a resourceful repository of new perspectives and directions in the theatre. In each one of the three plays that were analyzed and presented in this chapter, she made exemplary use of the elements of play and games through the technique of transformations, placing different concerns in the foreground each time. Thus, in *Keep Tightly Closed*, Terry vividly illustrates what Johan Huizinga claims with regard to the element of play: that "play" is not "ordinary" or "real" life, and that it is rather a stepping out of "real life into a temporary sphere of activity with a disposition all of its own," that only children can fully achieve (8). In this way, all three characters—Jaspers, Michaels, and Gregory—(and, through them, the audience as well) are given the opportunity to experience different selves and finally to cope with their true selves. By means of their self-conscious stepping out of "real" life, that of their prison (whether actual or psychological), they are enabled to shed new light on the conditions of their real life. In other words, their constant play of impersonation provides a prism through which their miserable real life is magnified, particularly their repressed sexuality under the weight of consumerism. The surrealist device of "one into the other," in the sense of a double plane of reality, is perfectly fitting here, as it is also in the case of *Calm Down Mother*.

In *Calm Down Mother*, moreover, Terry uses the device of multiple realities and thus of multiple truths in a slightly different manner. She links the reality of a scene with the new one that emerges out of it in a ritualistic manner, which she puts in the service of an explicit feminist agenda. In this way, she confirms Huizinga's statement about play: that it belongs "to the sphere of festival and ritual and lies outside the antithesis of wisdom and folly, and equally outside those of truth and falsehood, good and evil" (9). Indeed, the ritualistic and mystic aspects of play are present in this theatrical work and are stressed at several intervals by the chorus-like chanting of the three women that alternates their transformations. In its closing scene in particular, during which all three women celebrate their body parts in a funny way, in a peculiar dialogic mode, one gets the impression of a purely liberating, carnivalized scene in the Bakhtinian sense.

On the other hand, the ritualistic element of play is absent from *Comings and Goings*, which stresses instead another of its general characteristics as highlighted by Huizinga: its irrationality and its enchantment, with all its paraphernalia of beauty such as tension, balance, contrast, variation, solution, and reduction. All these features are put in the service of vividly illustrating the male–female relationship, which also ranges from irrationality and absurdity to enchantment. Terry, having thoroughly experimented with children's games, is convinced about the inexhaustible potential of the play element, and that is why she offers a new perspective in each one of her plays driven by the ludic element. She never ceased to believe in play and games, and always finds new ways of treating this subject matter. For instance, the game itself becomes the main subject matter in her play *Pro Game* (1974), in which a mother with her three sons gather around the TV to wallow in football. "During the course of the game the family eats, drinks, argues and overindulges while sexual politics stands on its head and consumerism kicks field goals" (Schmidman et al. 77). *Pro Game* was written "in reaction to the football fervor encountered when she arrived in Omaha" (Rose 288). Another of her plays, *Brazil Fado* (1977), shows an American couple on a high platform engaged in sexual sado-masochist games, while on the floor "a team of newspeople, movie stars, Brazilian peasants, and torture police enact recent violence in Brazil" (ibid. 289). Terry always finds inspiration in the play element, even in her most recent theatrical work after moving to Omaha in January 1974 to join artistic director Jo Anne Schmidman as playwright-in-residence at the Magic Theatre. There she materialized what she said in 1968 about the role of theatre artists: "to bring people together for an entertainment, a celebration, a living theatre to put down the fear and anguish that have got too many people in America by the throat" (ibid.). By mastering the onstage games at the alternative Omaha Magic Theatre Terry was able to bring back the fun and the laughter the audience needed, all the while bringing the latter face to face with its inner fantasies, fears, hopes, and desires. In the 1980s and the 90s, in particular, Terry kept playing with and to audiences' expectations through her actors' transformations in particular and her setting of the theatrical space, as she did for example in *Objective Love* (1980) and *Body Leaks* (1990) (see Figures 5.1 and 5.2). The former reworks the old issue of love and the relation between the two genders treated in *Comings and Goings* but this time in a more elaborated manner. Such elaboration is due to the use of multiple actors impersonating He and She and the use of two slide projectors that play with the alternation of a variety of plants and flowers on the two opposite sides of the stage, as well as due to the use of sound jam. Most of all, though, its ludic tone is guaranteed thanks to the game/pun "I object/Eye object" that eventually every actor plays on stage. The goal of the game is to move their favorite flowers-props (made either of paper, wood, silk, wire, ceramic etc.) to a place on the stage that satisfies their eyes and, in doing so, utter the phrase "Eye object," referring to the actual flower standing for an object for the actor's eye/view. As they make numerous attempts to make the perfect choice, the very phrase "Eye object" implies the sentence "I object." It is exactly on this theme/motif that the entire play unfolds ultimately bringing He and She to face each other as one another's respective "eye object" and therefore as the recipients of each other's objection, suggesting their gender-related inherent tensions and oppositions. In the end, He and She, along with all the actors who impersonate them, as if to show their multiple dimensions, agree that "their love is a frisbee." This metaphor, that successfully captures both the frivolous and agon-like relationship between the man and the woman who relate to each other, is prepared by another type of frisbee that endlessly occurs on the level of signifiers and which is reminiscent of the surrealist games encountered in the previous chapters. The entire scene prior to the falling of the curtain of this play is cited below to show how successfully Terry uses a combination of gaming strategies on stage, drawing on both the sports realm and the realm of dialogue:

> HE and SHE face each other. Each is the other's love object. They relate. The following lines are overlapped. But, time may be taken within some lines.
> SHE (*They tango*). You're as macho as split ends.
> HE (*Tango front. They turn to back wall*). You're as sweet as spiked heels.
> SHE. You're as strong as saliva.
> HE (*Tango front. They turn to back wall*). You're as weak as ocean waves.
> ACTOR 5. You're as attractive as Tequila.
> ACTOR 2. You're as handsome as gas and oil.
> ACTOR 4. You're as beautiful as soybeans.
> ACTOR 1. I respect you as much as cancer.
> ACTOR 3. I want you like water.
> ACTOR 4. Your ears are telephones.
> ACTOR 2. You look like withdrawal symptoms.
> HE. You come like a fire engine.
> SHE. You come like a marigold.
> ACTOR 3. Your teeth are a can opener.
> ACTOR 4. Your muscles are tire irons.
> ACTOR 2. Your tongue is calves liver.
> ACTOR 1. Your touch is a dirt bike.
> ACTOR 4. Your nails are Coke bottle caps.
> SHE. Your mind's as fast as a T-V commercial.
> HE. Your ass is Missouri marble.
> ACTOR 3. You talk like a robot car painter.
> ACTOR 4. You kiss like the Half-Price Store.
> ACTOR 2. You smell like cement.
> ACTOR 1. Your hair is astro turf after a mud slide.
> ACTOR 2. Your presence is crazy glue.
> ACTOR 5. Your eyes are methedrine.
> ACTOR 3. You're as smart as Mount Rushmore.
> ACTOR 2. Your blood is full of sharks.
> ACTOR 5. Your mind is the Yellow Pages.
> SHE. Loving you is a hangover.
> HE. Your will is cockroach eggs.
> ACTOR 4. Your laugh is the grave.
> ACTOR 2. Your nipples are vampire fangs.
> ACTOR 5. You're as funny as linoleum.
> ACTOR 1. Your brain has lost weight.
> ACTOR 3. Your skin is Hanscom Park.
> ACTOR 5. Your hugs are hamburger.
> ACTOR 4. You're as faithful as inter-stellar space dust.

ACTOR 2. You're as solid as moonlight.
ACTOR 1. You're as fast as rush hour traffic.
SHE. Your love making is a nest of cobras.
ACTOR 4. Your hips are a hydraulic jack.
ACTOR 3. Your tongue is a snail darter.
ACTOR 2. Your belly feels like aluminum foil.
ACTOR 1. You're as exciting as Sunday morning television.
HE. Your breath is air conditioning.
All actors suddenly sing. "Occupied Territory"
(*Song*)
This is occupied territory
We live in occupied territory.
Are you ready to live
Beyond your fingernail?
There is a vast body to behold—
That body is you. I implore you to swim into the
Mainstream of your own conscious being,
And live in your whole body, too.
Aren't you cramped there under that
Damp, dirty nail? Expand outward into your fist, and
Let your mind exist in
Your chest and rise upward to
The tip of your breast. Ahhhhhhhh yes she feels so good—
And you can feel you if you only would. This is a tiny game,
But it can extend when you are far from me.
Let me hold your hand
And you can live here safely in my land.
I won't give anyone your
Phone number.
But you can call me any time—
Night or day—
And we will—Fling our arms around each other—And lay and lay and lay
And lay and lay
And lay. (*Scene resumes as before*).
ACTOR 2. Your fingers are potato peelers.
ACTOR 3. You sing like airplanes.
ACTOR 5. You're armpits are the Henry Doorly Zoo.
ACTOR 1. Your hands are cowboy boots.
ACTOR 2. Your love making is butter and garlic spaghetti.
ACTOR 4. Your word is armed robbery.
ACTOR 2. Your eyes are grease pits.
ACTOR 3. Your face is a Norman Rockwell Christmas Plate.
ACTOR 5. You cook like Seventy-Second Street.
ACTOR 3. You taste like Comet cleanser.
ACTOR 2. Your mouth is a police car.
ACTOR 1. Your arms are roller coasters.
ACTOR 4. Your toes are whips.
ACTOR 3. Your legs are Carter Lake.
SHE. Your guts are the stock yards.
HE. You're full of Falstaff
(*a local beer*).
ACTOR 3. You're as reliable as the dollar.
ACTOR 2. Your cock is hair spray.
ACTOR 1. Your breasts are thumb tacks.
ACTOR 5. Your love is French fried.

ACTOR 2. Your love is Purina Cat Chow.
SHE & HE. Our love is a frisbee.
*HE and SHE each throw a frisbee into the audience. Smiling, the entire company throw
frisbees to the audience. Music up* (33–7).

"This is a tiny game" the song claims, yet it has redemptive skills. No matter
how logical the images that come out of the spontaneous metaphors uttered in
the above excerpt, one thing remains sure. Their relationship, when conceived
as a frisbee game, gains in authenticity and freedom, as it welcomes both the
calculated preparation and the abandonment to chance, both objectivity and
subjectivity and it involves everyone in the surrounding environment. The closing
scene is characteristic: by throwing frisbees to the audience, an immediate
invitation to play the game is addressed, one that is accompanied by music,
dance, and ritual festivity.

Likewise, in *Body Leaks*, Terry explains, they "played the central action against
one wall of the theatre, but continued around the audience with other actions
and special sections. The audience sat in three rows facing the main wall, but we
also ran around behind them. Many audience members, besides remarking on
aspects of the production, said that they also had the feeling of being hugged.
It made me very happy to hear that" (Communication of 17 February, 2011). This
belief in the cathartic role of the theatre is similar to Robert Wilson's claim about
live theatre as "a forum where people can come together and share something. ...
a place of exchange" (quoted in Morey and Pardo 40–41). After all, both of them
belong to the same generation of avant-garde American theatre artists, always
looking for new directions in their endeavors, and both were deeply influenced
by Antonin Artaud's ideas about the theatre, particularly his ideas about a "total
theatre" in the sense of an original unity of experience. A comparison of Wilson
and Terry reveals an amazing list of common goals and aspirations, while each
one retains his/her own distinct mark in his/her work.

Their main similarity is their common faith in the potential of the play
concept for the renewal of the stage experience, in particular as they have
explored it in children's games. Both worked with children for many years and
confirmed their findings about the benefit of transferring their patterns on
the stage. By adopting the ease with which children play at the same time
on two different planes, both real and imaginary, actors are liberated from
the constraints of reason and stage inhibitions. Furthermore, both Wilson
and Terry have been interested in the multifarious games that can be played
with language on the stage, as well as in those that operate on the level of
the actors' body movements. Wilson, a firm believer in language's intriguing
meaning, even in its dysfunction, is more prone to unearth its inexhaustible
potential on stage by pushing his experiments in all directions, from privileging
the acting of autistic or deaf-mute actors to the utmost exploration of silence
and that of language's materiality on stage. Terry, more interested in seeking
reason through an irrational and boisterous use of stage language, favors the
materiality of the body on stage for the sake of feminist issues. Both adopted
Surrealism's favorite technique of seemingly random juxtapositions and its
montage-like technique. Both experimented with one-act plays, but also with
huge stage productions, thanks to their well-rounded training in the world

of theatre.[13] They have also been critical toward American culture; Terry has perhaps been more overtly political, putting her work in the service of feminist issues, for example. As a result, her works, although they are performed worldwide, are more apt for an American audience compared to Wilson's works, which have a wider application.

One of the ways in which they are quite distinct from one another is in their attitude toward logic and its use in stage language. It seems that Terry never denies logic, even when her widely used technique of transformations suggests so; she may *challenge* logic only to re-appropriate it. On the contrary, Wilson is rather interested in an almost intuitive pre-logic, particularly as he investigates it through his experiments with deaf-mute or autistic children. In both cases, however, they strive to invent new games for dramatic writing, as pure representatives of postmodern drama, one that "identifies transformation as the nucleus of postmodern games of change and as a principal postmodern strategy in order to subvert fixed concepts of meaning, content, and truth, as well as rigorous orders of textual representations" (Schmidt 71). Whether given the title "theatre of transformations" or "theatre of images," their theatrical work is nourished by the concept of change and playfulness, a concept that we can trace back to the innocent game of Breton's *Nadja*. In my conclusion, I will identify more closely the poetics of play and games that initially took shape in the surrealist theatre and was inherited by the postmodern theatre.

5.1   From *Body Leaks* by Sora Kimberlain, Jo Ann Schmidman, Megan Terry, Omaha Magic Theatre. Excerpted from *Right Brain Vacation Photos: New Plays and Production Photographs, 1972–1992/Omaha Magic Theatre*, edited by Jo Ann Schmidman, Sora Kimberlain, Megan Terry; photographs by Megan Terry. 1st edition. Omaha, NE: Omaha Magic Theatre, 1992, 71

5.2 From *Body Leaks* by Sora Kimberlain, Jo Ann Schmidman, Megan Terry, Omaha Magic Theatre. Excerpted from *Right Brain Vacation Photos: New Plays and Production Photographs, 1972–1992/Omaha Magic Theatre*, edited by Jo Ann Schmidman, Sora Kimberlain, Megan Terry; photographs by Megan Terry. 1st edition. Omaha, NE: Omaha Magic Theatre, 1992, 94

Notes

1   Information released in an e-mail communication to me on February 17, 2011.

2   In the same e-mail communication Terry adds that both her parents were athletes. Her father played in the Rose Bowl for the University of Washington, while her mother, among many other games played golf, and was also a fabulous singer. She herself is still an avid football and baseball fan and she loved playing those games when she could.

3   Viola Spolin uses theatre games extensively and she describes them in detail in her books, *Improvisation for the Theater* and *Theater Games for Rehearsal*. Spolin's *Theater Game File* is a special selection of theatre games abstracted from *Improvisation for the Theater*, a few traditional children's games, and some of the author's unpublished games/exercises presented on separate cards in a file box as self-contained classroom workshops.

4   Elia Kazan used a similar technique in his films through which he elicited remarkable performances from his actors.

5   From now on I will refer to this play as *Keep Tightly Closed*.

6   Such ludic techniques might be reminiscent of the relevant techniques that the improvisational director John Cassavetes used, particularly in his film *Faces* (1968), in which life and art overlap. More specifically, *Faces* corresponds to a variety of versions of the director himself, as the following incident points out: "According to George

O'Halloran, there was, in fact, an enchanted evening during the making of the film when, with the whole male cast and crew present in his living room eating and drinking late at night, Cassavetes sat down at the piano and improvised a succession of serenades to each of them one after another, telling each how he was a version of himself—someone he had wanted to be or had been at some other point in his life; someone who had done things he wanted to do; someone who figured a wish, a dream or a secret part of him that no one else knew about" (Carney 134).

7   One might find Robert Altman's film techniques relevant here. The first chapter of critic Helene Keyssar's book, *Robert Altman's America*, is appropriately entitled "The Altman Signature: A World in Motion" (3).

8   The fact that we have three versions of the same mechanical transformation corresponds to each one of the three characters, representing thus each one's point of view. It is like a rotating game.

9   I think this term best illustrates what these transformational scenes convey in Terry's play. They convey different situations with the same underlying patterns.

10   These words uttered by Jaspers bring him closer to the existentialist philosopher Karl Jaspers for whom the issue of freedom was of the highest concern.

11   Such realization is in agreement with Stamos Metzidakis's conclusion about the similar, modern use of the word "hypocrite," attributed to the reader as "bearer of a mask" in Baudelaire's *Fleurs du mal*: "L'acte de lire en soi constitue ainsi déjà pour Baudelaire un acte hypocrite, un acte qui transforme inévitablement celui qui s'y livre, en comédien ou "porteur de masque" (le sens étymologique du mot 'hypocrite')" ("Baudelaire" 227). [The act of reading in itself constitutes thus already for Baudelaire a hypocritical act, an act which inevitably transforms he who delivers himself to the act of reading into a comedian or "bearer of a mask" (the etymological sense of the word "hypocrite").]

12   The use of the pronouns HE/SHE instead of names has a long tradition that dates back to Diderot's *Le Neveu de Rameau* (*Rameau's Nephew*, 1762), in which the author uses the personas of "moi"/"lui" (me/him) to convey the dialogue that takes place between the two parts. This use of the personal pronoun has the advantage of gaining in verisimilitude and at the same time conveying a sense of universality. In Terry's case, moreover, the use of he/she emphasizes gender differences as they are implicated in their different use of language. It must also be noted that the use of numbers instead of names to portray characters, as in woman#1, woman #2, and woman #3 in *Comings and Goings*, is a common choice in Terry's entire work and originates from the corresponding numbering of players in a team game like basketball whose rules Terry brought onstage.

13   Megan Terry (with Jo Ann Schmidman) presented the musical *Running Gag* at the Omaha Magic Theatre in 1979 and then they were invited to perform it during the 1980 Winter Olympic Games in Lake Placid, NY. The play was published by Broadway Play Publishing in 1983. Also, Robert Wilson's monumental 12-hour pageant *CIVILwarS: a tree is best measured when it is down* was commissioned to be performed at the Los Angeles Olympics Arts Festival in 1984, but it was cancelled due to lack of financial backing.

CONCLUSION

This study of the poetics of play and games in surrealist and post-surrealist theatre demonstrates the need to reconsider this much-misunderstood theatre. The primary focus has been to show that ludic theory is a valid path for re-examining and restoring surrealist theatre since the ludic principle corresponds perfectly to the quintessence of Surrealism: the defiance of bipolarities and binary thinking. Finding its best expression in the surrealist game "one into another," surrealist theatre emphasizes the possibility of the simultaneity of dream and reality on stage, in the same way that play simultaneously works on two planes—that of fantasy and reality. Another important reason for examining surrealist theatre in light of ludic theory is surrealist theatre's tendency to challenge the notion of rational thinking. Allowing room for nonsense in surrealist theatre is equivalent to acknowledging nonsense in children's games or the surrealist games. Yet such nonsense, in all cases, ultimately brings us to another kind of sense—one that is tied to the irrational, the marvelous, and the subconscious. More precisely, this new sense emerges from the new concept of dialogue that Surrealism invented, one that eschews mere communication and showcases, instead, the most audacious flights of the imagination in those involved, through the accumulation of surrealist images which are uninhibited by reason. This new dialogue-game is, in fact, one of the major contributions of Surrealism to the stage, as it re-orients it toward a non-mimetic organizational principle.

For all the above reasons, it is time to cease thinking of surrealist theatre in terms of Aristotle's aesthetic theory (as developed in his *Poetics*), which includes the six qualitative parts of plot, character, thought, diction, melody, and spectacle. Although all these elements can occasionally be found in surrealist plays, none of them are rigorously applied. Rather than a clear-cut plot that creates unity in a play, one finds a fragmented, montage-like assemblage of intense tableaus, irrationally juxtaposed in a manner very similar to cinematic technique and far from a linear, cause-and-effect relationship. Rather than well-rounded characters, we find caricatures: types or their transformations that challenge the notion of an unshaken identity and a stable reality. Instead of focusing on the characters' thoughts and ideas, surrealist plays highlight the intense, contradictory emotions displayed on stage. Instead of a coherent diction, surrealist plays encourage the most arbitrary diction, dictated at best directly by the subconscious. Rather than a traditional concept of melody, in surrealist plays, melody primarily arises from the characters' poeticized language. Rather than the diminished importance Aristotle attributed to spectacle, surrealist theatre elevates spectacle to become one of its most significant elements, with an emphasis on the image and the visual. Instead of a well-built dramatic action, one finds in surrealist theatre intense dramatic moments that engage the audience, not as spectators, but as active players. Rather than the traditional presence of a fourth wall, one sees constant interaction between the actors and the spectators, as if all those present are engaged in a game. In such interaction, what matters most is the element of desire that transforms everyone involved into a desiring subject, wholly engaged in the vast play-ground that forms both the stage and the auditorium, where the ambiance created is one of rite, ritual, or ceremony.

In tracing the ludic strategies in the work of several representatives of surrealist and post-surrealist theatre, it became clear that "play" in surrealist theatre functions as a figure of syllepsis, that is, as "a construction in which one word serves two others" (Preminger and Brogan 1250). Or, to borrow Riffaterre's definition, "[s]yllepsis is a word understood in two different ways at once, as meaning and significance" ("Syllepsis" 638). Thus, in surrealist theatre, *play* in the sense of a theatrical work should be considered identical with *play* in the sense of "ludic activity"—the theatrical praxis in surrealist theatre is inextricable from its playful activity. This conclusion obviously has many implications for surrealist theatre.

First, as stated above, it fulfills Surrealism's quintessential idea of the unification of the opposites as best exemplified in the surrealist game "one into another." Thus, surrealist theatrical works unfold within the sphere of ludic activity and, at the same time, one inevitably traces ludic activity within surrealist theatre. Second, the tautology on the level of signifier "play=play" stretches the limits of reason, as it makes full sense on the level of "signifiance." Furthermore, such tautology showcases in an exemplary way Breton's idea that Surrealism is mostly concerned with the problem of human expression. By amplifying the notion of "play," yet remaining in the sphere of the concrete, surrealist theatre automatically amplifies the paucity of reality; in fact, it challenges the notion of reality by revealing a new reality, able to lead to surreality, the meeting point of reality, dream, and imagination.

Third, and most of all, the play=play equation bears proof that surrealist theatre sought to return to the origins of theatrical creation, that is, to its ritualistic roots. In this ritual, all participants come freely to liberate themselves. They dare to confront their inner fears and experience multiple selves in order to find themselves. Thus, surrealist theatre is redemptive, initiative, and *methectic* rather than mimetic. The stage is redefined as an active play-ground and not as a place of representation; it entails the direct communication of the proscenium and the auditorium, while a transformation occurs in both the actors/players and spectators/players.

All these elements were detected in an embryonic stage in Nadja's game, which Breton felt constituted the idea-limit or further determinant of Surrealism. It was from this game that the reconstruction of Breton's ludic dramatic theory—

centering on a series of "one into another" games that corresponded to his vision of the marvelous—could begin. Nadja's game activated the mechanism of metaphor and thus unearthed a poeticized language and a series of juxtaposed images that puzzled Breton. Rendering himself a plaything of his memory, Breton's "wireless imagination" was triggered and he re-imagined a theatre where reality, dream, and imagination, as well as fluidity of the self, freely converge to materialize "surreality." As his re-imagined theatre was constructed in reaction to the entire Western realist and illusionistic theatrical tradition, he did not attempt to implement it on stage himself. He feared that staging this new idea of theatre would destroy its inherent liberating potential. In his hesitation, Breton became "tomorrow's player," since his ideas about theatre would only be implemented on stage by some of his successors, in some cases even unintentionally.

Thus, in this study, I have traced a variety of ways in which Breton's ludic dramatic theory was brought to the stage over a span of about 80 years. In some cases, it was done as an experiment directly linked to Breton's ideas, as in the case of Antonin Artaud, Roger Vitrac, and Nanos Valaoritis. In others, the connection with Breton and Surrealism was more indirect, as in the cases of postmodern artists Robert Wilson and Megan Terry. All of these playwrights experimented, to a greater or lesser degree, with the stage as a form of playground and thus created an outcome strikingly similar to that which Breton had imagined for it, that is, an activation of the "marvelous." This supreme category of surreality is manifested in each one of these playwrights' works, in the form of the four categories of games, i.e. *agon*, *alea*, *mimesis*, and *ilinx*—crazy love, objective chance, the experience of multiple selves, and the vertiginous form of the "one into another" game, respectively.

Artaud and Vitrac, in their joint endeavor the Théâtre Alfred Jarry, attempted to prove to Breton that surrealist theatre could indeed exist on stage, and be fruitful. Their project was based on the proviso that the stage be seen as a play-ground where a thrilling game takes place in which both actors and spectators play at their own lives. There is no separation between life and art for them; instead, art is in life and life is in art. Personally, I believe they succeeded in their goal, although Breton never endorsed their achievement.

A few decades later, Nanos Valaoritis, Breton's disciple, intrigued by the experiment of Vitrac and Artaud, undertook his own version of surrealist theatre. He hoped that his concentration on surrealist dialogue, as opposed to spectacle, would overcome his mentor's skepticism about the possibility of implementing surrealist theatre. Breton remained unmoved, declining an invitation to the premiere of *The Nightfall Hotel*. In his version of surrealist theatre, Valaoritis benefitted to the utmost from the creative potential of the repository of surrealist games, which he himself had practiced as an active member of the surrealist group. He proved that surrealist dialogue could also function as a new type of dramatic dialogue if seen as an end in itself. This experimentation with games fluctuates from the pole of improvisation (*paidia*) to that of the rule-bound (*ludus*) and constitutes a revolutionary act against the traditional Western conception of theatre.

Robert Wilson's work joined this surrealist legacy unintentionally through his experimentation with a broad gamut of ludic strategies; his work was even qualified as the "fulfillment of Surrealism's dream" by Louis Aragon. The ludic strategies Wilson employs operate on the level of language and the actors' bodies, and the play of light and shadow in the theatrical space. It is through this ludic principle that Wilson is able to show the materiality of language, to the point that it becomes an autonomous player/actor upon the stage.

Finally, Surrealism's transformational ludic principle culminates in Megan Terry's theatre *games*. In her pieces, one scene emerges out of another as if in a "one into another" game, yet achieved with a minimal change of setting. These transformational scenes allow for a simultaneous experience of multiple identities on the part of the actors, similar to Nadja's experience of multiple identities. The game of the "self" into the "other" and its reverse, is a clear indication of the fluidity of the self and of the possibility of achieving surreality, consisting in an actualized convergence of reality, dream, and imagination.

In conclusion, Surrealism's major contribution to theatre is the preeminence of the marvelous, evoked by dream and the employment of a non-communicative dialogue. Such a dialogue was made possible thanks to the activation of the ludic principle, where theme and form converge, constituting the originality of surrealist theatre. In other words, the uniqueness of surrealist theatre resides in its ludic and transformational, and thereby non-mimetic, character. Seen as play where all kinds of games are not only permissible, but highly desirable, surrealist plays sweep away the representational principle and all its paraphernalia, including its didactic goals. This new concept of theatre, initially imagined by Breton himself, was implemented on stage progressively thanks to the audacity of a few firm believers in Surrealism's ludic activity, and their fascination with the play concept itself. Postmodern theatre, then, is directly affiliated with surrealist theatre through the ludic principle. Seen as play, a free activity *par excellence*, surrealist and postmodern theatre alike emancipate the stage from the confines of the mimetic principle and embark on an endless experimentation governed by desire.

The influence, then, of surrealist theatre extends far beyond the theatre of the absurd or the existentialist theatre with which it has been generally associated. An expansion of this current project would confirm this thesis. There is much scope for further exploration of the entire corpus of each playwright featured in this study—all prolific writers. In every phase of their artistic creation they are guided by ludics. Likewise, a further exploration of a similar theatrical output by other important playwrights, who were not included in this project, would certainly provide further evidence for my thesis about the direct, ludic link between surrealist, post-surrealist, and postmodern theatre. The work of the ex-member of Surrealism Jean-Yves Tardieu, for example, would be relevant to this further project, particularly his *Poèmes à jouer* (*Poems to Play* or *Poems to Perform*) (1960), which includes his play *Les Amants du métro* (*The Lovers of the Metro*). Also, a comparison with the Theatre of the Absurd, including especially Artur Adamov's *Ping-Pong* (1955), would be a rich source of material. The work of Edward Albee, such as *The American Dream* (1961) or *Who's Afraid of Virginia Woolf?* (1962), and the most recent productions of Megan Terry and Robert Wilson, would also be relevant to this project. Most importantly, all the above would further support the idea that André Breton indeed became "tomorrow's player" when he re-imagined theatre on the basis of Nadja's game in 1928. His "wireless imagination" would bring together surrealist and postmodern theatre as "one into another," where play and its players freely encounter the marvelous and the surreal.

Works cited

Andreoli, Jean-Pierre. 1968. *Les Drames de Roger Vitrac et le théâtre d'avant-garde*. Diss. Université d'Aix en Provence.

Antle, Martine. 1988. *Théâtre et poésie surréalistes: Vitrac et la scène virtuelle*. Birmingham, AL: Summa Publications.

——. 1990. Towards Re-Presentation: Spatiality and Voice in Roger Vitrac's Surrealist Sketches. *Modern Language Studies* 20(2), 19–27.

——. 2001. *Cultures du surréalisme*. Paris: Acoria.

Apollinaire, Guillaume. 1946. *Les Mamelles de Tirésias*. Paris: Éditions du Bélier.

Aragon, Louis. 1926. *Le Paysan de Paris*. Paris: Gallimard.

——. 1928. *Traité du style*. Paris: Gallimard.

——. 1971. *Paris Peasant*, trans. Simon Watson Taylor. London: Jonathan Cape.

——. 1971. Lettre ouverte à André Breton. *Lettres françaises* 2 juin, 314–15.

Aristotle. 1982. *Aristotle's Poetics*, trans. James Hutton. New York: Norton.

Artaud, Antonin. 1968 (1927). *Le Jet de sang*, in *L'Ombilic des limbes*. Paris: Gallimard, 76–83.

——. 1976 (1932). The Theatre of Cruelty: First Manifesto, in *Selected Writings*, ed. Susan Sontag and trans. Helen Weaver. New York: Farrar, Straus & Giroux, 242–51.

——. 1976 (1933). An End to Masterpieces, in *Selected Writings*, ed. Susan Sontag and trans. Helen Weaver. New York: Farrar, Straus & Giroux, 252–59.

——. 1961. *Œuvres complètes*. Vol. II. Paris: Gallimard.

——. 1998. *Messages révolutionnaires*. Paris: Gallimard.

Auslander, Philip. 1980. Surrealism in the Theatre: The Plays of Roger Vitrac. *Theatre Journal* 32(3), 357–69.

Balakian, Anna. 1959. *Surrealism: The Road to the Absolute*. New York: The Noonday Press.

——. 1964. André Breton as Philosopher. Spec. issue of *Yale French Studies* 31, 37–44.

Baranska, Ewa. 1983. Deux auteurs et deux pièces surréalistes: *La Boule de verre* de Salacrou et *Le Jet de sang* d'Artaud. *Roczniki humanistyczne* 31(5), 33–47.

Barber, Richard W. 1986. *King Arthur: Hero and Legend*. New York: Saint Martin's Press.

Beachler-Severs, Carol. 1976. *Roger Vitrac and Surrealism in the Theater*. Diss. Case Western Reserve University.

Beaujour, Michel. 1967. Qu'est-ce que *Nadja*? André Breton (1896–1966) et le mouvement surréaliste. Spec. issue of *La Nouvelle revue française* 172 (April), 780–99.

Béhar, Henri. 1966. *Roger Vitrac: Un reprouvé du surréalisme*. Paris: A.G. Nizet.

——. 1967. *Étude sur le théâtre dada et surréaliste*. Paris: Gallimard.

——. 1980. *Vitrac: Théâtre ouvert sur le rêve*. Paris: L'Âge d'Homme.

——. 1989. The Passionate Attraction: Breton and the Theatre, in *André Breton Today*, ed. Anna Balakian and Rudolf E. Kuenzli. New York: Willis Locker & Owens, 13–18.

——. 1990. *André Breton: Le Grand indésirable*. France: Calmann-Lévy.

Bell, John. 1994. The Language of Illusion: An Interview with Robert Wilson. *Theater Week* 3 January, 17–24.

Benedikt, Michael and George E. Wellwarth. 1964. *The Avant-Garde Dada, and Surrealism. Modern French Theatre: An Anthology of Plays.* New York: E.P. Dutton.

Bennison, Martin John. 1971. *Aesthetic Principles in Representative Surrealist Plays.* Diss. University of Missouri-Columbia.

Berghaus, Günter. 2001. Artaud's *Jet de sang*: A Critical Post- Production Analysis. *Studies in Theatre and Performance* 21(1) (April), 4–17.

Bermel, Albert. 1972. Artaud as Playwright: *The Fountain of Blood* (*Le Jet de Sang*). *Boston University Journal* 20(3), 8–15.

Birringer, Johannes. 1993. Wilson's Vision. *Performing Arts Journal* 15(1), 80–86. [Online: JStor]. Available at   http://www.jstor.org/stable/3245800 [accessed: December 16, 2010].

Blank, Carla. 2003. Notes on Robert Wilson and Anna Deavere Smith, 1–8. [Online: Carlanotes]. Available at http://www.lib.berkeley.edu/MRC/carlanotes.html [accessed: December 11, 2003].

Bosnakis, Panayiotis. 2002. Το θεατρικό αρχείο του Νάνου Βαλαωρίτη (Nanos Valaoritis's Theatrical Archive). *Mandragoras*, 27 (March), 96–8.

Brandt, W. George, ed. 1998. *Modern Theories of Drama.* Oxford: Clarendon Press.

Brecht, Stefan. 1978. *The Original Theatre of the City of New York: From the mid-60s to the mid-70s. Book 1: The Theatre of Visions: Robert Wilson.* New York: Suhrkamp.

Breton, André. 1960. *Nadja*, trans. Richard Howard. New York: Grove Press.

——. 1964. *Nadja*. Paris: Gallimard.

——. 1972. *Manifestoes of Surrealism*, trans. Richard Seaver and Helen. R. Lane. Ann Arbor, MI: University of Michigan Press.

——. 1987. *Mad Love*, trans. Mary Ann Caws. Lincoln, NE: University of Nebraska Press.

——. 1988. *Œuvres complètes.* Vol. I. Paris: Gallimard.

——. 1992. *Œuvres complètes.* Vol. II. Paris: Gallimard.

Brunel, Pierre. 1978. Strindberg et Artaud. *Société de l'histoire du théâtre* 30, 346–58.

Burke, Mary Ann. 1974. *The Merveilleux as a Category of Esthetic Expression in a Selection of Medieval Works and in the Surrealist Novels of André Breton and Louis Aragon.* Diss. University of Wisconsin.

Caillois, Roger. 1961. *Man, Play, and Games*, trans. Barash Meyer. New York: The Free Press.

Camus, Marcel et al. 1986. *Orfeu Negro* (*Black Orpheus*, dir. Marcel Camus and Jacques Viot). Produced by Sacha Gordine. Videocassette. Lopert Films. Los Angeles, CA: Voyager.

Canney, Michael. 1966. Foreword. *Surrealism: A State of Mind, 1924–1965* [University of California, Santa Barbara. Art Gallery]. New York: Arno/Worldwide.

Capron, Marcelle. 1959. Review of *L'Hôtel de la nuit qui tombe*, by Nanos Valaoritis. *Le Combat* 29 April. No page.

Cardullo, Bert and Robert Knopf, eds. 2001. *Theater of the Avant-garde, 1890–1950: A Critical Anthology*. New Haven, CT: Yale University Press.

——. 2001. Artaud's Theater of Cruelty and the Spurt of Blood, in *Theater of the Avant-garde 1890–1950: A Critical Anthology*, ed. Bert Cardullo and Robert Knopf. New Haven, CT: Yale University Press, 375–77.

Carney, Ray, ed. 2001. *Cassavetes on Cassavetes*. London: Faber & Faber.

Carrouges, Michel. 1974. *André Breton and the Basic Concepts of Surrealism*, trans. Maura Prendergast. University, AL: University of Alabama Press.

Cauvin, Jean-Pierre. 1981. Literary Games of Chance: The André Breton Manuscripts. *The Library Chronicle of the University of Texas at Austin* 16, 16–41.

Caws, Mary Ann. 1981. *A Metapoetics of the Passage: Architextures in Surrealism and After.* Hanover, NH: University Press of New England.

Cohn, Ruby. 1964. Surrealism and Today's French Theatre. Spec. issue of *Yale French Studies* 31, 159–65.

——. 1979. Artaud's *Jet de sang*: Parody or Cruelty? *Theatre Journal* 31(3) (October), 312–18.

——. 1986. Godot's Games and Beckett's Late Plays, in *Auctor Ludens: Essays on Play and Literature*, ed. Gerald Guinness and Andrew Hurley. Philadelphia, PA: Benjamins, 183–90.

Conley, Katharine. 2001. Rev. of *Cultures du surréalisme* by Martine Antle. *SubStance* [Online] 30(3), 128–31. Available at *Project Muse* http://muse.jhu.edu/journals/substance/v030/30.3conley.html [accessed: 23 March 2005].

Dante. 1994. *The Inferno of Dante*, trans. Robert Pinsky. New York: Noonday Press.

Deák, František. 1974. Robert Wilson. *The Drama Review* 18(2) (June), 67–73.

De Beauvoir, Simone. 1968. *The Second Sex*, trans. H.M. Parshley. New York: Alfred A. Knopf.

Diderot, Denis. 1936. Paradoxe sur le comédien, in *Diderot's Writings on the Theatre*, ed. F.C. Green. Cambridge: Cambridge University Press, 249–317.

Dimensions of Dialogue. 1990. *Svänkmejer: Alchemist of the Surreal.* (dir. an Svänkmejer). Videocassette. Collector's edition. New York: IFEX International Video.

Durozoi, Gérard. 2002. *History of the Surrealist Movement*, trans. Alison Anderson. Chicago, IL: University of Chicago Press.

Ehrmann, Jacques. 1968. Homo Ludens Revisited. *Game, Play, Literature*, spec. issue of *Yale French Studies* 41, 31–57.

Esslin, Martin. 1961. *The Theatre of the Absurd*. New York: Anchor Books.

———. 1976. *Antonin Artaud*. New York: Penguin Books.

Fairbrother, Trevor. 1991. *Robert Wilson's Vision: An Exhibition of Works by Robert Wilson*. Boston, MA: Museum of Fine Arts.

Feldman, Peter. 1967. Notes for the Open Theatre Production, in *Viet Rock: Four Plays by Megan Terry*. New York: Simon and Schuster, 199–206.

Frank, Claudine, ed. 2003. *The Edge of Surrealism: A Roger Callois Reader*. Durham, NC: Duke University Press.

Freud, Sigmund. 1960. *Beyond the Pleasure Principle*, trans. and ed. James Strachey. New York: Norton.

Garrigues, Emmanuel. 1995. *Archives du surréalisme: Les Jeux surrealistes (mars 1921–septembre 1962)*. Paris: Gallimard.

Gershman, Herbert S. 1966. Toward Defining the Surrealist Aesthetic. *Papers on Language and Literature: A Journal for Scholars and Critics of Language and Literature* 2, 47–56.

Gide, André. 1922. *Les Caves du Vatican*. Paris: Gallimard.

Goldman, Laurence. 1998. *Child's Play: Myth, Mimesis and Make-believe*. Oxford: Berg.

Gooding, Mel. 2001. *Surrealist Games*. Boston, MA: Shambhala Redstone.

Gréa, Philippe. 2001. L'Un dans l'autre. Enigme et métaphore filée dans un jeu surréaliste. *Revue Romane* 45(1), 91–116.

Hardison-Londré, Felicia. 1996. *Speaking on Stage: Interviews with Contemporary American Playwrights*, ed. Philip Kolin and Colby H. Kullman. Tuscaloosa, AL: University of Alabama Press, 138–49.

Hartnoll, Phyllis, ed. 1967. *The Oxford Companion to the Theatre*. London: Oxford University Press.

Henriot, Jacques. 1989. *Sous couleur de jouer: la métaphore ludique*. Paris: José Corti.

Holmberg, Arthur. 1996. *The Theatre of Robert Wilson*. Cambridge: Cambridge University Press.

Hugo, Victor. 1963. Les Tables tournantes de Jersey: 1853–1855. *Œuvres dramatiques complètes*, ed. Jean-Jacques Pauvert. Paris: Societé française des presses suisses, 1619–1713.

———. 1991. *Les Fantômes de Jersey*, ed. Francis Lacassin. Monaco: Rocher.

Huizinga, Johan. 1938. *Homo Ludens*. Boston, MA: Beacon, 1955.

Innes, Christopher. 1993. *Avant-garde Theatre (1892–1992)*. London: Routledge.

Ionesco, Eugène. 1964. *Notes and Counter Notes*, trans. Donald Watson. New York: Grove Press.

———. 1974. *Tueur sans gage*. Paris: Gallimard.

Jarry, Alfred. 1961. *Ubu-roi*. New York: New Directions.

———. 1972. *Œuvres complètes*. Vol. I. Paris: Gallimard.

Keyssar, Helene. 1984. *Feminist Theatre: An Introduction to Plays of Contemporary British and American Women*. London: Macmillan.

———. 1991. *Robert Altman's America*. Oxford: Oxford University Press.

Knapp, Bettina. 1964. Artaud: A New Type of Magic. Spec. issue of *Yale French Studies* 31, 87–98.

Kornhaber, David. 2004. Modern Beginnings and Postmodern Endings: The "Failed" Dramas of Antonin Artaud. *Theatron* 2(2) (Spring), 48–58.

Kristeva, Julia. 1984. *Revolution in Poetic Language*, trans. Margaret Waller. New York: Columbia University Press.

——. 2004. From "The Subject in Process." *Antonin Artaud: A Critical Reader*, ed. Edward Scheer. London: Routledge, 117–24.

Lacan, Jacques. 1977. *Écrits: A Selection*, trans. Alan Sheridan. New York: Norton.

Larson, James Wallace. 1988. *Public Dreams: A Critical Investigation of the Plays of Megan Terry, 1955–1968*. Diss. University of Kansas.

Laxton, Susan. 2003. The Guarantor of Chance: Surrealism's Ludic Practices. *Papers of Surrealism* 1 (Winter). No page.

——. 2004. *Paris as Gameboard: Man Ray's Atgets*. New York: The Wallach Gallery. Diss. Columbia University.

Leavitt, Dinah L. 1981. Megan Terry: Interview, in *Women in American Theatre: Careers, Images, Movements: An Illustrated Anthology and Sourcebook*, ed. Helen Krish Chinoy and Linda Walsh Jenkins. New York: Crown Publishers, 285–92.

Lejeune, Philippe. 1989. *On Autobiography*, ed. Paul John Eakin and trans. Katherine Leary. Minneapolis, MN: University of Minnesota Press.

Levi, Peter. 1991. The Last Greek Surrealist. *The Spectator* 23 February. No page.

Levitt, Anette, S. 1976. Roger Vitrac and the Drama of Surrealism, in *Aeolian Harps: Essays in Literature in Honor of Maurice Browning Cramer*, ed. Donna G. Fricke and Douglas C. Fricke. Bowling Green, OH: Bowling Green University Press, 247–72.

Maillard-Chary, Claude. 1990. Melusine entre Sphinx et Sirène, ou la "queue prehensile" du désir rattrapé. *Cahiers du Centre de recherche sur le surréalisme (Paris III). Melusine.* XI, ed. Henri Béhar. Paris: L'Âge d'homme, 213–28.

Malpas, Simon. 2005. *The Postmodern*. London: Routledge.

Matthews, J.H. 1967. *André Breton*. New York: Columbia University Press.

——. 1970. Surrealism in the Sixties. *Contemporary Literature* 11(2) (Spring), 226–42.

——. 1974. *Theatre in Dada and Surrealism*. Syracuse, NY: Syracuse University Press.

Melzer Henkin, Annabelle. 1980. *Latest Rage the Big Drum: Dada and Surrealist Performance*. Diss. Ann Arbor, MI: UMI Research Press.

——. 1994 (1976). *Dada and Surrealist Performance*. Baltimore, MD: Johns Hopkins University Press.

Metzidakis, Stamos. 1978. L'Apothéose de l'erreur: Étude du jeu dans *Le Paysan de Paris* d'Aragon. *Rackham Literary Studies* 9, 7–13.

——. 1989. Breton and Poetic Originality, in *André Breton Today*, ed. Anna Balakian and Rudolf E. Kuenzli. New York: Willis Locker & Owens, 28–35.

——. 1989. Baudelaire et ses hypocrites lectures. *Orbis Litterarum* 44(3), 222–33.

——. 1995. *Difference Unbound: The Rise of Pluralism in Literature and Criticism*. Amsterdam: Rodopi.

——. 1996. Breton's Structuralism. *L'Esprit créateur* 36(4) (Winter), 32–42.

Moi, Toril, ed. 1986. *The Kristeva Reader*. New York: Columbia University Press.

Morel, Jean-Paul. 2004. Les Jeux surrealists, in *O Surrealismo*, ed. J. Guinsburg and Sheila Leirner. São Paulo: Editora Perspectiva, 773–81.

Morey, Miguel and Carmen Pardo. 2003. *Robert Wilson*. New York: D.A.P./Distributed Art Publishers.

Motte, Warren F. 1995. *Playtexts: Ludics in Contemporary Literature*. Lincoln, NE: University of Nebraska Press.

Muller, John P. and William J. Richardson. 1982. *Lacan and Language: A Reader's Guide to Écrits.* New York: International University Press.

Nadeau, Maurice. 1965. *The History of Surrealism*, trans. Richard Howard. New York: Macmillan.

Ollier, Nicole. 1988. Nanos Valaoritis: Métamorphose et surréalisme. *Annales du Centre de recherches sur l'Amérique Anglophone* 13, 151–61.

——. 1997. Nanos Valaoritis: The Cultural Cross-Breeding of a Cosmopolitan and Protean Writer. *Journal of Modern Greek Studies* 15 (May), 29–54.

Orenstein Feman, Gloria. 1975. *The Theater of the Marvelous: Surrealism and the Contemporary Stage*. New York: New York University Press.

Ovid. 1921. *Metamorphoses*. Vol. I. 1916, trans. Frank Justus Miller. Cambridge, MA: Harvard University Press.

Palau, Pierre. 1956. *Les Détraquées. Le Surréalisme, même* 1 (3ème trimestre), 73–120.

Pavis, Patrice. 1998. *Dictionary of the Theatre: Terms, Concepts and Analysis*. Toronto: University of Toronto Press.

——. 2003. *Analyzing Performance: Theater, Dance, and Film*, trans. David Williams. Ann Arbor, MI: University of Michigan Press.

Persels, Jeffrey Charles. 1991. *Sacred Anchors: Securing Signs of the Male in Early Modern French Texts, 1530–1550*. Diss. University of Virginia.

Pierron, Agnes. 1996. House of Horrors. *Grand Street*. [Online magazine]. Available at http://www.grandguignol.com/grandstreet.htm [accessed: June 29, 2011].

Piret, Pierre. 1998. *Victor ou les enfants au pouvoir* de Roger Vitrac: Une fiction créationniste, in *Le Mal dans l'imaginaire littéraire français, 1850–1950*, ed. Myriam Watthee-Delmotte and Metka Zupancic. Paris: L'Harmattan, 329–46.

Plato. 1888. *The Timaeus of Plato*, ed. R.D. Archer-Hind. London: Macmillan.

——. 1980. *The Laws of Plato*, trans. Thomas L. Pangle. New York: Basic Books.

Polizzoti, Mark. 1995. *Revolution of the Mind: The Life of André Breton*. New York: Farrar, Straus, and Giroux.

Preminger, Alex, T.V.F. Brogan, et al., eds. 1993. *The New Princeton Encyclopedia of Poetry and Poetics.* Princeton, NJ: Princeton University Press.

Riffaterre, Michael. 1978. *Semiotics of Poetry*. Bloomington, IN: Indiana University Press.

——. 1980. Syllepsis. *Critical Inquiry* 6(4) (Summer), 625–38.

——. 1983. *Text Production*, trans. Terese Lyons. New York: Columbia University Press.

Rimbaud, Arthur. 1972. *Œuvres complètes*, ed. Antoine Adam. Paris: Gallimard.

——. 1975. *Lettres du voyant (13 et 15 mai 1871)*, ed. Gerald Schaeffer. Paris: Minard.

Romero, Laurence. 1995. Poet from Another World: Robert Wilson in France. *The French Review* 68(3) (February), 487–500.

Rose, Phyllis Jane. 1981. Megan Terry. *Dictionary of Literary Biography: Twentieth-Century American Dramatists*, ed. John MacNicholas. Detroit, MI: Bruccoli Clark. Vol. 7(2), 277–89.

Russell Taylor, John. 1966. *The Penguin Dictionary of the Theatre*. Harmondsworth: Penguin Books.

Sartre, Jean Paul. 1966 (1947). *Huis clos*. Paris: Gallimard.

Schechner, Richard. 1967. The Playwright as Wrighter, in Megan Terry, *Viet Rock: Four Plays by Megan Terry*. New York: Simon and Schuster, 7–18.

——. 2003. Robert Wilson and Fred Newman: A Dialogue on Politics and Therapy, Stillness and Vaudeville, Moderated by Richard Schechner. *The Drama Review* 47(3) (Fall), 113–28.

Schlueter, June. 1990. Megan Terry's Transformational Drama: *Keep Tightly Closed in a Cool Dry Place* and the Possibilities of Self, in *Modern American Drama: The Female Canon*, ed. June Schlueter. Rutherford, NJ: Fairleigh Dickinson, 161–71.

Schmidman, Jo Ann, Sora Kimberlain and Megan Terry, eds. 1992. *Right Brain Vacation Photos: New Plays and Production Photographs, 1972–1992/Omaha Magic Theatre*, photographs by Megan Terry. Omaha, NE: Omaha Magic Theatre.

Schmidt, Kerstin. 2005. *The Theater of Transformation: Postmodernism in American Drama*. Amsterdam: Rodopi.

Schumacher, Claude, ed. 1989. *Artaud on Theatre*. London: Methuen Drama.

Schuster, Jean. 1969. Le Quatrième chant. *Le Monde* 4 Octobre.

Sewell, Elizabeth. 1952. *The Field of Nonsense*. London: Chatto & Windus.

Shank, Theodore. 2002. *Beyond the Boundaries: American Alternative Theatre*. Ann Arbor, MI: University of Michigan Press.

Shyer, Laurence. 1989. *Robert Wilson and His Collaborators*. New York: Theatre Communications Group.

Simon, Alfred. 1970. *Dictionnaire du théâtre français contemporain*. Paris: Librairie Larousse.

Situationist Manifesto. 1960. Trans. Fabian Thompsett. *Internationale Situationniste* 4 (June), 1–2. [Online]. Available at http://www.cddc.vt.edu/sionline/si/manifesto.html [accessed: June 29, 2011].

Slovenko, Ralph and James A. Knight, eds. 1967. *Motivations in   Play, Games and Sports.* Springfield, IL: Thomas.

Spariosu, Mihai I. 1989. *Dionysus Reborn: Play and the Aesthetic Dimension in Modern Philosophical and Scientific Discourse*. Ithaca, NY: Cornell University Press.

Spolin, Viola. 1972. *Improvisation for the Theater: A Handbook of Teaching and Directing Techniques.* Evanston, IL: Northwestern University Press.

———. 1985. *Theater Games for Rehearsal: A Director's Handbook*. Evanston, IL: Northwestern University Press.

———. 1989. *Theater Game File*. Evanston, IL: Northwestern University Press.

Suleiman Rubin, Susan. 2003. Surrealist Black Humour: Masculine Feminine. *Papers of Surrealism* 1 (Winter), 1–11.

Sundell, Nina. 1985. Robert Wilson: Medea and Parsifal, in Robert Wilson, *Robert Wilson: Medea e Parsifal disegni incisioni video*. Pesaro: Centro Stampa del Commune di Pesaro, 7–10.

Sutton-Smith, Brian. 1997. *The Ambiguity of Play*. Cambridge, MA: Harvard University Press.

Taylor, E. Victor and Charles E. Winquist, eds. 2001. *Encyclopedia of Postmodernism*. London: Routledge.

Terry, Megan. 1966. *Calm Down Mother: A Transformation for Three Women*. New York: Samuel French.

———. 1967. *Comings and Goings: A Theatre Game.* New York: Samuel French.

———. 1967. *Viet Rock; Comings and Goings; Keep Tightly Closed in a Cool Dry Place; The Gloaming, Oh My Darling: Four Plays by Megan Terry.* Intr. Richard Schechner. New York: Simon and Schuster.

———. 1978. *Brazil Fado*. Omaha, NE: Omaha Magic Theatre Press.

———. 1980. *Objective Love*. Electronic Edition by Alexander Street Press, 2011. [Online]. Available at http://solomon.wodr.alexanderstreet.com.ezpprod1.hul.harvard.edu/cgi-bin/asp/philo/navigate.pl?wodr.805 [accessed: May 18, 2011].

———. 1990. *Body Leaks*. Electronic Edition by Alexander Street Press, 2011. Also published in *Theatre Alive! An Introductory Anthology of World Drama*, ed. Norman A. Bert. Colorado Springs, CO: Meriwether Publishing, 1995. [Online]. Available at http://solomon.wodr.alexanderstreet.com.ezpprod1.hul.harvard.edu/cgi-bin/asp/philo/wodr/documentidx.pl?work_code=PL007973 [accessed: May 18, 2011].

The Theory of Moments and the Construction of Situations. 1960. Trans. Paul Hammond. *Internationale Situationniste* 4 (June), 1–2. [Online]. Available at http://www.cddc.vt.edu/sionline/si/moments.html [accessed: May 18, 2011].

Toloudis, Constantin. 1989. The Impulse for the Ludic in the Poetics of Raymond Queneau. *Twentieth Century Literature* 35(2) (Summer), 147–60.

Valaoritis, Nanos. 1957. *Henriette où est-elle passée?* (*Henriette Where Did She Go?*). Unpublished Play.

———. 1957. *Les Tables rondes*. Unpublished Play.

———. 1957. *L'Hôtel de la nuit qui tombe* (*The Nightfall Hotel*). Unpublished Play.

———. 1990. *Για μια Θεωρία της Γραφής* (*For a Theory of Writing*). Athens: Exantas.

———. 2001. Personal Interview. May 20.

———. 2006. *Για μια Θεωρία της Γραφής Β* (*For a Theory of Writing B*). Athens: Electra.

Vallaire, Stéphane. 1959. *Les Lettres françaises*. 7 May. No page.

Vitrac, Roger. 1948. *Théâtre*. Vol. II. Paris, Gallimard.

———. 2000. *Victor ou les enfants au pouvoir*, ed. Marie-Claude Hubert. Paris: Gallimard.

Walter, Sidney S. 1967. Notes for the Firehouse Theatre Production, in Megan Terry, *Viet Rock: Four Plays by Megan Terry.* New York: Simon and Schuster, 206–9.

Winspur, Steven. 1984. Wittgenstein's Semiotic Investigations. *The American Journal of Semiotics* 3(2), 33–57.

Wittgenstein, Ludwig. 1953. *Philosophical Investigations*, trans. G.E.M. Ansombe. Oxford: Basil Blackwell.

Wylie, Harold. 1979. Breton, Schizophrenia and Nadja. *The French Review*. Spec. issue 1 (Winter), 100–106.

Zeps, Betty S. 1967. Artaud's *Le Jet de sang* and His Theory of Drama. *Semi-gallian Blazoon* 1, 13–17.

Zinder, David G. 1976. *The Surrealist Connection: An Approach to a Surrealist Aesthetic of Theatre*. Diss. Ann Arbor, MI: UMI Research Press. 1980.

Index